THE

EPIC SONGS OF RUSSIA

BY

ISABEL FLORENCE HAPGOOD

WITH AN INTRODUCTORY NOTE

BY

PROFESSOR FRANCIS J. CHILD

GREENWOOD PRESS, PUBLISHERS
WESTPORT, CONNECTICUT

Originally published in 1886
by Charles Scribner's Sons, New York

First Greenwood Reprinting 1970

Library of Congress Catalogue Card Number 73-110841

SBN 8371-4507-4

Printed in the United States of America

INTRODUCTORY NOTE.

I CANNOT forbear to bespeak a welcome for this spirited and sympathetic version of the more important of the Great Russian Popular Heroic Songs. Besides the pleasure which may be got from it, it will help to an appreciation of that large class of our fellow-creatures, in the past and in the present, who have been educated by tradition and not by books, and who, though living on oats, feel and cherish poetry not less than those who have been nursed in comfort and schooled in literature. The songs and tales of this class have now been collected from Siberia to the Azores, from Iceland to Cyprus, and more or less all the earth over. The pampered world of cultivated readers has made new and refreshing acquisitions from the inheritance of the poor and simple, and has reason to respect and admire those whom, at best, they pitied for their destitution of intellectual solaces and delights. Though this book is meant for the general reader, it cannot fail to be most acceptable to students of popular tradition who have been so unfortunate as to neglect Russian; for nothing of the same kind and compass has, so far as I know, been published in any language of Western Europe. The translator has said in her introduction all that I should otherwise have felt called to say, and has left it for me only to express the obligation, which I for one feel to her, for undertaking this work, and the wish that it may meet with the reception which I think it deserves.

F. J. CHILD.

PREFACE.

THOROUGH study of the epic poems of Russia, (*bylinas*) as of other branches of folk-lore, is not to be thought of at the present day, without the aid of the comparative method, which must begin in the circle of the other Slavic literatures, Bulgarian, Servian, etc.

It has not seemed to me advisable to enter upon so vast a subject in this volume, which is intended for popular reading. I hope that the brief notes in the Appendix will suffice to give a general idea of the historical foundation of the *bylinas*, and of the relationship which exists between them and the epic poems of other nations.

As it is extremely improbable that a complete translation of these Songs will ever be published, a word of explanation is necessary with regard to the method I have pursued. — Of each Song many versions exist, varying in number from three to three dozen or more. Some of these, though mere fragments, contain important facts. Others are rendered inordinately long by the repetition of speeches, the multiplication of details, or the interpolation of passages from other songs. In very few instances is the story complete; and when complete, many characteristic details are lacking. Literal rendering of such a vast and puzzling mass of poems, which are numbered by the hundred, and in their printed form, cover thousands of pages, is manifestly impossible. Eclecticism is the only solution of the difficulty, for the descriptive method conveys no adequate idea of either style or story. I have consulted all the variants. The style I have preserved as nearly as possible, deeming the action sufficiently rapid and forcible to sustain the old-fashioned language. I venture to think that the result would satisfy the peasant-minstrels themselves.

I have simplified the spelling of the proper names as much as possible, and of the very few Russian words employed, and have accented all, in order that the pronunciation may not mar the reader's pleasure.

The theory that the epic songs are of purely legendary origin, and not nature myths, is gaining ground. If this view is accepted, the very slight distinction between the Elder and the Younger heroes immediately disappears. It has seemed best, however, to retain that division, since it is customary in Russia and necessary to the proper understanding of any reference to the subject. The mythological explanation will be found interesting from its ingenuity, whichever view may eventually prevail.

For the *bylinas* I am indebted to the Collections of Kirshá Daniléf, Sakárof, Rýbnikof, Kiryéevsky, Bezónof, Hilferding, and the Ethnographical Bulletin of the Natural History Society of Moscow University; for my notes, to works on these Songs by Orest Miller, Schepping, Máikof, Busláef, Galakóf, and other recognized Russian authorities.

ISABEL FLORENCE HAPGOOD.

Boston, August, 1885.

TABLE OF CONTENTS.

	PAGE
INTRODUCTION	1

THE ELDER HEROES.

VOLGÁ VSESLÁVICH THE WIZARD	23
VOLGÁ AND MIKÚLA SELYANÍNOVICH THE VILLAGER'S SON	28
HERO SVYATOGÓR	33

THE CYCLE OF VLADÍMIR, OR OF KÍEF.

ILYÁ OF MÚROM THE PEASANT HERO, AND HERO SVYATOGÓR	39
QUIET DÚNAÏ IVÁNOVICH	48
STAVR GODÍNOVICH THE BOYÁR (NOBLE)	65
ILYÁ OF MÚROM AND NIGHTINGALE THE ROBBER	77
BOLD ALYÓSHA THE POPE'S SON	88
THE ONE AND FORTY PILGRIMS	98
ILYÁ IN DISGUISE	110
DOBRÝNYA THE DRAGON-SLAYER, AND MARÍNA	116
IVÁN GODINÓVICH	124
DOBRÝNYA AND THE ADVENTURE OF THE PAVILION	135
CHURÍLO PLENKÓVICH, THE FOP	139

TABLE OF CONTENTS.

	PAGE
Ilyá and the Boon Companions	148
Diuk Stepánovich	151
Vasíly the Drunkard and Tzar Bátyg	178
Ilyá and Idol	183
Dobrýnya and the Dragon	188
Iván the Merchant's Son and his Horse	201
Ilyá of Múrom and Falcon the Hunter	206
Sweet Mikáilo Ivánovich the Rover	214
Nightingale Budímirovich the Sailor Hero	232
Danílo the Huntsman and his Wife	240
Ilyá and the Adventure of the Three Roads	246
Dobrýnya and Alyósha	253
Ilyá of Múrom and Tzar Kálin	269
Tzar Solomon and Tzarítza Solomónida	282

THE CYCLE OF NÓVGOROD.

Vasíly Busláevich the Brave of Nóvgorod	295
Merchant Sadkó the Rich Guest of Nóvgorod	313

APPENDIX.

The Alátyr Stone	327
Volgá Vsesávich	329
Volgá and Mikúla	332
Svyatogór	334
Ilyá of Múrom	336
The Fair Sun Prince Vladímir	341
Quiet Dúnai Ivánovich	342
Stavr Godínovich	343
Bold Alyósha Popóvich	344

TABLE OF CONTENTS. xiii

	PAGE
DOBRÝNYA THE DRAGON-SLAYER	346
IVÁN GODINÓVICH	349
CHURÍLO PLENKÓVICH	350
DIUK STEPÁNOVICH	351
VASÍLY THE DRUNKARD AND TZAR BÁTYG	352
SWEET MIKÁILO IVÁNOVICH THE ROVER	353
NIGHTINGALE BUDÍMIROVICH	355
TZAR SOLOMON AND TZARÍTZA SOLOMÓNIDA	356
VASÍLY BUSLÁEVICH	357
MERCHANT SADKÓ THE RICH GUEST OF NÓVGOROD	357

THE EPIC SONGS OF RUSSIA.

INTRODUCTION.

THE highest stage of development reached by popular song is the heroic epos — the rhythmic story of the deeds of national heroes either historical or mythical. In many countries these epics were committed to writing at a very early date. In Western Europe this took place in the Middle Ages, and they are known to the modern world in that form only, their memory having completely died out among the people.

To this rule, there are two striking exceptions. — At the beginning of the present century, the old heroic songs were sung in the Faroë Islands, and that in a much more antique form than is preserved in the later, Middle Age versions. The second exception is still more remarkable. Russia presents the phenomenon of a country where epic song, handed down wholly by oral tradition for nearly a thousand years, is not only flourishing at the present day in certain districts, but even extending into fresh fields.

Amid the vast swamps and forests of Northern Russia the *bylínas*[1] are sung to-day by scores of peasants, men

---

[1] *Bylína*, from *byt*, to be: i.e., the story of something which has actually occurred, in contradistinction to the account of a purely imaginary event.

and women, old and young, to whom they have descended through countless generations of ancestors, and whose belief is as implicit in the *bogatýrs*[1] whose deeds they celebrate as was the belief of the first of those ancestors.

It is only within the present century, — within the last twenty-five years in fact, — that the discovery has been made that Russia possesses a national literature which is not excelled by the finest of Western Europe.

About the middle of the last century, Kirshá Daniléf made a collection of songs among the workmen at the Demídof mines in the Government of Perm. It is not known who this Kirshá Daniléf was. An incomplete edition published from his manuscript in 1804 created some interest as a curiosity. In 1818 a more complete edition was issued; and the attention of students having been directed to the subject, various songs were written down by different persons, as occasion offered. A collection was also published in German at Leipzig in 1819, which contained some epic songs not since found. It was left, however, for Petr Rýbnikof, to arouse general

---

[1] The etymology of *bogatýr*, a hero, is uncertain. Some authorities refer it to a word current among various Turko-Mongolian tribes, *bagadour, batour, bator, bagadar*, which is applied to a hero who has thrice penetrated first and alone into the ranks of the enemy. The title is thereafter affixed to his name. But the Mongolians had borrowed the word from the Sanskrit, where it already denoted a person endowed with good luck, a successful person — and success constitutes an inseparable attribute of all heroes. A more purely Russian theory is that which derives it from *bog*, god, through the intermediate form *bogátyi*, rich, as in Latin *dives*, rich, is immediately related to *divus, godlike*, i.e. endowed with an abundance of wonderful powers and gifts. In Little Russia, *bogatýr* is still used to denote a rich man, and sometimes a hero. In the ancient Chronicles, the heroes do not bear the name of *bogatýrs* until 1240, but are called *ryezvetzý*, bold, daring men, or *udaltzý*, braves, the title still applied to the heroes of the Nóvgorod cycle.

INTRODUCTION. 3

attention and enthusiasm. In 1861-62 appeared the first two volumes of his great collection made on the shores of Lake Onéga. They were greeted with so much amazement and even incredulity, that Rýbnikof appended to his third volume a detailed account of his journeyings and of the peasants from whose lips he had written down his songs. The publication of these songs marked an epoch in the literature of Russia.

Petr N. Rýbnikof was a government official who was stationed at Petrzavodsk on the western shore of Lake Onéga. Conversing in 1859 with some of the older inhabitants of the town, he learned that many curious and ancient customs, traditions and songs were preserved among the villagers of the Olónetz Government. In confirmation of the statement he was referred to two poems which had been published in the government journals. In the course of that year, he succeeded in obtaining some manuscript songs, which had been written down at the dictation of a peasant tailor known as "The Bottle." He then set to work to collect monuments of popular poetry, but at first found only historical and spiritual songs and laments.

In 1860 he was ordered to collect certain statistics, and this afforded him an opportunity to pursue his search among the people themselves. At Shungsk Fair he succeeded, with the aid of the police, in finding a couple of *kalíky* or psalm-singers, and persuaded them to sing all they knew. As very few of these *kalíky* sing "worldly songs," i.e., *bylínas*, his hopes were again frustrated. He continued to hear much of "The Bottle," who in the pursuit of his calling roamed over the whole of the trans-Onéga region. But although, in search of him, Rýbnikof made two journeys across

Lake Onéga on the ice in severe winter weather, and one in summer on a leaky boat, it was not until 1863 that he succeeded in finding him. — Before this, however, he had heard many an epic song from other singers.

Knowing the distrust with which an official inspires the peasants, he dressed himself like a man of the people, and took passage on a market-boat returning to Pudóga, where "The Bottle" lived. Though it was May, the ice was not out of the lake, and it was bitterly cold. Contrary winds forced them to put in at an island covered with woods and swamps, only twelve versts from their starting-place, after having labored at the oars all night. The dirty hut of refuge was already crowded with peasants, weather-bound like themselves, so Rýbnikof made himself some tea by a fire which was burning in the open air, and lay down on the ground to sleep. He was awakened by strange sounds. About three paces from him sat a group of peasants and an old man with a great white beard, bright eyes, and a kindly expression of countenance. From the old man's lips flowed a wondrous song, unlike any which Rýbnikof had ever heard, lively, fantastic, gay, growing now more brisk, again breaking off suddenly, and suggesting in style something very ancient and long forgotten by living men. That song finished, the old man began another — the famous lay of Sadkó the Merchant of Nóvgorod. Thoroughly aroused now, Rýbnikof knew that this was his long-sought epic. Many a one did he thereafter listen to, sung by rhapsodists with fine voices and masterly diction, but none of them ever produced upon him the fresh and overwhelming impression made by old Léonty Bogdanóvich with his poor, cracked voice and imperfect versions.

Thanks to Bogdanóvich, Rýbnikof was enabled to find a great number of singers, and to overcome their habitual distrust of *chinóvniks* (officials) sufficiently to induce them to sing all the songs they knew. In this manner he succeeded in collecting over 50,000 verses. — But this collection was far from exhausting the rich hoards of epic poetry treasured up in the region about Lake Onéga. In 1870 Alexander F. Hilferding, impelled by a desire to see something of the peasantry and to hear some of the remarkable rhapsodists described by Rýbnikof, undertook a journey to certain districts recommended by the latter. But he did not pause there; penetrating to the North and East of the Olónetz government, he found, apparently, the very home of epic poetry in the XIX. century. In less than two months he had made a collection of *bylínas* even larger than Rýbnikof's, containing 318 songs.

The region is but little known, and a condition of things prevails which cannot differ much from that of epic days. The peasants on the borders of Lake Onéga have a comparatively enviable lot. They have intercourse with St. Petersburg, and are not entirely cut off from the world. But further to the North and East, in Kenózero, Vygózero and Vadlózero, the peasant's lot is hard indeed. There lie forests, swamps, and again forests. The only means of communication between the hamlets which dot this vast wilderness is afforded by the scattered lakes. There are no carts,— they cannot be used on the marshy roads; sledges are employed even in summer, or *voloki* — long poles, one end of which is fastened to the horse collar, while the other end, with board attached to bear the load, drags on the ground. Where water communication is lacking, the peasant must go on horseback, making his own path through the dense forest. The cultivation, with great labor, of tiny clearings in the forest, and fishing in autumn, form the only means of livelihood, so that all are obliged to add some trade — hunting wild animals, teaming to the White Sea in winter, and so forth. The women and girls work equally hard, and the peasant is happy if, by their united labors, they manage to escape starvation. Oats prepared in various ways form the chief article of food, for they cannot raise either cabbages, onions, cucumbers or buckwheat.

"The condition of things is growing worse," says Hilferding in 1870. Some bureaucrat took it into his head that the interests of the Treasury demanded the preservation of the Northern forests; consequently, the peasants were forbidden to make their little clearings, in spite of the fact that they used only the land which was covered by a stunted growth of birches and alders, and did not touch the valuable wood, for the simple reason that the soil on which grow pines and larches is not fit for crops.

This prohibition has had the curious effect in one district of introducing epic songs, where they had not been previously known. Agriculture is not favorable to the preservation of epic poetry, the singers coming almost entirely from the ranks of the tailors, shoemakers and net-makers. When, therefore, this community was forced to abandon agriculture, it took to making fine nets, — and to learning epic songs.

Two of the causes which have aided in the preservation of epic poetry in these remote districts, long after its disappearance from other parts of Russia, are liberty and loneliness. These people have never been subjected to the oppressions of serfdom, and have never lost the ideal of free power celebrated in the ancient rhapsodies. In these forest fastnesses they have never felt the influences of change, — conditions remain as in epic times. Even education has hardly left a trace. A man who can read and write is very rare.[1] Faith in antiquity and marvels is thus preserved. All the singers and most of their hearers believe implicitly in the *bylínas*, for when doubt enters, epic poetry dies. When Hilferding made the minstrels repeat slowly and with pauses, in order to enable him to write down their songs, they and the peasants present would interpolate remarks which showed their entire faith in the incidents narrated. If, as sometimes happened, a slight doubt was expressed as to whether a hero could wield a club of sixteen hundred pounds (forty *poods*), or annihilate forty thousand men with his own hand, the rhapsodists explained matters very simply: "People were not at all then as they are now."

The singing of the poems is not now a profession, as it was in ancient Greece, in Europe during the Middle Ages, and as it is in Little Russia at the present day, where the *Kobzárs* still exist. It has remained a domestic diversion for people whose voices and memories permit them to learn the old songs.

The singing of religious songs or *stíks* is of a professional character, however, and the *kalíky perekózhie*, or wandering-psalm-singers, mostly blind men or cripples, use it as a means of livelihood.

That there were professional minstrels in Russia in the Middle Ages, there can be no doubt. The Chronicles

---

[1] Out of seventy singers, Hilferding found only four or five who could read and write.

8   *INTRODUCTION.*

mention them at the Court of Saint Vladímir's grandson. The Church also denounced *skomoroki* (buffoons), fiddlers and players, and the singing of devilish (i.e. worldly) songs, before the Tatar conquest. If, as is probable, these "devilish songs" included the epic songs, we may assume that they were not originally composed for the common people, but were sung before the higher classes and the royal body-guard. The manner in which the exploits of the guard are magnified and those of the Prince belittled would seem to indicate that these songs were preëminently an entertainment for the body-guard. The minstrels also exercised their art before the Prince — if we can trust the evidence of the poems themselves.[1]

However this may be, the present minstrels all belong to the peasant class, and are nearly all well-to-do, as talent for practical affairs seems to accompany a taste for epic poetry. Many of them would accept nothing from Rýbnikof and Hilferding; and when the former offered a kerchief to the daughter of Ryabínin, one of the best singers, the minstrel at once presented an embroidered towel, saying that it was customary for friends to exchange gifts at parting. As an instance of the esteem in which *bylína* singing is regarded by the peasants, it is related of this Ryabínin, that his comrades would take turns in doing his share of the work on the fishing-boat, on condition that he should sing to them. The aged bard also, from whom many of the present generation learned their songs, was in the habit of saying when asked to sing: "Give me a *poltína* (half a ruble), and I will sing you a *bylína*." The half ruble

---

[1] See "Stavr Godínovich," and "Dobrýnya and Alyósha."

was always forthcoming; but he was a very fine singer and the only one who demanded any thing from his fellows.

So long as schools and trade do not penetrate to this secluded region, there is no danger of epic poetry dying out. Memory is the chief factor; creative power, which undoubtedly exists (though it is supposed to have become extinct after Peter the Great's day), does not come into play. As a man has received his song, so he sings it, with all the obsolete words, sometimes quite unintelligible. If asked the definitions of these words, he will answer simply, "it is always sung so," unless the words chance to be included in his provincial vocabulary. In this manner have been preserved details of nature on the Dniepr, — the "plume grass," the "open plain," the "aurochs" (now extinct), of which the North Russian peasant knows nothing whatever. Yet not a few local touches are introduced; — the mossy marshes and little lakes over which the hero gallops and picks his way, the fitting out of ships and the saddling of horses, all details dear and familiar to these lake-dwellers, are enlarged upon.

One of the most striking results of local influence is seen in the preservation of the *polyánitza*. This has become so foreign an idea in the rest of Russia, that when Rýbnikof's first volume was published even the savants did not know the meaning of the word. It was defined as a "bold fellow who gallops about seeking adventures;" and even Dahl in his great dictionary gives it as "a band of desperadoes or robbers." But any peasant in North-eastern Olónetz will explain that in ancient times heroic deeds were performed indifferently by men and women, the men being called *bogatýrs* and the women *polyánitzas*.

Fine or poor, all the rhapsodists preserve the distinct characters in their songs perfectly. Never once does Vladímir depart from the rôle assigned him, of a good-natured, but not always just, ruler; Dobrýnya is always courteous, Alyósha bold and cunning, Churílo foppish. Thus the story is always preserved intact. But in spite of the singers' assertions that they sing things exactly as they have learned them, two men who sing the same poem, which they have learned from the same person, will tinge it with their own distinct personalities to a marked degree. Thus, with some singers, the heroes are distinguished for their piety; other singers tone down the fiercest speeches in accordance with their own mild dispositions. Some render their songs inordinately long — two or three hours — by the multiplication of details and the repetition of whole passages, in true epic fashion. Yet with all these modifications, which render these ancient songs almost as much a living product of the nineteenth century as of the tenth, each song possesses as distinct a character as any of the epic lays which crystallized into a literary form in the Middle Ages and faded out of the memories of the people.

A regular tonic versification forms one indispensable property of these epic poems; irregularity of versification is a sign of decay, and a complete absence of measure the last stage of decay. The common measure of the *bylína* is trochaic with a dactylic ending, of five or six feet, which with characteristic elasticity can be lengthened to seven or contracted to four. A longer or shorter measure than these is an evidence of decay. The measure varies with the subject to some extent. For example, Ryabínin sang the lay of *Stavr* in trochaic

INTRODUCTION. 11

measure with a dactyl, *Mikáilo Rover* in pure trochaic, and *Volgá and Mikúla* in anapæsts.

The airs to which they are sung, or chanted, are very simple, consisting of but few tones, yet extremely difficult to note down. Each singer has an air of his own (perhaps two), to which he sings all the songs in his repertory, modifying it according to the subject and sentiment, with the greatest skill. Rýbnikof and Hilferding often dropped their pens and listened in amazement and admiration to the skill of these untutored minstrels.

It is interesting to trace the different stages of decay in an epic poem ending in the *skázka* (tale).

The epic poem has strictly defined characteristics; names historical or pseudo-historical are given to places and persons, the style is determined, the rhythm fixed within certain limits. A weakening of these characteristics makes of the epic a *pobyválchina* or *starína* (old tale); further deterioration brings it to the class of *kazácheskiya* (Cossáck songs); next comes the class of the *molodyétzkiya* (young men's songs), then the *bezimyániniya* (nameless songs), then the *skázka* or prose tale. At each step of this descending scale, it loses more and more of the definiteness of time and place as well as the names of the actors, until in the *skázka*, all definite rules of construction, all indications of distinct locality, vanish.

The epic songs proper are broadly divisible into three groups: the cycle of Vladímir or Kíef, that of Nóvgorod, and that of Moscow, preceded by three songs of the Elder Heroes. With regard to the first two, and the Kíef cycle in particular, authorities on the origin of Russian literature differ widely. One writer endeavors to prove that the Russians, while preserving the traditions common to all Aryan races in their Ceremonial Songs, entirely forgot the common Aryan stock of heroic legends. He assumes that these legends came back to them much later by appropriation from peoples of Turko-Mongolian race, who had become acquainted with epic traditions through Buddhism. This theory is analogous to that propounded by the distinguished Orientalist Benfey, with regard to European tales. According to this view, there is in Russian nothing but the crippled skeleton of foreign tales, to which have been added a few historical and geographical names and psychical traits furnished to various heroes by over-zealous students, who approached the subject with preconceived notions.

That the epic songs possess a family likeness to the heroic legends of other Aryan races, is not denied by any one; and this likeness is particularly strong in the case of the Rig-Veda, the Ramayana, the Edda and the Celtic epics. But about this *epic skeleton*, so to speak, a living body has grown up which is as characteristically national as any of those mentioned. The examples cited from Tatar and Mongolian sources by the author of the theory above referred to, are in most cases extremely far-fetched. His views have been combated by distinguished students of comparative mythology, and this wholesale appropriation from Eastern myths cannot be regarded as established. A comparison of these epic songs with the ancient Chronicles shows that the heroes are thoroughly Russian, and that the pictures of manners and customs which they present are valuable for their accuracy.

The point of departure for the mythologies of all

INTRODUCTION.   13

Aryan races must be sought in the phenomena of Nature. These were first personified as gods, and when each of these gods became divided into two or more individuals, according to their various attributes, these attributes, now entirely independent personages, were called the sons and grandsons of the gods. The localization of these Nature-myths began in heathen times. They were attached to various places, historical events and persons. With the introduction of Christianity this localization became more decided, and the ancient objects of worship were transformed, now into heroes, again into house demons or sorcerers, and fell under the ban as evil spirits or were merged with the new saints.

Prince Vladímir Svyatoslávich introduced Christianity into Russia in 988. It was not only established as the State religion, but the people, at Vladímir's command, accepted the new faith, permitted their idols to be destroyed and themselves to be baptized by thousands forthwith. Though they had idols representing the powers of Nature which they worshipped, there were neither temples nor priests to interfere with this summary change. But their old beliefs could not be so readily set aside, and finding themselves thus provided with two faiths, they solved the difficulty in the most natural manner, — by subjecting their heathen gods to baptism also. Thus, for instance, Perún the Thunderer became Ilyá (Elijah) the Prophet, the hero Ilyá of Múrom of the Songs. This furnishes the key to the cycle of Vladímir, and shows how the epithet "two-faithed," often applied to the Russian people by their old writers, was earned.

Side by side with the cycle of Vladímir and the heroes of Kíef, and sung by the same rhapsodists, flourishes the Nóvgorod cycle, with its Braves (*udaltzý*). Much more restricted than either the Kíef or the Moscow cycle, it consists practically of but two songs.

Nóvgorod was one of the greatest cities of the North, a Slavic Venice, long before the other Russian towns had emerged from obscurity. It had extensive commercial relations with Western Europe and the Orient, and of this feature of Nóvgorod the Great, *Sadkó the Merchant* is the epic representative. Of the perpetual war waged against the Chouds, Scandinavians and other tribes, no trace remains in the songs which survive; but the memory of the civil war which raged between the patricians and the common people, between the two quarters of the town separated by the Volkóf, is perpetuated in the song of *Vasíly Busláevich*.

This cycle is not so rich in the ancient poetry of the Elements as the Kíef cycle, and compared with that, it is far more definite, practical and closer to history.

In the two cycles already considered, the heroic epos, the historical fate of the people is reflected in its most salient features and essential spirit. — But there exist among the people epic songs which are more justly entitled to the general appellation bestowed upon all similar productions, *bylínas* — records of what has been. The actors in these songs are connected with well-defined epochs, with real events, and not only bear historic names like the heroes of the Kíef and Nóvgorod cycles, but frequently perform the feats assigned to them by history.

Epic marvels have not wholly disappeared from these songs of what is termed the Moscow or Imperial cycle, and at times heroic, supernatural feats are narrated, evidently copied from the earlier cycles. These Moscow songs are inferior in force, and approach in style the "Old" or "Nameless Songs." The pre-Tatar period is not represented, and the cycle proper begins with Iván the Terrible; and ends with the reign of Peter the Great, when the power of composing epic songs is supposed to have disappeared. Iván and Peter are the most prominent figures. As the period extending from the Kíef cycle to Iván is not rich in song, so likewise there is a great gap of a hundred years before Peter the Great, in which the songs are in no way remarkable, notwithstanding the many striking events which would seem to have afforded fitting subjects for the popular muse.

Fantastic as are some of the adventures in these songs, there is always a solid historical foundation. The same process which unites (Saint) Vladímir Svyatoslávich and Vladímir Monomáchus in one person, is pursued with Iván the Terrible. To this much-married Tzar are attributed many deeds of his grandfather Iván III. (his father being ignored), and other persons; and he is always represented in a rather favorable light. The conquest of Siberia, the taking of Kazán and Astrakhan, the wars against Poland, the Tatars of the Crimea, etc., are the principal points about which are grouped the songs referring to Iván's reign.

Richard James, Almoner to the English Embassy to Moscow in 1619, only fourteen years after the brief reign of the False Dmítry, noted down many of the songs which were already current upon that event, and another collection of contemporary lays was made by Kalaidóvich in 1688. These are the first instances of the Russian national songs being reduced to writing. Many of those noted by James are reprinted in P. V.

Kiryéevsky's great work in six volumes, which is very rich in songs of the Moscow cycle.

The epic Peter the Great bears but a faint resemblance to the historical Peter. His wars offered fine subjects for the singers, but they incorporated many a detail from the ancient myths of Dobrýnya the Dragon Slayer and Ilyá of Múrom in their songs about the battle of Poltáva.

The composition of epic poetry did not entirely cease until after the French invasion of 1812; though the songs of that epoch are much inferior to those of the ancient days, are utterly devoid of poetry, and merit attention only as curious mementos of the times. A more detailed account of the Moscow cycle is unnecessary, as it will not be represented in this volume. Its methods can be observed in the songs of the semi-mythical epoch, where they appear at their best. These poems are sung in the same regions as those of the first two cycles, and also to a greater extent than the latter in the central governments of Túla and Saratof.

In support of the theory that the poems of the Vladímir and Nóvgorod cycles were not original creations but derived from Turko-Mongolian sources, its advocates point to the fact that in the Government of Kíef and Southern Russia, where they should have originated if of Russian composition, none are now to be heard, while in Siberia and the governments of Archangel, Simbírsk, Perm, Olónetz (especially the latter), on the Don, and at the mouths of the Vólga, they abound. This, they claim, proves that the epic songs came from the wandering hordes of Siberia. A more simple and natural explanation of this phenomenon is furnished by the history of the Kíef region.

INTRODUCTION.   17

— The lays of Vladímir were composed in the x.,
xi., and xii. centuries. There are several reasons for
assigning them to this epoch. — They all represent
Russia as Christian, united under the rule of Vladímir,
and in constant (generally hostile) contact with the
Tatars. The action is almost exclusively confined to
Kíef or its environs, and among the other towns men-
tioned (all belonging to the Kíef epoch) Moscow is not
included. This confines them between the limits of
988 (when Christianity was introduced by Vladímir
Svyatoslávich) and 1147 when Moscow first appears in
the Chronicles, Yúry the son of Vladímir Monomáchus
having built the first houses on the present site of the
Kremlin. Most of the heroes are, moreover, mentioned
in the Chronicles, and none of them can have lived later
than the beginning of the xiii. century.

Further proof is furnished by the "Word of Ígors
Troop"[1] (*Slova o plkou Igorevye*), — Russia's famous
written epic poem and the only one which was com-
mitted to writing earlier than the xvii. century. — In
1185, Ígor, Prince of Nóvgorod-Syéversky, undertook
a campaign of retaliation against the Polovtzý, a no-
mad tribe of Turko-Finnish extraction living on the
shores of the Don. This poem which is founded on
that expedition bears internal evidence of having been
composed during the lifetime of the principal actors in
the drama. It is supposed to have been committed to
writing in the xiv. or xv. century. The unknown
author announces in the first lines, his intention of sing-

---

[1] The original manuscript discovered in 1795, was destroyed at the
burning of Moscow in 1812. A MS. copy preserved among the papers
of Catherine II., and the text printed from the original in 1800 alone
survive.

ing in the "present style"—the style of the *bylínas*—
"and not in that of Boyan," evidently a poet of repute
at that time. This shows that these songs were in
vogue as early as 1185. As the only epic poem which
has been transmitted to us in writing, the "Word"
is of the greatest value and interest, but it differs so
radically from the *bylínas* (in spite of the author's
intention) that it lies without the scope of the present
work.

The epic songs are the work of the people alone;
they present no traces of individual character, their
heroes are more mythical than historical. The "Word,"
on the other hand, is the work of a poet, who has
succeeded in coloring it strongly with his own personality; its heroes are simple men, with no trace of the
supernatural, the event chronicled is historical, and the
poem forms an organic whole. — In the songs layers of
poetry as well as of history are discernible, and it has
been suggested that a system of *poetical paleontology*
might be applied to them.

There seems thus to be sufficient ground for assuming that the songs of the Kíef cycle (and those of the
Elder Heroes) were already in existence when, in the
x. and xi. centuries, Vladímir and Yaroslávl were
founded, and the great movement of the South Russian population towards the North and the East began.
This movement continued to increase, particularly during the xii. century, when the seat of empire was
removed to Vladímir. It is easy to see how the songs
would be carried by this emigrating population from
the South to the points which became later the centre
of Great Russia; and how, still later, the development
of new needs and forms of life in the Russia of Mos-

cow, removed the Kíef songs to the borders of the country together with other relics of antiquity.

The devastation of Southern Russia by the Tatars in the XIII. century, and the decay of its civilization under the Lithuanian sway in the XIV. and XV., obliterated these poems from popular memory. When, in the XVI. century, the population of Southern Russia organized itself anew in the forms of the Cossáck communes, it fabricated for itself a fresh cycle of epic legends, which finally replaced those of Kíef. Thus, in Little Russia, where they originated, these epic songs are sung no longer, though a dim hint or a name may be found now and then in the Ceremonial Songs, and the *Kobzárs*[1] celebrate the deed of a new race of Cossáck heroes. But in the lonely wildernesses of the North-east, where circumstances have called forth no great or warlike deeds, the ancient paladins of Prince Vladímir's court have no rivals, and the emigrants have cherished the songs and legends which recall their fair Southern home of yore.

This progress of the epic poems ever further towards the North, recalls the famous migration of the Norse epos to Iceland, where it was committed to writing in the Middle Ages, affords a reasonable explanation of the present home of epic song, and renders the Siberian theory superfluous.

---

[1] Professional minstrels who accompany their songs on the *kobzá* or *bandúra,* a twelve-stringed instrument, resembling a mandolin in shape.

THE ELDER HEROES.

EPIC SONGS OF RUSSIA.

VOLGÁ VSESLÁVICH THE WIZARD.

THE red sun sank behind the lofty mountains, behind the broad sea, stars studded the clear heavens; then Volgá Vseslávich was born in Holy Mother Russia, the son of Márfa Vseslávievna and a Dragon.

Mother Earth trembled, the wild beasts fled to the forests, the birds flew up to the clouds, and the fish in the blue sea scattered. At an hour and a half old, Volgá spoke thus to his lady mother: "Swathe me not in cocoon-like bands, neither gird me about with silken bonds. But swathe me, mother mine, in strong steel mail; on my head set a helm of gold; in my right hand put a mace, a heavy mace of lead, in weight three hundred poods."[1]

In due course Lord Volgá learned all wisdom and all cunning, and divers tongues. When he

---

[1] A pood is about forty pounds.

attained to fifteen years[1] he collected a body-guard, bold and good — thirty heroes, save one; and he himself was the thirtieth. To them Lord Volgá spoke:

"Good and brave druzhína[2] mine! listen to your atamán.[3] Weave snares of silk, spread them on the damp earth, amid the dusky forest, and take martens, foxes, wild beasts and black sables for the space of three days and three nights."

His good body-guard hearkened to their elder brother, to their chief, and did the thing commanded: but no single beast could they take. Then Lord Volgá transformed himself into a lion, and trotted over the damp earth to the gloomy forest, headed off the martens, foxes, the wild beasts and black sables, the far-leaping hares and little ermines, capturing as many as he would.

Again, on a day, Lord Volgá was in Kíef town, with his nine and twenty heroes; and he said to them:

"Good my body-guard! twine now mighty cords. Make them fast to the topmost crests of the trees in the dark forest; and catch therewith geese, swans, clear falcons, and little birds of all the various sorts. And this ye shall do for the space of three days and nights."

---

[1] In some versions, *twelve* years, the epic age of martial maturity.

[2] From *drug*, a friend; a body-guard where all were like brothers. See Appendix: *Volgá Vseslávich.*

[3] Hetman, Cossack chief.

And when they did so, and caught nothing, Lord Volgá turned himself into an ostrich-bird, and turned all back, geese, swans, clear falcons and lesser birds.

Again he ordered his good body-guard to take axes of stout metal, and build oaken vessels, and to knot silken nets, wherewith to take salmon, dolphins, pikes, flat fish and precious sturgeons, for three days and as many nights. And when they could not, he transformed himself into a pike, and drove all the fishes back.

And being again in Kíef town, with his body-guard, Lord Volgá spoke: "Brave and good druzhína mine! Whom shall we send to the Turkish land, to learn the Tzar's mind,—what the Tzar thinketh, whether he meaneth to come against Holy Russia? If we send an old man, there will be long to wait; if a young one, he will sport with the maidens, he will divert himself with the young damsels, and hold converse with the old crones, and so also we shall have long to wait. Plain is it then that Volgá himself must go."

Then Volgá became a little bird, and flew above the earth, and came speedily to the Turkish land. There he alighted over against the Tzar's little window, and listened to the secret talk between the Tzar and his Tzarítza.

"Aï, my Tzarítza Pantálovna! I know what I know. In Russia the grass groweth not as of yore, the flowers bloom not as of old; plainly, Volgá is no longer among the living."

To this the Tzarítza Pantálovna made answer:

"And thou my Tzar, thou Turkish Sántal! the grass still groweth as of yore in Russia, and the flowers blossom as was their wont. Last night and in my dreams I saw a little titmouse fly from the East, and from the West a black raven. They flew against each other in the open plain, and fought. The little bird tore the black raven asunder, and plucked out his feathers, and scattered all to the winds."

Then Tzar Sántal the Turk made answer: "I am minded to march against Holy Russia shortly. Nine cities will I take and bestow upon my nine sons, and for myself I will fetch a rich furred cloak."

"Thou shalt never take nine cities," quoth Pantálovna, "for thy nine sons, nor shalt thou fetch for thyself a rich furred cloak."

"Thou old devil!" spake Tzar Sántal the Turk, "thou hast but slept and dreamed."

Therewith he smote her upon her white face, and, turning, smote the other cheek, and flung the Tzarítza upon the floor of brick; and yet a second time he flung her.

"Nay, but I shall go to Holy Russia!" quoth he, "and I shall take nine cities for my nine sons, and a rich furred cloak for my own wearing."

Then Lord Volgá Vseslávich transformed himself to a little ermine, crept into the armory, turned back into a goodly youth, snapped the stout bows, broke the silken cords, all the fiery arrows, and the locks upon the weapons, and drenched all the powder in the casks. Again Lord Volgá turned himself into a gray wolf, and galloped to the stable, and tore open the throats of all the good steeds therein. When that was done, Lord Volgá flew back to Kíef town, to his good body-guard, in the form of a little bird.

"Let us go now, my bold, good guards, to the Turkish land," he said.

So they rode thither, and took all the Turkish host captive.

"Let us now divide the prisoners," quoth Lord Volgá. What lot was dear, and what was cheap? Sharp swords were rated at five rubles, weapons of damascened steel at six rubles: — and but one lot was exceeding cheap — the women. Old women were valued at a quarter of a kopék, young women at half a kopék, and beauties at a copper farthing.

VOLGÁ AND MIKÚLA SELYANÍNOVICH THE VILLAGER'S SON.[1]

COURTEOUS Prince Vladímir, of royal Kíef town, gave to his beloved nephew Volgá, three cities, Kurtzóvetz, Oryekóvetz, and a third, Krestyánovetz. For Volgá had traversed many lands, many hordes; he had collected gifts in tribute from all Tzars and kings, and had brought them to glorious Kíef town, to his uncle, Prince Vladímir. Much gold had he collected and silver and great pearls, and yet more of Arabian bronze, which darkeneth never, nor corrodeth, and is more precious than gold or pearls or silver.

Now, in those three glorious cities given him by his uncle Vladímir, dwelt stiff-necked people, who obeyed no man, neither gave gifts nor tribute to any. Then young Volgá Vseslávich assembled his good body-guard, and set out to take possession of his towns. — As they rode over the open plain, Volgá heard a husbandman ploughing. The plough screamed, the share grated against the stones. Volgá rode in quest of the husbandman. A whole day he rode until evening, and heard the plough

---

[1] See Appendix for mythological signification, etc.

grate ever through the plain; but dark night o'ertook him on the way, and he found not the man. A second day he rode toward that husbandman until dusk, and yet a third; and on the third day he came upon the man driving his plough, and casting the clods of earth from side to side of the furrow. The husbandman ploughed up damp oaks, stumps and great stones; and his nightingale mare was named " Raise-her-head;" for she could lift it to the clouds. His plough was of maplewood, his reins of silk, the share of damascened steel with fittings of silver, and the handles of pure gold. His curls waved over his brows of blackest sable, his eyes were falcon clear; his shoes were of green morocco with pointed toes; and under the hollow of his foot, sparrows might fly. His hat was downy, and his caftan was of black velvet.

Lord Volgá spoke these words: " God aid thee, husbandman, in thy ploughing and tilling!"

" Art thou come, Volgá Vseslávich, with thy troop?" answered the husbandman. " Ridest thou far, Volgá? Whither leadeth thy course, with thy good guard?"

" I go to take possession of three towns which courteous Prince Vladímir, my uncle, hath given to me. Kurtzovétz, Oryékovetz, and Krestyánovetz."

" Ho, Volgá Vseslávich! Robbers dwell there. Two days ago I was in that town, bearing two sacks of salt, of a hundred poods each, upon my nightingale mare, and they demanded toll; and for all I gave them they would still have more. Then I began to thrust them back by thousands; he who was standing is now sitting, he who was sitting now lieth, and he who then lay will stand no more forever.[1]"

Then spoke Volgá: "Husbandman! come thou with me as my comrade."

The husbandman at that, loosed the silken reins, turned his mare from the plough and mounted the good steed, and they rode forth.

But the husbandman soon paused in thought.

"Ho, there, Volgá!" quoth he; "I have left my plough in the furrow. Command now thy men to turn it from the furrow, scrape the soil from the share, and cast it into a willow bush, that robbers find it not, — that none discover it save those to whom it will yield service, — my brother peasants."

So Volgá despatched five of his mighty youths, and they twisted the handles all about, but could not draw that plough of maple-wood from the furrow.

Then Volgá sent thither ten men, and again his whole body-guard; but the strength of them all

---

[1] Something resembling this occurs in *Doon de Mayence*. Doon, who has been reared far from men, does not even know the meaning of money, and when the ferryman demands toll, he pays his way with blows.

was not enough to loose the share, shake off the earth and toss it into the willow bush.

Then the husbandman rode up on his nightingale mare, grasped the plough of maple-wood with one hand, shook the soil from the share, tossed it to the clouds, saying:

"Farewell my plough! Never more shall I till with thee."

Then they mounted their good steeds and rode, and came to the famous town of Kurtzovétz, to Oryékovetz, and to the little burgh of Krestyánovetz.

Thereupon the common folk assembled in throngs and gave them great battle. And those peasants were very cunning rogues. They reared a treacherous bridge. But the youthful heroes were yet more cunning, and first sent forward their great force upon that bridge of staffwood. Then the bridge broke, and all that host fell into the little river, and began to drown and to be in sorry plight. Volgá and the husbandman urged their good steeds across that little stream, the Volkof, and the brave chargers leaped it. Then they began to do honor to the peasants, to give them due guerdon and to lash them with their whips. And when they had chastised these peasants at their good pleasure, they rode back whence they came.

And the peasants began to be submissive from that hour, and to pay their just tribute.

The husbandman rode in front, and Volgá essayed to overtake him; yet spur on as he would, he could barely keep in sight. Raise-her-head's tail spread far abroad, her mane waved in the breeze, and she went at a walk; but Volgá's horse galloped at full speed. Raise-her-head paced, and Volgá's steed was left far behind. Then Volgá waved his cap and shouted. When the husbandman perceived it, he restrained his nightingale mare, the while Volgá spoke thus:

"Halt, thou husbandman! If that mare were but a stallion, I would give for her five hundred rubles."

"Thou art but foolish, Volgá," the husbandman made answer: "I bought this mare as a foal from her mother's side for five hundred rubles; and were she a stallion she would be priceless."

"By what name art thou called, husbandman, and what is thy patronymic?" asked Volgá.

"Now ho, thou Volgá Vseslávich!" the husbandman made answer; "I will plough for rye and stack it in ricks, I will draw it home and thresh it, brew beer and give the peasants to drink: — and the peasants shall call me Young Mikúla Selyanínovich, the Villager's Son."

HERO SVYATOGÓR.[1]

HERO SVYATOGÓR saddled his good steed, and made ready to ride afield. As he traversed the open plain, he found none with whom to measure the strength which flowed so fiercely through his veins. Weighed down with might, as with a heavy burden, he spoke:

"Would there were a ring fixed in the heavens — I would drag them down! If there were but a pillar firm set in damp mother earth, and a ring made fast thereto, I would raise the whole earth and twist it round!"

And as he went his way over the wide steppe, he was aware of a traveller there, and rode after him, but could by no means overtake him. He rode at a trot, and the wayfarer was ever before him; — at full gallop, and the man still went on before. Then cried the hero:

"Ho there, thou wayfarer! pause a little, for I cannot overtake thee on my good steed."

So the wayfarer halted, took a small pair of pouches from his shoulder and cast them on the damp earth.

---

[1] See Appendix: *Svyatogór.*

"What hast thou in thy pouches?" said Svyatogór.

"Lift them from the earth, and thou shalt see," quoth the man.

Then Svyatogór sprang from his good steed, and seized the pouches with one hand, — and could not raise them. Then he essayed both hands; — a breath alone could pass beneath, but the hero was sunk to his knees in the earth, and blood, not tears, streamed down his white face.

"What lieth in thy wallet?" said Svyatogór then. "Lo! my strength hath not begun to fail me, yet I cannot lift this weight."

"The whole weight of the earth lieth therein," the man made answer.

"And who art thou? What art thou called, and what is thy patronymic?"

"I am Mikúlushka [1] Selyanínovich, the Villager's Son."

"Tell me then, Mikúlushka, inform me, how I may know the fate decreed by God?"

"Ride on the straight way, until thou come to the fork of the road. At the parting of the way, turn to thy left hand, send thy horse at full speed, and thou shalt come to the Northern Mountains. In those mountains, beneath a great tree, standeth a smithy; and of the smith therein do thou inquire thy fate."

---

[1] *Ushka* is the diminutive termination.

Then Svyatogór rode three days as he had been commanded, and so came to the great tree and the smithy, where stood the smith forging two fine hairs.

Quoth the hero: "What forgest thou, smith?" The smith made answer: "I forge the fates of those that shall wed."

"And whom shall I wed?"

"Thy bride is in the kingdom by the sea, in the royal city; thirty years hath she lain on the dung-heap."

Then the hero stood and thought: "Nay: but I will go to that kingdom by the sea, and will slay my bride."

So he went to the royal city of that kingdom by the sea, and came to a miserable hut and entered. No one was there save a maiden lying on the dung-heap; and her body was like the bark of fir-trees. Svyatogór drew forth five hundred rubles, and laid them on the table, and with his sharp sword, he smote her on her white breast. Then he departed from that kingdom, and the maiden woke and gazed about her. The fir-bark fell from her limbs, and she became a beauty such as was never seen in all the world nor heard of in the white world.

On the table lay the five hundred rubles, and with this money she began to trade. When she had accumulated untold treasure of gold, she built dark red ships, freighted them with precious wares and sailed forth upon the glorious blue sea. And when she was come to the great city, to the Holy Mountains, and began to barter her precious wares, the fame of her beauty spread through all the town and kingdom, and all men came to look upon her and marvel at her fairness. Hero Svyatogór came also to gaze upon her beauty — and loved her, and began to woo her for himself.

After they were married, he perceived a scar upon his wife's white bosom, and inquired of her: "What scar is that?"

And his wife made answer: "An unknown man came to our kingdom by the sea, and left five hundred rubles of gold in our hut. When I awoke, there was a scar upon my bosom, and the fir-bark had fallen away from my white body. For before that day, I had lain for thirty years upon the dung-heap."

Then Svyatogór the hero knew that none may escape his fate, nor may any flee upon his good steed from the judgment of God.

THE CYCLE OF VLADÍMIR, OR OF KÍEF.

ILYÁ OF MÚROM THE PEASANT HERO, AND HERO SVYATOGÓR.

IN the hamlet of Karachárof, by Múrom town, dwelt Ilyá[1] the old Cossáck. Thirty years he sat upon the oven, having neither arms nor legs, because of his grandfather's sin.

And when thirty years were past, in summer, at the time of haying, his father and mother went forth to clear the forest-girdled meadows, and left Ilyá alone in the cottage. Then there came to him three wayfarers — Christ and two of his apostles, in the guise of poor brethren, strolling psalm-singers, and besought him that he would give them to drink.

"Alas! ye wayfarers, aged men, dear friends!" said Ilyá; "full gladly would I give you to drink: but I cannot rise, and there is none in the cottage with me."

And the men made answer: "Arise, and wash thyself; so shalt thou walk and fetch us drink."

Then he arose and walked; and having filled a cup with kvas,[2] brought it to the aged men.

---

[1] For historical and mythological points, see Appendix: *Ilyá of Múrom*.

[2] A sourish liquor made from rye-meal.

They received it, drank, and gave it again to Ilyá, saying:

"Drink now after us, Ilyá, son of Iván." When he had drunk, the old men said: "How is thy strength now, Ilyá?"

Ilyá answered: "I thank you humbly, ye aged men. I feel a very great strength within me, so that I could even move the earth."

Then the men looked each upon the other, and said: "Give us to drink yet again." And Ilyá did so. And when they had drunk, they gave the cup to him the second time, and inquired: "How is it with thee now, Ilyá?"

"The strength I feel is very great," said Ilyá, "yet but as half the former strength."

"Thus let it be," spoke the men: "for if we give thee more, mother earth will not bear thee up." And they said: "Go forth now, Ilyá."

So Ilyá set his cup upon the table, and went forth into the street with all ease; and the aged men said:

"God hath blessed thee, Ilyá, with this strength of His. Therefore, defend thou the Christian faith, fight against all infidel hosts, bold warriors and daring heroes, for it is written that death shall not come to thee in battle. Stronger than thee there is none in the white world, save only Volgá, (and he will take thee not by might but by craft), and Svyatogór, and, stronger yet, beloved of damp mother earth, Mikúla Selyanínovich, the Villager's Son. Against these three contend thou not. Live not at home, — labor not; but go thou to royal Kíef town." And therewith the men vanished.

Then Ilyá went forth to his father, in the clearing, and found him with his wife and laborers reposing from their toil. He grasped their axes and began to hew; and what his father with the laborers could not have done in three days, that Ilyá achieved in the space of one hour. Having thus felled a whole field of timber, he drove the axes deep into a stump, whence no man could draw them.

When his father with wife and laborers woke, and beheld the axes, they marvelled, saying: "Who hath done this?" Then came Ilyá from the forest, and drew the axes from the stump; and his father gave thanks to God that his son should be so famous a workman.

But Ilyá strode far over the open plain; and as he went, he beheld a peasant leading a shaggy brown foal, the first he had seen. What the peasant demanded for the foal, that Ilyá paid. — For the space of three months, he tied the foal in the stall, feeding it with the finest white Turkish wheat, and watering it from the pure spring. After these months were past, he bound the foal for three nights in the garden, anointing it with three dews. When that was done, he led the foal to the lofty paling, and the good brown began to leap from side to side, and was able to sustain Ilyá's vast weight; for he had become a heroic steed. — All this Ilyá did according to the commands of the aged psalm-singers who had healed him.

Then Ilyá saddled his good steed Cloudfall, prostrated himself, and received the farewell blessing of father and mother, and rode forth far over the open plain.

As he rode, he came to a pavilion of white linen, pitched under a damp oak; and therein was a heroic bed, not small, for the length of the bed was ten fathoms, and the breadth six fathoms. So he bound his good steed to the damp oak, stretched himself upon that heroic bed and fell asleep. And his heroic slumber was very deep; three days and nights he slept. On the third day, good Cloudfall heard a mighty clamor toward the North. — Damp mother earth rocked, the dark forests staggered, the rivers overflowed their steep banks. Then the good steed beat upon the earth with his hoof, but could not wake Ilyá, and he shouted with human voice:

"Ho there, Ilyá of Múrom! Thou sleepest there and takest thine ease, and knowest not the ill fortune that hangeth over thee. Hero Svyatogór cometh to this his pavilion. Loose me now, in the open plain, and climb thou upon the damp oak."

EPIC SONGS OF RUSSIA.

Then sprang Ilyá to his nimble feet, loosed his horse and climbed into the damp oak.

And lo! a hero approached; taller than the standing woods was he, and his head rested upon the flying clouds. Upon his shoulder he bare a casket of crystal, which, when he was come to the oak, he set upon the ground and opened with a golden key. Out of it stepped his heroic wife; in all the white world, no such beauty was ever seen or heard of; lofty was her stature and dainty her walk; her eyes were as those of the clear falcon, her brows of blackest sable, and her white body was beyond compare.

When she was come forth from the crystal casket, she placed a table, laid a fair cloth thereon and set sugar viands; and from the casket, she also drew forth mead for drink. So they feasted and made merry. And when Svyatogór had well eaten, he went into the pavilion and fell asleep.

But his fair heroic wife roamed about the open plain, and so walking, espied Ilyá upon the damp oak.

"Come down now, thou good and stately youth," she cried: "descend from that damp oak, else will I waken Hero Svyatogór and make great complaint of thy discourtesy to me."

Ilyá could not contend against the woman, and so slipped down from the oak as she had commanded.

And after a space, that fair heroic woman took

Ilyá and put him in her husband's deep pocket, and roused the hero from his heavy sleep. Then Svyatogór put his wife in the crystal casket again, locked it with his golden key, mounted his good steed, and rode his way to the Holy Mountains.

After a little, his good steed began to stumble, and the hero to beat him upon his stout flanks with a silken whip. Then said the horse in human speech:

"Hitherto I have borne the hero and his heroic wife; but now I bear the heroic woman and two heroes. Is it a marvel that I stumble?"

Thereupon Hero Svyatogór drew Ilyá from his deep pocket, and began to question him: — who he was and how he came in the pocket. And Ilyá told him all the truth. When he heard it, Svyatogór slew his faithless heroic wife; but with Ilyá he exchanged crosses, and called him his younger brother.

And as they talked together, Ilyá said: "Full gladly would I see Svyatogór that great hero; but he rideth not now upon damp mother earth, nor appeareth among our company of heroes."

"I am he," quoth Svyatogór. "Gladly would I ride among you, but damp mother earth would not bear me up. And furthermore, I may not ride in Holy Russia, but only on the lofty hills, and steep precipices. Let us now ride among the crags, and come thou to the Holy Mountains with me."

Thus they rode long together, diverting themselves; and Svyatogór taught Ilyá all heroic customs and traditions.

On the way, Svyatogór said to Ilyá: "When we shall come to my dwelling, and I shall lead thee to my father, heat a bit of iron, but give him not thy hand."

So when they were come to the Holy Mountains, to the palace of white stone, Svyatogór's aged father cried:

"Aï, my dear child! Hast thou been far afield?"

"I have been in Holy Russia, father."

"What hast thou seen and heard there?"

"Nothing have I seen or heard in Holy Russia, but I have brought with me thence a hero." The old man was blind, and so said:

"Bring hither the Russian hero, that I may greet him."

In the mean while, Ilyá had heated the bit of iron, and when he came to give the old man his hand in greeting, he gave him in place of it, the iron. And when the old man grasped it in his mighty hands, he said: "Stout are thy hands, Ilyá! A most mighty warrior art thou!"

Thereafter, as Svyatogór and his younger brother Ilyá journeyed among the Holy Mountains, they found a great coffin in the way; and upon the coffin was this writing: "This coffin shall fit him who is destined to lie in it."

Then Ilyá essayed to lie in it, but for him it was both too long and too wide. But when Svyatogór lay in it, it fitted him. Then the hero spoke these words:

"The coffin was destined for me; take the lid now, Ilyá, and cover me." Ilyá made answer: "I will not take the lid, elder brother, neither will I cover thee. Lo! this is no small jest that thou makest, preparing to entomb thyself."

Then the hero himself took the lid, and covered his coffin with it. But when he would have raised it again, he could not, though he strove and strained mightily; and he spoke to Ilyá: "Aï, younger brother! 'Tis plain my fate hath sought me out. I cannot raise the lid; do thou try now to lift it."

Then Ilyá strove, but could not. Said Hero Svyatogór: "Take my great battle sword, and smite athwart the lid." But Ilyá's strength was not enough to lift the sword, and Svyatogór called him:

"Bend down to the rift in the coffin, that I may breathe upon thee with my heroic breath." When Ilyá had done this, he felt strength within him, thrice as much as before, lifted the great battle sword, and smote athwart the lid. Sparks flashed from that blow, but where the great brand struck, an iron ridge sprang forth. Again spoke Svyatogór:

"I stifle, younger brother! essay yet one more

blow upon the lid, with my huge sword." Then Ilyá smote along the lid — and a ridge of iron sprang forth. Yet again spoke Svyatogór:

"I die, oh, younger brother! Bend down now to the crevice. Yet once again will I breathe upon thee, and give thee all my vast strength."

But Ilyá made answer: "My strength sufficeth me, elder brother; had I more, the earth could not bear me."

"Thou hast done well, younger brother," said Svyatogór, "in that thou hast not obeyed my last behest. I should have breathed upon thee the breath of death, and thou wouldst have lain dead beside me. But now, farewell. Possess thou my great battle sword, but bind my good heroic steed to my coffin; none save Svyatogór may possess that horse."

Then a dying breath fluttered though the crevice. Ilyá took leave of Hero Svyatogór, bound the good heroic steed to the coffin, girt the great battle sword about his waist, and rode forth into the open plain.

And Svyatogór's burning tears flow through the coffin evermore.

QUIET DÚNAÏ IVANOVICH.

QUIET[1] Dúnaï Ivánovich roamed long from land to land, and in his wanderings, came at length to the kingdom of Lithuania. Three years did Dúnaï serve the King of that land as Equerry, three years as Grand Steward, three as Lord High Seneschal, and yet three more as Groom of the Chambers.

The King loved the youth and gave him meet guerdon; and the young Princess Nastásya favored him and kept him in her heart.

On a certain day, the King made a great feast and banquet; and the Princess would have kept the youth from it. "Go not to this worshipful feast, Dúnaï," she said. "There will be much eating and drunkenness, and thou wilt boast of me, the fair maid. And so shalt thou lose thy head, Dúnaï."

But Dúnaï heeded not her warning and went to the feast. When all were well drunken, and the feast waxed merry, they began to brag.[2] And

---

[1] Dunaï signifies not only the Danube, but any river, and *quiet* or *peaceful* is always the accompanying adjective. See Appendix.

[2] Bragging was very popular — in ancient times, and is often met with in ballads of Northern lands. A very amusing set of brags or gabs, occurs in the *chanson de geste* "Charlemagne's Journey to Jerusalem."

Dúnaï spoke much, boasting of his many wanderings, of the King's favor and rewards, and of how the young Princess Nastásya kept him ever in her heart.

The King liked not this brag, and cried in a loud voice: "Ho there, ye pitiless headsmen! Seize this quiet Dúnaï by the white hands, by his golden ring; lead him into the open plain, and cut off his turbulent head."

Then Dúnaï besought his keepers to lead him past Nastásya's dwelling, and before he was come to it, he cried softly:

"Sleepest thou, Nastásya? Wakest thou not? Lo, they are leading Dúnaï to the open plain." And when he was over against her window he shouted at the top of his voice:

"Sleepest thou, Nastásya? Wakest thou not? Dúnaï goeth to his death. Forgive!"

With that great shout the palace quaked; Princess Nastásya woke, and ran forth into the spacious court of the palace, in a loose robe without a girdle, and cried in piercing tones:

"Ho there, ye pitiless headsmen! Take treasure as much as ye will, and release Dúnaï in the open plain. Then go seek in the royal pot-house[1] an accursed Tatar, some vile wretch whom ye may

---

[1] *Kabák*. An interpolation of the 16th century. The pot-houses were called *royal* or *imperial* because, until recently, the crown derived its revenue from them.

render drunk with wine. Cut off his turbulent head, and bear it to the King in place of Dúnaï's."

The headsmen hearkened to the Princess's words, released Dúnaï, and bore the drunkard's head to the King of Lithuania.

But Dúnaï traversed the open plain and came to Kíef town. There he entered the royal pothouse, and drank away his hat from Grecian land, all his flowered garments, his shoes of morocco, and all that he had.

And as Dúnaï sat thus over his horns of liquor, it chanced on a day, that courteous Prince Vladímir[1] made a great and honorable feast, to many princes, boyárs (nobles) and mighty Russian heroes, where they sat eating bread and salt, carving the white swan, and quaffing sweet mead, and green wine.

The long day drew towards its close, the red sun sank to even, and all was merry at the feast when the guests began their brags. One vaunted his good steed and one his youthful prowess, this knight his sharp sword and that his deeds of might; the wise man praised his aged father or mother, the foolish his young wife or sister.

Then through the banquet hall paced Fair Sun Prince Vladímir, wrung his white hands and shook his yellow curls. No golden trumpet pealed, nor

---

[1] See Appendix for Vladímir in his historical and mythological aspects.

silver pipe trilled sweet, but Prince Vladímir spoke: "Boast not, brothers; glory not in your prowess nor in good steeds nor golden treasure. Have not I also red gold, pure silver, fair round pearls? But in this may ye glory: All at my feast are wedded, save one, your Prince. I only am unwed. Know ye not of some Princess, who is my equal? Lofty of stature must she be, of perfect form, her gait delicate and graceful, like the peacock; a faint flush in her face like to a white hare, and eyes of the clear falcon must she have, yellow hair, brows of blackest sable, and swan-speech entrancing. So shall I have one with whom I may think my thoughts, and take counsel, and ye my mighty princes, heroes and all Kíef one to whom ye may pay homage."

Then all at meat fell sad and silent, and none spoke a word. The great fled behind the lesser, the lesser hid behind the small, and from the small came no reply.

At length there stepped forth from behind the oven, a bold, brave youth, Dobrýnya Nikítich, saying:

"Our liege, Prince Vladímir! grant me to speak a word without speedy death or distant exile, and chastise me not therefor."

"Speak, then, Dobrýnya Nikítich," said Vladímir, "God will forgive thee."

Then spoke Dobrýnya, and wavered not: "I

know a fitting mate for thee, a princess, and all thou hast described is she — a beauty such as exists not elsewhere in all the white world. I have not seen her, but her fame I have heard from my brother in arms, my cross-brother, mighty Dúnaï Ivánovich. He sitteth now in the great royal pot-house over his horns, and hath not the wherewithal to come to thy honorable feast."

Then spoke Vladímir: "Take my golden keys, open my iron bound chests, take treasure as thou requirest, and go, Dobrýnya, to the royal pot-house, ransom Dúnaï's raiment, and conduct Dúnaï to our honorable feast."

So Dobrýnya took gold, and went to the pot-house. "Ho there, ye innkeepers and usurers!" he cried, "take what ye will, and restore Dúnaï's garments."

When this was done, Dobrýnya told Dúnaï how he was bidden to Vladímir's feast; and Dúnaï made answer: "Lo! with drunkenness and hunger my turbulent head is broken."

So they poured him a cup of green wine, in weight a pood and a half.[1] This Dúnaï grasped in one hand and drained at one draught. Then the good youths set out; and as they passed through Kíef, maids and wives thrust heads and shoulders

---

[1] Sixty pounds. The vessels of liquor drunk by the heroes are rain-bearing clouds.

from the windows crying: "Whence come such fair youths as these?"

When they came to the palace of white stone, to the fair banquet hall, Dúnaï crossed himself as prescribed, did reverence as enjoined, on two, three, and four sides, to all the Russian heroes and to Prince Vladímir in particular. And they gave Dúnaï a seat at the oaken board, in the great corner,[1] the place of honor.

As he feasted, Fair Sun Vladímir began to inquire of Dúnaï, and poured out green wine into a great cup of crystal from the East, set in a rim of gilt, and brought it to quiet Dúnaï. The measure of that cup was a bucket and a half, and its weight a pood and a half. Quiet Dúnaï took the cup in one hand, and quaffed it at a breath. Then Fair Sun Vladímir poured an aurochs' horn of sweet mead, a pood and a half, and after that a measure of the beer of drunkenness. These also quiet Dúnaï drained at one draught, and intoxication showed itself in his head. Nevertheless he stepped forward without staggering, and spoke without confusion:

"I know a bride fit to mate with thee, royal Vladímir. Twelve full years I served in yonder

---

[1] The corner is the place of honor in the East; the most illustrious tombs stand in the corners of the churches, and at the Coronation banquet, the Emperor dines alone in one corner of the ancient *térem* (palace) known as the gold room. The kings of France sat in the left-hand corner of the apartment to hold their *beds of Justice*.

land of Lithuania, and the King's Majesty hath two great and fair daughters. The eldest, Princess Nastásya, is no mate for thee; she rideth ever over the open plain seeking adventures. But the younger, the Princess Apráxia, sitteth at home in a fair chamber embroidering a kerchief in red gold. Behind thrice nine locks she sitteth, and thrice nine guards, in a lofty castle, that the fair red sun may not scorch her nor the fine and frequent rains drop on her, nor the stormy winds breathe on her; — that she may be seen of few."

"Aï, my Russian heroes!" spoke Prince Vladímir then: "Whom shall we send to far-off Lithuania?"

And a hero made answer: "Fair Sun Vladímir! we have not been in strange and distant countries, nor seen strange people. It is not meet that we should go. Send quiet Dúnaï Ivánovich; he hath served as ambassador, and viewed many lands. He talketh much; therefore send him to do thy wooing."

Then spake Prince Vladímir: "Go thou, my Dúnaiushka, to that brave Lithuanian realm, and woo the Princess Apráxia for me with fair words."

"Lord," said Dúnaï, "it is not meet for a youth to go alone."

"Take then a host of forty thousand, and treasure, as much as thou requirest: and if the King give not his daughter willingly, then fetch her by force."

"I need no host to wage battle, nor golden treasure to barter," quoth Dúnaï. "I will essay heroic force and royal threat. Grant me but my beloved comrade, Dobrýnya Nikítich, — he is of good birth, and understandeth how to deal with people. And give us two good colts which have never borne saddle or bridle. And write thou a scroll, that our wooing of the Princess Apráxia for our Prince Vladímir is honorable."

All these things Fair Sun Vladímir did. Then Dúnaï and Dobrýnya went forth from the palace, and saddled their steeds; put on them plaited bridles of parti-colored silks, and silken saddle-cloths, and upon these, felts, and then the saddles, their small Cherkessian saddles, and secured them with twelve girths with silver buckles, — the stirrup buckles were of gold. Then they arrayed and armed themselves; put on their little caps from the Sorochínsky land,[1] forty poods in weight, took their maces of damascened steel, their stout bows, their silken whips, mounted their good steeds and rode through the narrow lanes of Kíef. And the good steeds galloped at will.

But when they reached the highway out of Kíef, they urged their good steeds on, spurring their brisk flanks, and smiting them with their braided whips of silk. Past deep lakes they rode, through forests dreaming still in primeval denseness; and

---

[1] Saracen land.

so came to the brave land of Lithuania, and to the royal palace.

There quiet Dúnaï asked no leave of gate-keepers nor porters, but flung wide the barriers and led the horses into the spacious court, bidding Dobrýnya stand there and guard them. So Dobrýnya took the bridles in his left hand, and in his right, his little elm-wood club from Sorochínsky.

"Stand thou here, Dobrýnya," spake quiet Dúnaï then, "and look towards the royal audience hall; when I shout, then will be the time to come."

Then quiet Dúnaï entered the royal hall where sat the King, crossing himself and saluting as prescribed by custom.

"Hail, little father, King of brave Lithuania!"

"Hail, little Dúnaï Ivánovich! Whither leadeth thy path? Art thou come to show thyself or to view us? Twelve years thou didst serve us faithfully; art thou now come to fight against us, or to serve us as of yore? — Yet eat thy fill, fair youth, and drink as good seemeth to thee." Then the King seated him at the great table in the place of honor, giving him sweet viands and mead, and began again to inquire his errand.

"My errand is good," Dúnaï made answer. "I come to woo thy daughter Apráxia for the Fair Sun, Prince Vladímir." Then he laid the scroll on the oaken table.

The King looking upon it, tore the black curls

from his head and cast them on the brick floor, as he spoke in wrath :

"Stupid in sooth is Vladímir of Royal Kíef, in that he sent not as wooer a wealthy peasant, a good lord or a mighty hero! But he must needs send me some noble's serf! Ho there, my trusty servants! Take this Dúnaï by his white hands, seize him by his golden ring, by his yellow curls; lead him to the deep dungeons for his discourteous speech. Shut him in with oaken planks, with iron gratings, and above sprinkle orange-tawny sand. Let his food be water and oats alone, until he shall bethink himself and gain his senses."

Quiet Dúnaï hung his turbulent head, and dropped his clear eyes to the floor; then raised his small white hand and smote the table with his fist. The fair liquors all were spilled, the dishes rolled away, the tables fell together, and the railed balconies of the palace sat awry. The Tatars all were terrified, the King fled to his lofty tower, and covered himself with his cloak of marten skins.

Then quiet Dúnaï leaped over the golden chair (for he perceived that the matter was not a light one), seized one Tatar by his heels, and began to slay the rest.

"This Tatar is tough," he cried; "he will not break; the Tatar is wiry, he will not tear."

Dobrýnya at that shout, began to lay about him,

and slew five hundred Tatars with his own right hand.

Then the King's trusty servants fled to him from his princely court: "Aï, little father, King of brave Lithuania! Thou knowest not the evil that is come upon thee. Into thy royal court no falcon clear hath flown, no raven black hath fluttered, but a bold and goodly youth hath ridden. In his left hand he graspeth the silken bridles of two good steeds, in his right he holdeth a club of elm-wood filled with lead. Wheresoever he waveth that club, the Tatars fall before it. He hath slain them all, to the last man, and none is left to continue the race!"

Then the King of Lithuania cried: "Aï, quiet little Dúnaï Ivánovich! Forget not my hospitality of yore! Sit thou at one table with me, and let us consider this wooing of Prince Vladímir. Take my elder daughter."

"I will not," said quiet Dúnaï, and ceased not to slay.

"Take then the Princess Apráxia, if thou wilt!" said the King when he saw that.

Then quiet Dúnaï went to the lofty castle, and began to knock off the locks and to force open the doors. He entered the golden-roofed tower, and came to where the most fair Princess Apráxia was pacing her chamber, clad in a thin robe without a girdle, her ruddy locks unbound, and no shoes upon her feet.

"Aï, Princess Apráxia! wilt thou wed with Prince Vladímir?" said Dúnaï.

And she made answer: "These three years I have prayed the Lord that Prince Vladímir might be my husband."

Then quiet Dúnaï Ivánovich took her by her small white hands, by her golden ring, and kissed her sugar lips for that sweet speech, and led her forth to the spacious court.

There the King met them, and said: "Take also the Princess's dowry." So thirty carts were laden with red gold, pure silver, fair round pearls and jewels.

Then they mounted their good steeds, and rode over the glorious, far-reaching, open plain.

Dark night overtook them on the road. So the good youths pitched a linen pavilion, and lay down to sleep. They placed their good steeds at their feet, their sharp spears at their heads; at their right hands lay their stout swords, at their left their daggers of steel.

The good youths slept and slumbered, enjoying the dark night. Nothing saw they, and nothing did they hear, not even the Tatar riding across the plain.

They rose while it was still very early, and set out upon their way. And the Tatar rode in pursuit, his steed all covered with the mire of the way.

Then Dúnaï was aware of the knight in the way,

and sent Dobrýnya on to Kíef town in Holy Russia, with the fair Princess Apráxia, but remained himself in the open plain to meet that stout, bold adversary.

When the Tatar perceived that he was pursued in turn, and that Dúnaï had overtaken him, he began to smite Dúnaï with his spear, and to say to himself: "Halt, Tatar, on the open plain; roar, Tatar, like a wild beast; whistle, Tatar, like a serpent!"

So the Tatar roared and whistled;—the pebbles were scattered over the plain, the grass withered, the flowerets drooped, and Dúnaï fell from his good steed. But quickly sprang Dúnaï to his nimble feet, and fought the Tatar knight, with mace, far-reaching spear and sharp sword, until all were broken or dulled, and he had overcome his adversary. Then he drew his dagger, and would have pierced him to the heart.

"Tell me now, accursed Tatar," cried Dúnaï, "and conceal it not: What is thy birth and tribe?"

"Sat I on thy white breast," quoth the Tatar, "I would inquire neither tribe nor family, but would stab thee."

Then Dúnaï sat upon his foe's white breast, and would have pierced it, but his tender heart was terrified, and his arm stiffened at the shoulder: for the bosom was that of a woman.

"How now, fair Dúnaï! knowest thou me not?

Yet we trod one path, sat in one bower, drank from one cup! And thou didst dwell with us twelve full years. — But loud-voiced men have come from Holy Russia, while I was from home, and have stolen away my sister. And her I seek."

"Aï, Princess Nastásya!" cried quiet Dúnaï, and raised her from the damp earth by her white hands, and kissed her sugar mouth. "Let us go to Kíef town, and receive the wonder-working cross, and take the golden crowns."[1]

So he placed her upon his good steed, took from her her mace of steel and her sharp sword, and mounting, led her horse behind them.

Thus they came to Kíef town, to God's church: and in the outer porch, they met Fair Sun Prince Vladímir and the Princess Apráxia who were come thither to be married. The sisters greeted each other, and Nastásya received baptism. Then they were married, the younger sister first, as was meet, and the elder afterwards. And great was the marriage feast which courteous Prince Vladímir made for himself and for quiet Dúnaï Ivánovich.

— Three years they lived in mirth and joy: and in the fourth year, courteous Prince Vladímir made again a great and honorable feast. When all had well drunken, they began to make brags. Dúnaï Ivánovich bragged also. "In all Kíef town," quoth

---

[1] Be married: referring to the crowns held over the heads of bride and groom during the marriage ceremony.

he, "is no such youth as quiet Dúnaï. — From the Lithuanian land he drew forth two white swans; he married himself, and gave another also in marriage."

Princess Nastásya answered him: "Is not thy boast empty, Dúnaiushka? Not long have I dwelt in this town, yet much have I learned. Fair is Churílo Plenkóvich, daring Alyósha Popóvich, and courteous young Dobrýnya Nikítich;" and so she praised the different heroes, yet spake no word of praise for Dúnaï, who had praised himself.

"Neither in deeds of knightly exercise are the heroes lacking," quoth the Princess, "and even I can shoot somewhat. Let us now take a stout bow, and let us set a sharp dagger in the open plain, a full verst[1] away, and before it, a silver ring. Let us shoot through the silver ring at the sharp dagger in such wise that the arrow may fall into two equal parts against the dagger, into two parts alike to the eye and of equal weight."

Quiet Dúnaï was both ashamed and wroth at this, and said: "Good, Nastásiushka! let us go to the plain, and shoot our fiery darts."

So they went forth. Nastásya sent a burning arrow; it passed through the ring, and falling upon the sharp blade, was parted in twain; and both the parts were exactly equal.

Then Dúnaiushka shot; the first arrow he sent

---
[1] Two-thirds of a mile.

too far, the second fell short, the third flew wide of the mark and was never found again.

Quiet Dúnaï waxed very wroth thereat, and aimed a burning arrow smeared with serpent's fat at Nastásya's white breast. Then she besought him:

"Aï, fair Dúnaï Ivánovich! forgive my foolish woman's words. Better will it be for thee to punish me. Let this be thy first reprimand: take thy silken whip, dip it in burning pitch, and chastise my body. And for the second reprimand: bind me by my woman's hair to thy stirrups, and send thy horse at speed over the wide plain. — Bury me to the breast in the damp earth, — beat me with oaken rods, — torture me with hunger, — feed me with oats, and so keep me three full months. — But grant me only to bear thy son, and leave a posterity behind me in the world. For such a child there is not in all the town. His little legs are silver to the knee, his arms to the elbow are of pure gold; upon his brow gloweth the fair red sun, upon his crown shine countless stars, and at the back of his head the bright moon beameth."

Dúnaï heeded not her speech, but sent his burning arrow into her white breast, and took out her heart with his dagger. And his son was as she had said.

Then Dúnaï's heroic heart burned within him for grief and remorse. "Where the white swan fell," he cried, "there also shall fall the falcon bright." Then he placed the hilt of his dagger on the damp earth, and fell upon its sharp point with his white breast. And from that spot flowed forth straightway two swift streams; the greater was the river Don, the lesser the Dniepr, Nastásya's river. Nastásya's river flowed to the Kingdom of Lithuania, and thence to the Golden Horde. The Don, twenty fathoms deep and forty wide, ran past Kíef town. Where they met, two cypress trees sprang up, and twined together, and on their leaves was written: "This marvel came to pass for the wonder of all young people, and the solace of the old."

Thus the Song of quiet Dúnaï forever shall be sung, for the peace of the blue sea and the hearing of all good people.

STAVR GODÍNOVICH THE BOYÁR (NOBLE).

COURTEOUS Prince Vladímir made a great feast in royal Kíef town, and summoned thereto all his princes, boyárs, mighty heroes and bold polyánitzas:[1] likewise many merchants and strangers.

Among these last was young Stavr Godínovich from Chérnigof. Softly he mounted the steps, and lightly paced through the antechambers, as he crossed himself and bowed low on all sides, and to Prince Vladímir and his daughter in particular.

The red sun inclined to even, and all the youths were merry with drink, so that they waxed boastful. The heroes vaunted their good steeds, heroic strength or golden treasure, the merchants their Siberian fox pelts, and black sables. — But Stavr sat alone, eating and drinking nothing, and making no brag. As Prince Vladímir paced the banquet hall, he espied Stavr sitting thus; and he poured out a cup of green wine and brought it to him, inquiring wherefore he neither ate nor drank.

"Thou tastest not my white swan," he said, "neither makest thou any brag. Hast thou, then,

---
[1] Female warriors.

no towns with their suburbs, villages with their hamlets, nor even so much as a good mother or a praiseworthy young wife, of whom thou mayest boast?"

"Stavr hath enough whereof to boast, Prince Vladímir of royal Kíef," quoth Stavr. "What petty outpost is this Kíef of royal Vladímir, forsooth? Stavr's spacious court is no worse than the whole of Kíef town. His palace covers seven versts, his halls and chambers of white oak are hung with gray beaver skins; the ceilings with black sables. His floors are of silver only — his hasps and hinges of steel. Thirty youths also hath Stavr, master shoemakers all; — they sew shoes, pausing not. Stavr weareth a pair a day, and yet another day, perchance: then are they taken to the market place, and sold to princes and nobles for their full worth. And yet more hath Stavr whereof to boast: — thirty young tailors — masters of their trade, who make ever new caftáns, so that Stavr weareth his garments but a day, or at the most, two days, and then selleth them in the market to princes and nobles at a great price. — But Stavr will not brag. — And yet more hath Stavr — a golden-coated mare, whose cost was five hundred rubles. On the best of her foals Stavr rideth, and the worst he selleth at great prices to princes and boyárs. Hence Stavr's golden treasure is never exhausted. Yet one thing hath Stavr whereof he will boast, a young wife, Vasilísa Mikúlichna:[1] she could buy and sell all Kíef town, deceive all these princes and nobles, and drive even Fair Sun Vladímir from his senses."

Then all at the feast fell silent at this word. Prince Vladímir liked not the discourteous speech, and his nobles cried:

"Fair Sun Vladímir, Prince of royal Kíef! Let us now thrust this churl into a cold dungeon, and let his young wife deceive us all, princes and nobles, drive thee, Prince Vladímir, from thy wits, and deliver Stavr from his prison."

So Vladímir gave command that iron fetters should be placed on Stavr's hands and feet, and that he should be led to a dungeon forty fathoms deep, with iron doors and locks of steel, where his food should be oats and water.

But Stavr's serving-man mounted his master's good steed and rode in haste to Chérnigof, to Stavr's palace of white stone, and his young wife.

Now Vasilísa Mikúlichna had made a great banquet for the wives of the merchants and rulers of the town, and so the man found them feasting.

When her husband's man told her all that had befallen in Kíef, the young wife rose from her bench of oak, and said:

"Time is it, my welcome guests, to betake yourselves to your own homes and dwellings."

---

[1] Daughter of Mikúla the Villager's Son, and sister of Nastásya, Dobrýnya's wife, according to the peasant singer.

Then she seated herself in her folding chair, and for the space of three full hours she meditated how she might release her husband.

"Untold treasure of gold will not ransom Stavr," she said, "nor may he be released by mighty heroic strength. Stavr must be saved by woman's wiles."

Then she wrote a letter to show that she was an ominous ambassador from the Island of Kodól, in the land of Ledenétz, come on an honorable mission to Fair Sun Prince Vladímir, to sue for the hand of his fair daughter Beauty.[1] After that she hastened to her heroic chamber, and summoned her tiring-women: "Aï, my trusty maids, make haste and cut off my ruddy braid, fetch me an ambassador's apparel, and saddle me a heroic steed."

In very great haste they sheared off her ruddy locks in fashion like a man's, dressed her in black velvet breeches and the garments of an ambassador, and led forth her horse.

Then she summoned a body-guard of forty good youths, and they mounted and rode with her.

When they had traversed half the way, a stern messenger came riding towards them from Kíef town, and as they came together they saluted, palm kissing palm. Then the messenger began to inquire of Vasilísa whence this bold and goodly youth was come and whither he was going.

She told him that she was sent by the stern King

---

[1] Zapava, or Zabava.

Yetmanuíla Yetmanuílovich, to collect tribute for twelve years, — three thousand rubles for each year.

In turn the messenger told her, that he was on his way to seal up Stavr's palace, and to fetch his young wife to Kíef. Then spoke the good youths of Vasilísa's guard:

"We have been at Stavr's palace, and there is no one therein: for his young wife hath departed to the distant land, to the Golden Horde."

So the messenger turned back to Kíef, and out-riding them, told Prince Vladímir privately that a threatening ambassador,[1] Vasíly Mikúlich, was on his way to Kíef from a far-off land.

Prince Vladímir was sore troubled thereat, and the people made haste to sweep the streets, and to lay pine-trees in the muddy ways, so that they might be passable. Then they waited outside the gates, for the coming of the ambassador from the stern King Yetmanuíla Yetmanuílovich from the far-off land of Ledenétz.

But when Vasíly Mikúlich came, he passed not the gates: — he leaped the city walls, past the corner towers, and came to the spacious princely court. There he sprang from his good steed, thrust the butt-end of his far-reaching spear into the earth, flung his silken bridle over the golden spike at its point, and entered straightway the fair,

---

[1] Vasilísa appears as a Tzarévich in some versions.

royal halls, asking leave of none, but flinging wide the doors.

There Vasilísa bowed on all sides, and to Prince Vladímir in particular, laid her letter on the oaken table, and demanded the hand of his daughter [1] in marriage.

Prince Vladímir rose to his nimble feet, took the letter in his white hands, broke the seal and scanned each word narrowly, then spake:

"'Tis well, Vasíly Mikúlich. I will give thee Beauty to wife. I go now to take counsel with my daughter."

But when he came to his well-loved daughter, Beauty said: "What art thou minded to do, dear father? wilt thou give a maiden in marriage to a woman? For I have marked this Vasíly Mikúlich. No threatening ambassador is he — but a woman, by all the signs. When he walketh in the courtyard, 'tis like a duck swimming; his speech is a woman's pipe, his gait in the royal halls is mincing; when he sitteth upon the wall-bench, he presseth his feet close one to the other; his little hands are white, his fingers delicate, and upon them the marks of rings still linger."

"That we shall see," quoth Vladímir: "for I will now prove this ambassador. I will have the steam bath prepared for him after his journey. If

---

[1] Evidently the same Beauty (Zapava) who figures in other *bylínas* as Vladímir's niece.

he be in truth a mighty hero, then will he come to the bath with me: but if he be a woman, he will not come."

So the bath was heated, and Vladímir went to invite Vasíly Mikúlich.

"Wilt thou steam thyself with me, after the road, good youth?" he said. And Vasíly replied:

"My soul burneth to do that. Pleasing will it be after my journey."

Now, Prince Vladímir was royally apparelled, and while he was busy with putting off his garments, Vasilísa hastened to the bath, wet her head, and came forth as Vladímir entered.

"With great speed hast thou steamed thyself, Ambassador Vasíly Mikúlich! Why didst thou not await my coming?"

"Thou art at home and at leisure, Prince Vladímir, but I am a traveller; my business brooketh no long delay in the bath. I am come to woo. Give me thy young daughter to wife."

"I will take counsel with the maiden," quoth Vladímir, and went to his daughter.

But Beauty said: "Wilt thou make thyself a laughing-stock for all Russia, my father, and wed thy daughter to a woman? For, by all signs, she is no man."

"I will prove her yet once more, my dear daughter," quoth Vladímir, and went to Vasíly.

"Is it pleasing to thee to shoot a match with my young men, Vasíliushka Mikúlich?"

"My soul longeth for that," she answered. Then they went forth upon the open plain, and began to shoot at a damp oak, a full verst distant. The arrow of one good youth flew past, another good youth shot short, a third shot wide of the mark. Some shot fair, but all the fiery arrows which were lodged in that tree by heroic hands did but make the damp oak quiver, as in stress of weather.

Then Vasíly Mikúlich spoke:

"Ho there, Prince Vladímir! I will have none of these heroic bows. I have by me a little travelling bow, with which I adventure out upon the open plain." Then came bold and goodly youths from the white pavilion without the walls, where she had left her body-guard. Five men bore the first end, and as many more the last, and thirty stout youths dragged along the quiver of burning arrows. — Then she took an arrow in her small left hand, — an arrow of steel, drew the great bow to her ear, and took aim at the damp oak. The cord of the stout bow sang, Vladímir crept about, and all his heroes stood as though stifled with stove gas. The firm dart screamed, lodged in the damp, ringbarked oak, and shivered it into splinters. Thereupon Prince Vladímir spat to one side, and said as he went away: "I will prove this ambassador yet once again. If he be a woman, he will refuse a wrestling match."

So he assembled thirty good youths and bold, in his spacious court, and spoke this word:

"Aï, Vasíly Mikúlich! doth thy soul burn to wrestle with my men?"

"In sooth, Fair Prince Vladímir, are there any with whom I may wrestle?" the ambassador made answer. "Since my childhood have I run the streets, and many a bout have I wrestled with the children in sport." Then Vasíly stepped forth into the court, grasped two heroes in one hand, three in the other, and knocked their skulls together, so that there was no soul left in them. Vladímir began to entreat her:

"Curb thy heroic heart, young Vasíly Mikúlich, I pray: spare at least a remnant of our people."

Vasíly answered: "I came on an honorable mission — to woo thy beloved daughter. If thou wilt now give her with honor, with honor will I take her; but if not, I will take her without honor, and I will beat in thy sides."

Then Prince Vladímir went no more to ask his daughter Beauty's pleasure in this matter, but betrothed her forthwith to the stern ambassador, and ordered a noble banquet and wedding feast.

On the third day of the feast, when the time drew near for them to fare to God's church and be married, Vasíly grew sad and exceeding sorrowful.

Then Prince Vladímir began to inquire of him why he was not merry.

Vasíly made answer: "I know not why my soul is heavy. My father hath died, perchance, or my dear mother. Hast thou then no good youths, no players upon the gúsly[1] of maple-wood, who may solace us?"

But when the harp-players were summoned, and played and sang songs of the olden days and of the present, and of all times, Vasíly was still sad, and said:

"Where is now Stavr Godínovich from our land? He is a master player upon the harp of maple-wood, and none but he can cheer my spirit."

Then Prince Vladímir said to himself: "If I summon not Stavr, I shall anger the ambassador; but if I summon him, he will be carried away."

Nevertheless he dared not offend Vasíly, and sent for Stavr, to the princely banquet-hall.

Stavr strung his harp, and began to pluck the strings. One string he strung from Kíef, and one from Tzargrád,[2] the third from far Jerusalem. He played great dances, and sang songs from over the blue sea.

Then Vasíliushka, the stern ambassador, began to sleep and dream,[3] and to say: "Aï, Fair Sun

---

[1] A sort of recumbent harp of four octaves.
[2] Constantinople.
[3] Among the ancient Slavs this was regarded as the highest compliment which could be paid to a musician.

Prince Vladímir; let Stavr go' to my white pavilion, and view there my body-guard, and walk in the open fields." This Vladímir would fain have refused, yet dared not anger the man; and so allowed it.

When they were come to the open plain and the pavilion, Vasilísa said: "Dost thou not know me, Stavr?" And he answered: "After that dungeon, I cannot recall far distant years."

"Aï, thou stupid Stavr! Knowest thou not thy young wife Vasilísa Mikúlichna?"

"Yea, her I should know after thirteen years."

"Foolish Stavr! thou hast not known me after scant three months."

Then she went into the pavilion, put off her manly garb, and donned her own raiment; and coming forth she took Stavr by his white hands, kissed his sugar mouth, called him her beloved husband. Then he knew his young wife, and said: "What will Fair Sun Vladímir do to us now? Let us mount and ride swiftly hence!"

But Vasilísa said: "Not so: we must not steal away in this fashion from royal Kíef. Let us rather go to Prince Vladímir."

When they came to the royal palace, Stavr said: "Aï, thou Fair Sun Prince Vladímir! I have made good my boast; for thou hast betrothed thy daughter to my young wife."

Then was Prince Vladímir shamed, and spoke

this word: "With reason did Stavr boast of his young wife, Vasilísa Mikúlichna! May God forgive thee thy former offence! But boast no more of thy young wife, and trade evermore in our good city of Kíef without tax."

But Stavr and Vasilísa mounted their good steeds, and rode to the glorious town of Chérnigof, to their lordly villages and palace of white stone. No more did Stavr frequent lordly banquets, and never more bragged he of his young wife, but dwelt thenceforth and took his ease in Chérnigof.

ILYÁ OF MÚROM AND NIGHTINGALE THE ROBBER.

YOUNG Ilyá of Múrom, Iván's son, went to matins on Easter morn. And as he stood there in church, he vowed a great vow: "To sing at high mass that same Easter day in Kíef town, and to go thither by the straight way." And yet another vow he took: "As he fared to that royal town by the straight way, not to stain his hand with blood, nor yet his sharp sword with the blood of the accursed Tatars." His third vow he swore upon his mace of steel: "That though he should go the straight way, he would not shoot his fiery darts."

Then he departed from the cathedral church, entered the spacious courtyard and began to saddle good Cloudfall, his shaggy bay steed, to arm himself and prepare for his journey to the famous town of Kíef, to the worshipful feast, and the Fair Sun Prince Vladímir of royal Kíef. Good Cloudfall's mane was three ells in length, his tail three fathoms, and his hair of three colors. Ilyá put on him first the plaited bridle, next twelve saddlecloths, twelve felts, and upon them a metal bound Cherkéssian saddle. The silken girths were twelve in number

— not for youthful vanity but for heroic strength; the stirrups were of damascened steel from beyond the seas, the buckles of bronze which rusteth not, weareth not, the silk from Samarcand, which chafeth not, teareth not.

They saw the good youth as he mounted, — as he rode they saw him not; so swift was his flight, there seemed but a smoke-wreath on the open plain, as when wild winds of winter whirl about the snow. Good Cloudfall skimmed over the grass, and above the waters; high over the standing trees he soared, the primeval oaks, yet lower than the drifting clouds. From mountain to mountain he sprang, from hill to hill he galloped; little rivers and lakes dropped between his feet; where his hoofs fell, founts of water gushed forth; in the open plain smoke eddied, and rose aloft in a pillar. At each leap Cloudfall compassed a verst and a half.

In the open steppe, young Ilyá hewed down a forest and raised a godly cross, and wrote thereon:

"Ilyá of Múrom, the Old Cossáck, rideth to royal Kíef town, on his first heroic quest."

When he drew near to Chérnigof, there stood a great host of Tatars, — three Tzaréviches, each with forty thousand men. The cloud of steam from the horses was so great, that the fair red sun was not seen by day, nor the bright moon by night. The gray hare could not course, nor the clear falcon fly, about that host, so vast was it.

When Ilyá saw that, he dismounted, and falling down before good Cloudfall's right foot, he entreated him:

"Help me, my shaggy bay!" So Cloudfall soared like a falcon clear, and Ilyá plucked up a damp, ringbarked oak from the damp earth, from amid the stones and roots, and bound it to his left stirrup, grasped another in his right hand, and began to brandish it. "Every man may take a vow," quoth he, "but not every man can fulfil it."

Where he waved the damp oak, a street appeared; where he drew it back, a lane. Great as was the number that he slew, yet twice that number did his good steed trample under foot: not one was spared to continue their race.

The gates of Chérnigof were strongly barred, a great watch was kept, and the stout and mighty heroes stood in council. Therefore Ilyá flew on his good steed over the city wall (the height of the wall was twelve fathoms), and entered the church where all the people were assembled, praying God, repenting and receiving the sacrament against sure approaching death. Ilyá crossed himself as prescribed, did reverence as enjoined, and cried:

"Hail, ye merchants of Chérnigof, warrior-maidens and mighty heroes all! Why repent ye now, and receive the sacrament? Why do ye bid farewell thus, to the white world?"

Then they told him how they were besieged by

accursed Tatars, and Ilyá said: "Go ye upon the famous wall of your city, and look toward the open plain."

They did as he commanded, and lo! where had stood the many, very many foreign standards, like a dark, dry forest, the accursed Tatars were now cut down and heaped up, like a field of grain which hath been reaped.

Then the men of Chérnigof did lowly reverence to the good youth, and besought him that he would reveal his name, and abide in Chérnigof to serve them as their Tzar, King, Voevóda,[1] — what he would; and that he would likewise accept at their hands, a bowl of pure red gold, a bowl of fair silver, and one of fine seed pearls.

"These I will not take," Ilyá made answer, "though I have earned them, neither will I dwell with you either as Tzar or peasant. Live ye as of old, my brothers, and show me the straight road to Kíef town."

Then they told him: "By the straight road it is five hundred versts, and by the way about, a thousand. Yet take not the straight road, for therein lie three great barriers: the gray wolf trotteth not that way, the black raven flieth not overhead. The first barrier is the lofty mountains; the second is the Smoródina river, six versts in width, and the

---

[1] Originally this signified a war chieftain.

Black Morass; and beside that river, the third barrier is Nightingale the Robber.

"He hath built his nest on seven oaks, that magic bird. When he whistleth like a nightingale, the dark forest boweth to the earth, the green leaves wither, horse and rider fall as dead. For that cause the road is lost, and no man hath travelled it these thirty years."

When Ilyá the Old Cossáck heard that, he mounted his good steed, and rode forthwith that straight way. When he came to the lofty mountains, his good steed, rose from the damp earth, and soared like a bright falcon over them and the tall dreaming forests. When he came to the Black Morass, he plucked great oaks with one hand, and flung them across the shaking bog for thirty versts, while he led good Cloudfall with the other. When he came to Mother Smoródina, he beat his steed's fat sides, so that the horse cleared the river at a bound.

There sat Nightingale the Robber (surnamed the Magic Bird), and thrust his turbulent head out from his nest upon the seven oaks; sparks and flame poured from his mouth and nostrils. Then he began to pipe like a nightingale, to roar like an aurochs, and to hiss like a dragon. Thereat good Cloudfall, that heroic steed, fell upon his knees, and Ilyá began to beat him upon his flanks and between his ears.

"Thou wolf's food!" cried Ilyá, "thou grass-bag! Hast never been in the gloomy forest, nor heard the song of nightingale, the roar of wild beast, nor serpent's hiss?"

Then Ilyá brake a twig from a willow that grew near by, that he might keep his vow not to stain his weapons with blood, fitted it to his stout bow, and conjured it: "Fly, little dart! Enter the Nightingale's left eye, come forth at his right ear!"

The good heroic steed rose to his feet, and the Robber Nightingale fell to the damp earth like a rick of grain.

Then the Old Cossáck raised up that mighty robber, bound him to his stirrup by his yellow curls, and went his way. Ere long they came to the Nightingale's house, built upon seven pillars over seven versts of ground. About the court-yard was an iron paling, upon each stake thereof a spike, and on each spike the head of a hero. In the centre was the strangers' court; and there stood three towers with golden crests, spire joined to spire, beam merged in beam, roof wedded to roof. Green gardens were planted round about, all blossoming and blooming with azure flowers, and a fair orchard encircled all.

When the Magic Bird's children looked from the latticed casements, and beheld a hero riding with one at his stirrup, they cried: "Aï, lady mother! Our father cometh, and leadeth a man at his stirrup for us to eat."

But Eléna, the one-eyed, Nightingale's witch daughter, looked forth and said: "Nay, it is the Old Cossáck Ilyá of Múrom who rideth, and leadeth our father in bonds."

Then spoke Nightingale's nine sons: "We will transform ourselves into ravens, and rend that peasant with our iron beaks, and scatter his white body over the plain." But their father shouted to them that they should not harm the hero.

Nevertheless, Eléna the witch ran into the wide courtyard, tore a steel beam of a hundred and fifty poods weight from the threshold, and hurled it at Ilyá. The good youth wavered in his saddle, yet being nimble, he escaped the full force of the blow. Then he leaped from his horse, and took the witch on his foot: higher flew the witch then than God's temple, higher than the life-giving cross thereon, and fell against the rear wall of the court, where her skin burst.

"Foolish are ye, my children!" cried the Nightingale. "Fetch from the vaults a cart-load of fair gold, another of pure silver and a third of fine seed pearls, and give to the Old Cossáck, Ilyá of Múrom, that he may set me free."

Quoth Ilyá: "If I should plant my sharp spear in the earth, and if thou shouldst heap treasure about it until it was covered, yet would I not release thee, Nightingale, lest thou shouldst resume thy thieving. But follow me now to glorious Kíef town, that thou mayest receive forgiveness there."

Then his good Cloudfall began to prance, and the Magic Bird at his stirrup to dance, and in this wise came the good youth, the Old Cossáck, to Kief, to glorious Prince Vladímir.

Now, fair Prince Vladímir of royal Kíef was not at home; he had gone to God's temple. Therefore Ilyá entered the court without leave or announcement, bound his horse to the golden ring in the carven pillar, and laid his commands upon that good heroic steed: "Guard thou the Nightingale, my charger, that he depart not from my stirrup of steel."

And to Nightingale he said: "Look to it, Nightingale, that thou depart not from my good steed; for there is no place in all the white world where thou mayest securely hide thyself from me!"

Then he betook himself to the Easter mass. There he crossed himself and did reverence as prescribed, on all four sides, and to the Fair Sun Prince Vladímir in particular. And after the mass was over, Prince Vladímir sent to bid the strange hero to the feast, and there inquired of him from what horde and land he came, and what was his parentage. So Ilyá told him that he was the only son of honorable parents. "I stood at my home in Múrom, at matins," quoth he, "and mass was but just ended when I came hither by the straight way."

When the heroes that sat at the prince's table heard that, they looked askance at him.

"Nay, good youth, liest thou not? boastest thou not?" said Fair Sun Vladímir. "That way hath been lost these thirty years, for there stand great barriers therein; accursed Tatars in the fields, black morasses; and beside the famed Smoródina, amid the bending birches, is the nest of the Nightingale on seven oaks; and that Magic Bird hath nine sons and eight daughters, and one is a witch. He hath permitted neither horse nor man to pass him these many years."

"Nay, thou Fair Sun Prince Vladímir," Ilyá answered; "I did come the straight way, and the Nightingale Robber now sitteth bound within thy court."

Then all left the tables of white oak, and each outran the other to view the Nightingale, as he sat bound to the steel stirrup, with one eye fixed on Kíef town and the other on Chérnigof from force of habit. And Princess Apráxia came forth upon the railed balcony to look.

Prince Vladímir spoke: "Whistle, thou Nightingale, roar like an aurochs, hiss like a dragon."

But the Nightingale replied: "Not thy captive am I, Vladímir. 'Tis not thy bread I eat. But give me wine."

"Give him a cup of green wine," spake Ilyá, "a cup of a bucket and a half, in weight a pood and a half, and a cake of fine wheat flour, for his mouth is now filled with blood from my dart."

Vladímir fetched a cup of green wine, and one of the liquor of drunkenness, and yet a third of sweet mead; and the Nightingale drained each at a draught. Then the Old Cossáck commanded the Magic Bird to whistle, roar and hiss, but under his breath, lest harm might come to any.

But the Nightingale, out of malice, did all with his full strength. And at that cry, all the ancient palaces in Kíef fell in ruins, the new castles rocked, the roofs through all the city fell to the ground, damp mother earth quivered, the heroic steeds fled from the court, the young damsels hid themselves, the good youths dispersed through the streets, and as many as remained to listen died. Ilyá caught up Prince Vladímir under one arm and his Princess under the other, to shield them; yet was Vladímir as though dead for the space of three hours.

"For this deed of thine thou shalt die," spake Ilyá in his wrath, and Vladímir prayed that at least a remnant of his people might be spared.

The Nightingale began to entreat forgiveness, and that he might be allowed to build a great monastery with his ill-gotten gold. "Nay," said Ilyá, "this kind buildeth never, but destroyeth alway."

With that he took Nightingale the Robber by his white hands, led him far out upon the open plain, fitted a burning arrow to his stout bow, and shot it into the black breast of that Magic Bird. Then he struck off his turbulent head, and scattered his bones to the winds,[1] and mounting his good Cloudfall, came again to Prince Vladímir.

Again they sat at the oaken board, eating savory viands and white swans, and quaffing sweet mead. Great gifts and much worship did Ilyá receive, and Vladímir gave command that he should be called evermore Ilyá of Múrom the Old Cossáck, after his native town.

---

[1] A Little Russian legend states that Ilyá in his wrath chopped Nightingale into poppy seeds; and from those poppy seeds come the sweet-voiced and harmless nightingales of the present day.

BOLD ALYÓSHA THE POPE'S SON.

FROM famous Rostóf, that fair town, rode forth two mighty heroes, like two bright falcons soaring. Alyósha[1] Popóvich (the pope's dear child) and Akím[2] Ivánovich were they hight. Shoulder to shoulder rode the warriors, heroic stirrup pressed to stirrup.

And as they roamed the open plain, they saw nothing, — no birds flying overhead, nor beast fleet coursing o'er the plain. They found but three broad roads lying upon the steppe, and where these ways met, a burning stone and a writing thereon.

Then said young Alyósha: "Thou, brother Akím Ivánovich, art learned in the lore of schools. Look now upon this writing on this stone, and interpret to me its meaning."

So Akím leaped from his good steed, and looked upon the writing, and found the three broad ways depicted therein.

The first way lay to Múrom, the second to

---

[1] A diminutive formed from Alexander, through Alexéi. See Appendix.
[2] Popular for Joachim.

Chérnigof, the third to Kíef town and courteous Prince Vladímir.

Said Akím: "Ho, there, brother, young Alyósha Popóvich! Which way doth it please thee to ride?"

And young Alyósha answered: "Better will it be for us to go to Kíef town, to courteous Prince Vladímir."

So they wheeled their good steeds about, and rode to Kíef town.

Ere they reached the Safat river, they halted amid green meadows (for Akím must needs feed the horses). There they pitched two pavilions, for Alyósha desired greatly to sleep. And when young Akím had hobbled the good steeds, and loosed them in the green meadow, he lay down likewise in his own pavilion to slumber.

The autumn night passed. Alyósha awoke right early, rose, washed himself in the dews of dawn, dried himself upon a white cloth, and prayed God toward the East. Then young Akím went to the good steeds, and led them to the Safat stream to water them, for Alyósha had commanded him to saddle them with speed; and when this was done they mounted, and made ready to go to Kíef town.

As they rode, there met them in the way a wandering psalm-singer. His foot-gear was woven of the seven silks, soled with pure silver, and the faces were studded with red gold. His long mantle was of sable, his hat from Sorochínsky, from the Grecian land; his travelling whip weighed thirty poods, his cudgel moulded of heaviest lead weighed fifty. He spoke this word:

"Hail, bold and goodly youths! I have seen Tugárin the Dragon's Son. His stature is three fathoms, and the breadth across his shoulders is a full fathom; the space between his eyes is an arrow's length. The horse beneath him is like a wild beast; from his throat flames flash, from his ears, smoke riseth in a pillar."

Then bold Alyósha Popóvich bade the psalm-singer yield his pilgrim garb, and receive Alyósha's heroic raiment in exchange. So the pilgrim refused not, but gave his garments to Alyósha, and put on the heroic raiment. And with speed did Alyósha array himself, as a wandering Kalyéka,[1] took the staff of fifty poods and a dagger of damascened steel, lest he should have need of it, and went to the Safat river. There he found Tugárin Dragon's Son, roaring in a huge voice: the green oaks trembled, and Alyósha could hardly walk for that roaring.

When young Tugárin beheld the pilgrim, he demanded of him, what he had seen or heard of young Alyósha, Pope's Son, for he would fain

---

[1] Pilgrim, psalm-singing beggar: the professional singers of religious songs are known as *kalyéky perikózhie*, wandering psalm-singers.

thrust him through with his lance, and burn him with fire.

Pilgrim Alyósha answered: "Come nearer; for I hear not what thou sayest." Then, when Tugárin drew near, Alyósha set himself against him, brandished his staff about his head, and smote Tugárin's tempestuous head, and broke it. Tugárin fell to the damp earth, and Alyósha sprang upon his black breast: whereupon young Tugárin besought him:

"Hail, thou wandering psalm-singer! Art thou not young Alyósha Popóvich? If thou be he in very truth, let us now swear brotherhood."

But Alyósha trusted not his enemy. He smote off his turbulent head, drew off his flowered garments (their value was one hundred thousand rubles), put them all on himself, mounted his good steed, and set out for his white pavilion.

But when Akím and the pilgrim beheld him, they were sore afraid; they mounted their good steeds, and rode toward Rostóf town. But young Alyósha followed and outrode them. When Akím Ivánovich saw that, he turned about, drew forth his battle-mace of thirty poods, and flung it behind him (for he thought from the garments it had been young Tugárin Dragon's Son), and struck Alyósha's white breast, thrusting him from his Cherkessian saddle.

Alyósha fell to the damp earth. Then Akím

sprang down from his good steed, and would have pierced his white breast, but perceived thereon a wondrous cross of gold, and so said to the pilgrim:

"This thing hath come upon me for my sins — that I should slay mine own brother!" Then began they both to shake and rock Alyósha, and gave him liquor from beyond the sea; and therewith he became whole again, and they fell to converse among themselves, and to changing of raiment. The wandering psalm-singer put upon him once more his pilgrim's habit, Alyósha took again his heroic garments, and laid Tugárin the Dragon's Son's flowered apparel in his saddle-bags. Then they mounted their good steeds, and rode to Kíef town to courteous Prince Vladímir.

When they came to the princely court, they lighted down from their good steeds, bound them to the oaken pillars, and entered the fair hall. There they prayed to the Saviour's picture, touched their foreheads to the ground, doing homage to Prince Vladímir, Princess Apráxia, and on all four sides. Courteous Prince Vladímir inquired their names and their country, and Alyósha made answer:

"Lord, I am called Alyósha Popóvich: I come from Rostóf, and am son to the aged pope of the cathedral."

Then Vladímir rejoiced, and said: "Hail, young Alyósha Popóvich! According to thy lineage, seat thyself in the great place, the fore corner; or in the second, the heroic place, on the oaken bench over against me; or in the third place, wheresoever thou desirest."

Alyósha seated himself not in the great place, but with his comrade on the beam of the oven-bench. And after a little space, lo! twelve mighty heroes bare in Tugárin the Dragon's Son on a great sheet of pure gold,[1] and seated him in the great place beside the Princess Apráxia. Then they fetched sugar viands, honeyed drinks, and all foreign liquors, and all began to eat, drink, and make merry.

But Tugárin Dragon's Son ate not his bread with honor; he thrust a whole loaf into his cheek (and they were monastery loaves of vast size). And not with honor did Tugárin drink: he gulped a whole cup down at a swallow, and the measure of that cup was a bucket and a half.

Then spoke up bold Alyósha Popóvich: "Ho there, courteous lord, Prince Vladimir! What lout is this that is come to the court, what untutored fool? For he sitteth not honorably at thy table, but layeth his hand upon the Princess Apráxia, kisseth her on her sugar mouth, and jeereth at thee, Prince. My lord and father had an old dog, that dragged himself with labor under

---

[1] Bodies have been found in the *kurgáns* or mounds, between sheets of pure gold; but these belong to ancient Scythian times.

the table, and choked himself with a bone. My father took him by the tail, and flung him out of the court-yard. And I will do the same to Tugárin."

Tugárin blackened like a night in autumn, and Alyósha was like the bright moon.

And again the cooks were cunning, and fetched savory viands and a white swan, which the Princess essayed to carve; and so doing, she cut her left hand. Then she wrapped it in her sleeve, let it hang beneath the table, and said: "Ah, ye heroes and nobles! Fain would I carve the white swan, were it not that I am still more fain to gaze upon this sweet youth, Tugárin Dragon's Son."

As she spoke, Tugárin seized the white swan, and suddenly swallowed it whole, and therewith yet another great round loaf. Alyósha said:

"Courteous Lord Vladímir! What boor and unpolished dullard is this that sitteth here? He thrusteth whole loaves into his cheek, and maketh but a mouthful of a white swan. My lord and father, Pope Fédor of Rostóf, had a miserable old cow. With pain she dragged herself to the court-yard, and broke into the kitchen, where she drank a keg of spiced small beer, — and burst. Pope Fédor took her by the tail, and swung her upon the hill. — So also will I do to Tugárin the Dragon's Son."

At this word, Tugárin turned black as an autumn night, plucked out his steel dagger, and flung it at Alyósha. But Alyósha was nimble, and Tugárin could not touch him. Akím Ivánovich seized the dagger, and said to Alyósha:

"Wilt thou cast it at him thyself, or dost thou command me to hurl it?"

"I will neither cast it, nor command thee. To-morrow I will meet him, I will lay a great wager with him — not of a hundred rubles, nor yet of a thousand; — but my tempestuous head shall be my stake."

Then sprang all the princes and nobles to their nimble feet, and backed Tugárin. The princes staked a hundred rubles, the nobles fifty each, the peasants five. And the trading guests who chanced there, staked on Tugárin all their three vessels, and all the foreign merchandise that stood on the swift Dniepr. Alyósha's only backer was the ruler of Chérnigof.

Then Tugárin rose in haste, went forth, mounted his good steed, spread his paper wings, and flew through the air.

The Princess Apráxia sprang to her nimble feet, and began to upbraid Alyósha Popóvich.

"Thou villager, thou rustic lout! thou wouldest not let my sweet friend tarry!"

But Alyósha heeded not her words; he rose, and, having called his comrade, hastened forth.

They mounted, and rode to the Sáfat river, and pitched their white pavilions; preparing to rest, they loosed their horses in the green meadow. All that night Alyósha slept not, but besought God with tears: "Fashion, O God, a threatening cloud, send a cloud with rain and hail!"

Alyósha's prayers came to Christ the Lord. God sent the cloud, and wet Tugárin's paper wings, so that he fell like a dog upon the damp earth. Then Akím came and told Alyósha that he had seen Tugárin stretched upon the earth; and Alyósha arrayed himself with speed, mounted his good steed, took his sharp sword, and rode against Tugárin the Dragon's Son.

When Tugárin beheld Alyósha, he roared in a piercing voice: "Ho there, young Alyósha Popóvich! Shall I burn thee with fire, or trample upon thee with my horse, or impale thee upon my lance?"

"Hail, young Tugárin Dragon's Son," Alyósha answered, "thou didst lay a great wager with me, to contend and fight in single combat; but now there is neither strength nor daring left in thee against me." Then, when Tugárin glanced behind him, Alyósha sprang forward with speed, and hewed off his head. As the head fell upon the damp earth, it was like a beer-kettle.

Then Alyósha leaped from his good steed, uncoiled the cord from his horse, pierced Tugárin's ears, bound the head to his horse; and having brought it to Kíef in this fashion, he flung it into the midst of the royal courtyard.

When Prince Vladímir beheld Alyósha, he entered his fair hall, seated himself at his richly decked table, and bade the banquet proceed for Alyósha.

After it had continued for a space, Prince Vladímir spoke: "Ho, young Alyósha Popóvich! In one moment thou hast given me solace. Dwell henceforth in Kíef town, I pray thee, and serve me, Prince Vladímir, and I will reward thee with love, and with all my heart."

This prayer bold young Alyósha Popóvich disregarded not, and began to serve Vladímir with loyalty and truth.

But the Princess said: "Thou villager and rustic lout! Thou hast parted me and my dear friend, young Tugárin the Dragon's Son."

Thereto Alyósha made answer: "Little mother, Princess Apráxia, I had almost called thee then by the name which thou hast merited."

THE ONE AND FORTY PILGRIMS.

On the open plain many great and mighty heroes assembled, forty bogatýrs and one; and the one was young Kasyán Mikáilovich, their atamán.

They halted in a green meadow, dismounted from their good steeds, and sat down in a circle to hold counsel together; and began to tell exploits.

They told whither one bold and goodly youth had journeyed, how a certain other had been in many lands and hordes, which one had slain the accursed Tatars, and which the infidels forever accursed.

When young Kasyán Mikáilovich heard the discourse of these mighty heroes, he addressed them thus: "Greatly have ye sinned against God, ye mighty warriors! For many turbulent heads have ye slain without avail, and have shed hot blood. Are ye therefore agreed to what I shall propose? Better is it for us now, to disperse our great host, and go to Jerusalem city to pray God in the holy sanctuary, to kiss the grave of the Lord, and to bathe in Jordan river, that our sins may be forgiven. But it behooveth us to lay upon ourselves a great vow, ye mighty heroes! — not to rob nor steal, not to yield to woman's charms, nor stain our knightly hands with blood.

"And if any shall offend against this vow, then shall his nimble feet be hewn off at the knee, his white hands at the elbow; his clear eyes shall be plucked from his brow, and his tongue torn out with pincers; and he shall be buried to the breast in damp mother earth."

This in no wise terrified the heroes, and they all agreed thereto. Then they loosed their good steeds upon the silken grass, to roam the open plain, and donned palmer's weeds. Over their heroic shoulders they threw their beggar's pouches of black cut velvet, embroidered in red gold, and strewn with fair seed-pearls. On their heads they set caps from the Grecian land, and in their white hands they took staves of precious fishes' teeth.[1] Their raiment was like the poppy in hue, and each bore in his hand a precious antaventa stone. By day they journeyed by the fair sun's light; by night these stones and the jewels woven into their foot-gear of the seven silks, lighted them on their way.

In this wise wandered the good youths from horde to horde, and so drew near to glorious Kíef town. In the open plain they met the Fair Sun Prince Vladímir, hunting the white swan, geese,

---

[1] Walrus tusk: greatly esteemed in the Archangel Government, and used for fine carvings.

and small gray migratory ducks, foxes and hares, martens and sables black.

When Prince Vladímir drew near, the pilgrims shouted in piercing tones: "Vladímir, Prince of Royal Kíef! give alms to the wandering psalm-singers. We will not take a ruble, nor yet a ruble and a half; but whole thousands must thou give, yea, forty thousand well told!"

Then Prince Vladímir lighted down from his good steed, and greeted them, beseeching them to sing him the spiritual song of Eléna, for he was fain to hear it from them.

So the pilgrims thrust their staves into the damp earth, and hung their pouches thereon, and standing in a circle, as is the custom with wandering psalm-singers, they sang the psalm of Eléna in a half voice.

— Mother earth trembled, the water in the lakes surged, the gloomy forests shook, and on the mountains the damp oaks bowed. Vladímir could neither stand nor sit nor lie. "Enough of this psalm of Eléna, good youths!" he cried. So the wandering psalm-singers took their velvet pouches, and made ready to pursue their journey.

Said Prince Vladímir then: "I have with me neither bread nor salt nor golden treasure. But go ye to Kíef, to my Princess Apráxia; she will give you food and drink and lodging. Go, therefore, to my princely palace, and say that the Fair

Sun Prince Vladímir sent ye from the open plain."

So they journeyed a day, and yet another day, and came to glorious Kíef town: there they sought the spacious courtyard of the palace, and besought alms for Christ's sake. At their piercing cry, the domes tumbled from the lofty castles, the crowns from the trees; mother earth quaked, and the liquors in the cellars grew thick.

The Princess Apráxia heard that great shout, and thrust herself out of the lattice window to her waist, quivering exceedingly with terror. Then she sent the stewards and cupbearers to greet young Kasyán Mikáilovich and his companions, and bid them enter.

When the pilgrims mounted the fair porch, step bent to step, and the new ante-chamber sagged beneath their tread. They crossed themselves as enjoined, prayed to the Saviour's picture, did reverence as prescribed to three sides and to four, and in particular to the Princess Apráxia.

The Princess bade them welcome, and commanded fair cloths to be laid on the oaken tables with all speed, sugar viands to be brought, and honeyed drinks. Then all sat down to meat: the pilgrims, the Princess Apráxia, with her nurses and duennas, and her fair handmaidens. Young Kasyán Mikáilovich sat in the great place of honor, and from his youthful countenance as from the fair red sun, rays streamed. The stewards and cup-bearers hastened to and fro, bearing fair meats and drinks.

They feasted long, even until the fair sun sank in the west. Then the pilgrims were led to chambers where they might repose; but the Princess Apráxia herself led young Kasyán to a fair chamber apart, where stood a couch of smooth boards with bed of down, heavy cushions, and a coverlet of rich black sables.

And when all were asleep in the palace, save young Kasyán who was praying God, the Princess Apráxia came to him, and told him of her love.

But young Kasyán recounted to her the great vow which he had taken, and bade her tempt him not, but go thence.

Nevertheless she came again, and yet the third time; then the good youth seized his stout cudgel and brandished it, and bade her begone, or he would smite her until she fell upon the brick floor. At that she was troubled, and went thence; but when Kasyán had fallen into a deep sleep, the Princess crept down from the glazed oven, took his pouch of rich velvet, ripped it open and placed therein the silver bratína,[1] from which the Prince

---

[1] A peculiar sort of bowl or loving-cup which was passed round the table at the beginning of a feast. These cups are usually globular in form, with a lip like a band contracting inwards, which generally bears an inscription in Slavonic characters, such as: "Cup for going the round; pour into it that which refreshes the mind, corrupts the morals, and divulges all secrets;" "I am the slippery path of truth," etc.

was wont to drink, on his return from the field; then she sewed up the velvet again so that it might not be perceived.

The next morning very early, the one and forty pilgrims arose, washed themselves very white, put on their shoes, and prayed to God. The Princess commanded the oaken tables to be served; and when the pilgrims had eaten and drunk their fill, they prayed God for the Fair Sun Prince Vladímir, returned thanks to the Princess Apráxia, swung their heroic pouches on their heroic shoulders, bowing low, and set out for Jerusalem.

A little space after their departure, Fair Sun Vladímir came from the open plain, and sat down to eat and drink. Then the cupbearers began to search for the royal bratína, through all the palace, and Vladímir said:

"Which of you hath taken the royal cup?"

The Princess Apráxia made answer in their stead: "Aï, Fair Sun Prince Vladímir! there came hither from the open plain, sent by thee, forty psalm-singers and one. Is it not they, perchance, who have carried off the royal cup? For they lodged here one night, and are but lately departed hence. They have taken thy royal cup!"

Then Prince Vladímir gave command in haste, that his mighty heroes should ride after the pilgrims. But Ilyá of Múrom warned him:

"Aï, Fair Sun Vladímir! these be no wandering

psalm-singers, but one and forty heroes bold, and whom have we to send against them?"

"Let us send bold Alyósha Popóvich," quoth Vladímir. So Alyósha was despatched, and bidden to speak them fair.

But Alyósha was not courteous by nature, and when he came up with them, and beheld them sitting, eating bread and refreshing themselves, he cried:

"Ho there! ye are not wandering psalm-singers, but forty thieves and robbers! Yield now peaceably the royal cup which ye have stolen!"

Then sprang young Kasyán Mikáilovich to his nimble feet, grasped his travelling cudgel, and flourished it widely.

"Did we go to Kíef town for your royal bratína?" quoth he. "Nay, but I will give thee the cup."

Alyósha beheld with great terror that there was nothing to be done, and, wheeling his good steed about in haste, returned again to Kíef. To Prince Vladímir he said that the brigands had set upon him when he asked for the royal cup, and had nearly unhorsed him, so that he had escaped with difficulty.

Again spoke the Old Cossáck: "Heed not that daring fool Alyósha, Prince Vladímir! for I know well how he addressed them. There is none for us to send but Dobrýnya Nikítich: lo! he knoweth how to petition with courtesy."

So Dobrýnya gat to horse, and when he came upon the forty and one sitting on the open plain, eating and refreshing themselves, he cried:

"Hail, ye forty pilgrims and one! I beseech your hospitality."

"Come hither, good youth," they answered, "sit with us, eat our bread and salt."

"Aï, ye pilgrims," quoth Dobrýnya: "how shall I tell you, good youths? There is a great tumult amongst us of Kíef. — For the royal cup of gold is lost; without it, the Prince will not taste his mead. I pray you, therefore, good youths, search your pouches, lest it may have strayed into them through error."

Then each looked upon the other, and knew not what to do. Said young Kasyán Mikáilovich:

"Dear comrades, pious pilgrims! open your pouches, and show them to this youth."

All the pilgrims rose to their nimble feet, took their pouches, and showed to young Dobrýnya: but the royal cup was not in them. Last of all, young Kasyán Mikáilovich opened his pouch, and lo! the princely cup was there. Then all were exceeding wroth, and in great amaze, and said:

"What shall we do with thee now, young Kasyán Mikáilovich? lo, it was thyself who didst impose that great vow."

"Beloved comrades," young Kasyán made answer, "I did not steal the royal cup: this thing

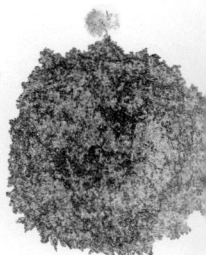

hath the Princess Apráxia contrived because I would not yield to her. Nevertheless, do ye now the thing commanded, and break not your solemn vows."

Then they all wept and began to take leave of him; and though it was very grievous to them, they fulfilled their vow. They hewed off his nimble feet to the knee, his white arms to the elbow, plucked his clear eyes from his brow and his tongue from his mouth, and buried him to the breast in damp mother earth. Then they bade him farewell, as a dead man, and betook themselves to Jerusalem.

Young Dobrýnya Nikítich looked on at all their deed, then rode thence with all speed, bearing the royal cup, and came to Kíef town, to Prince Vladímir's spacious court, gave the cup to the Fair Sun, and related the marvel he had seen; and how they had not stolen the royal cup, which was found upon them by mistake. But he told not what the Princess Apráxia had done. From that hour the Princess Apráxia fell ill with grief, and lay on the great dung-heap. But Prince Vladímir and many of his heroes made ready to go and view that great marvel.

But before them came Mikóla[1] of Mozháisk to young Kasyán Mikáilovich, and restored his nimble feet, his white hands, his clear eyes, and his tongue:

---

[1] St. Nicholas.

he put breath also into Kasyán's white breast, set him on his nimble feet, and spake this word: " Go thy way, young Kasyán Mikáilovich! thou shalt find thy friends at their first halting-place. The Lord hath sent me to thee, good youth, because thou wert wrongfully slain, not having stolen the royal cup. Go now to Jerusalem, pray God in the sanctuary, kiss the Lord's grave, bathe in Jordan river. And when thou art come again to this our land, build a cathedral church to Mikóla of Mozháisk; for I am he."

Then the hoary-headed old man vanished. Young Kasyán went his way, and overtook his companions late at night. He found them eating bread, and marvelling that they had executed him. But when they beheld him fairer than before, with his long curls hanging to his waist, and knew that the Lord and none other had been his help, they rejoiced with great joy.

When Prince Vladímir and his heroes came to the spot where Kasyán had been slain, and found the deep pit wherein he had been sunk to the breast, but found him not, they were in great amaze, and returned to Kíef town.

After the forty pilgrim-heroes and one had made their pilgrimage to Jerusalem, they returned again to where they had left their good steeds roaming, and rode to Kíef town, to Fair Sun Vladímir's spacious court, where they asked alms in Christ's name, that they might have the wherewithal to dine.

Prince Vladímir heeded their mighty shout which shook the palace, and bade them enter, and eat his bread. But they answered:

"Nay, we will not enter thy palace, for the Princess Apráxia is there, and she will again lay the royal cup in our young Kasyán Mikáilovich's pouch."

So they told Vladímir what the Princess had done when they had lodged there, and how the good youth whom they had slain, had nevertheless accompanied them to Jerusalem. Then Prince Vladímir sent his stewards and cupbearers to make obeisance to them and entreat them to enter.

When they obeyed, Prince Vladímir saluted young Kasyán courteously, and Kasyán inquired how it fared with the Princess Apráxia; — if she were well. Thereto Vladímir made reluctant answer, "Let us not go to her for a week or two." Young Kasyán heeded not his speech, but went straightway with the Prince to her chamber; and as they went the Prince held his nose, but Kasyán cared not for the odor. They opened the doors of the fair chamber, and flung wide the little lattice casements. The Princess prayed to be forgiven; thereupon young Kasyán breathed upon her with his holy breath, laid his holy hand upon her and pardoned her, and she was solaced; for she had suffered much, lying in shame a full half year.

Then young Kasyán returned with Prince Vladímir to the banquet-hall, prayed before the Saviour's picture, and sat down with his comrades at the richly adorned tables. They ate and drank and refreshed themselves; and when they would have pursued their journey, courteous Prince Vladímir besought them urgently to abide yet a day with him.

Young Princess Apráxia also came forth from her retreat, arrayed herself with speed, and adorned herself, and came to the table with her nurses, ladies in waiting and fair handmaidens. Young Kasyán she saluted without shame or confusion, though her sin lay in her mind, and Kasyán waved his small right hand over the sugar viands, hedging them about with the sign of the cross, and a blessing.

When all had feasted their fill, they saddled their good steeds, and having taken leave of courteous Prince Vladímir and of each other, they rode each to his own country.

And none of these forty heroes and one ever again roamed the open plain seeking adventures, nor stained their white hands with blood.

When young Kasyán Mikáilovich came to his own land, he raised a cathedral church to Mikóla of Mozháisk, and began to pray constantly to God, and to repent of his sins.

ILYÁ IN DISGUISE.

ON a day, as Ilyá rode in the open plain, he communed thus with himself: "Lo, I have been in many lands, but 'tis long since I was in Kíef town; I will ride thither, and learn what is doing there."

When he came to the palace in the royal city, Prince Vladímir was holding a merry feast. Ilyá entered straight the banquet-hall, crossed himself as prescribed, did reverence as enjoined, bowing on all four sides, and to the Fair Sun Prince Vladímir and the Princess Apráxia in particular. But Vladímir knew him not.

"What is thy name and tribe?" he asked; "and what thy patronymic?"

And Ilyá made answer: "Bright Vladímir, Fair little Sun! I am called Nikíta from beyond the Forest."

"Ho there, thou brave and free little fellow! Sit down with us now, to eat bread and to feast: there is yet a little place yonder at the lower end of the table; the other places are all filled. For prince-nobles, rulers, rich merchants and bold warrior-maids hold feast with me to-day, and sixty great Russian heroes."

The Old Cossáck liked not this speech, — that he should break bread at the lower end of the table; and he said this word: "And ho, thou Fair Sun Prince Vladímir! Thou eatest, feastest with the crows thyself, yet seatest me with the little crows? Nay! but I will not eat bread with nursling crows!"

This speech in turn pleased not the Fair Sun Prince. He sprang to his nimble feet, clouding over like the dusky night, and roared as he had been a wild beast.

"Ho there, ye mighty Russian heroes! Will ye hear yourselves called crows — yea, and little crows? — Seize the fellow, ye heroes, three by each arm; lead him into the spacious court, and there strike off his turbulent head."

They led him forth; but Ilyá waved one hand, and three heroes lay dead; he waved the other hand, and the other three fell dead likewise.

Then Prince Vladímir commanded that twelve should seize him; and with them it fared the same. Then twelve grasped him, with six more behind; and these eighteen met their fate likewise, for Ilyá's heroic heart burned within him when he was thus led out with ignominy.

He fitted an arrow to his stout bow. "Fly, my shaft, about the princely windows," he conjured it; "bear off all the golden spires, and the wonder-working crosses on God's temples."

Then he gathered up all the spires and crosses, went to the royal pot-house, sold the precious spires for countless treasure, and began to drink up the imperial roofs in green wine. He assembled also all the hangers-on of the pot-house, sots, and all who could drink green wine, led them into the kabák, and bade them help him drink the princely spires.

"What will the Prince do," said they, "when he knoweth that we are drinking his royal spires?"

"Drink, boon companions! care ye not for that. To-morrow I shall reign as Prince in Kíef town, and ye shall be my chiefs."

— Fair Sun Vladímir of royal Kíef perceived that a great misfortune was at hand, and knew not who it might be that was come thus to town. But young Dobrýnya Nikítich spoke up: "I know all the mighty heroes save one, — the Old Cossáck Ilyá of Múrom. Of him I have heard that his death is not decreed in battle. This is no Nikíta from beyond the Forest. It is Ilyá of Múrom. Thou hast not known, Vladímir, how to welcome thy guest on his coming, nor honor him at his going."

"Whom shall we send to bid him to an honorable feast?" said Vladímir in amaze. "Bold Alyósha Popóvich will not know how to bid him, and Churílo Plenkóvich is good for nothing but to strut among the maids and women. We must send a clever man, who can read and write, one whose discourse is reasonable. Go thou, therefore, Dobrýnya Nikítich; beat thy forehead against the brick floor, against damp mother earth, before him, and say: 'Prince Vladímir hath sent me to thee, thou Old Cossáck, Ilyá of Múrom, to bid thee to a worshipful feast. He knew thee not, good youth, and for that cause alone did he place thee at the lower end of the board to eat his bread. But now he entreateth thee to him with heartiness and great joy, and commands thee not to bear ill will for what is past. For thy place, which was the worst of all shall now be the best, to wit, in the great corner.'"

Then Dobrýnya thought within himself: "Shall I not go to sudden death at Ilyá's hands? But if I obey not Fair Sun Prince Vladímir, it will fare ill with me."

So he betook himself to the imperial pot-house, where sat Ilyá of Múrom drinking and carousing with the brawlers.

"It is better that I should approach him from behind!" thought Dobrýnya. And so he did, and seized Ilyá by his mighty shoulders, and delivered his message.

"Happy art thou, young Dobrýnya Nikítich," quoth the Old Cossáck, "in that thou camest upon me from behind. Hadst thou approached me from the front, thou shouldst have become ashes ere now! Now go, and say these words to thy Fair Sun Prince: 'Let strict ukases be promulgated throughout all the towns of Kíef and Chérnigof, that all the pot-houses and drinking places of whatever sort be opened freely for the space of three days, that all the people may drink green wine without price. And whoso drinketh no green wine, let him quaff the beer of drunkenness; and he who drinketh that not, sweet mead; that all may know that the Old Cossáck Ilyá of Múrom is come to famous Kíef town.' Let this be done, and let an honorable banquet be made, or the Prince shall reign no longer than until to-morrow's morn!"

Then quickly, quickly, very, very quickly and with speed ran Dobrýnya to Prince Vladímir, and quickly, very, very quickly were the stern ukases issued, and a mighty banquet prepared.

And vast multitudes assembled in the pot-houses, not to eat or drink, but to view the Old Cossáck.

When Ilyá came to the princely palace, he did reverence to all, and to the Prince and Princess in particular. Then Vladímir rose to his nimble feet, and spoke: "Ho there, thou Old Cossáck Ilyá of Múrom! Here is a place for thee beside me, either on my right hand or my left, and yet a third place — wherever it pleaseth thee to sit." Therewith he took Ilyá by his white hands, and kissed him on his sugar mouth.

And as they sat on the four-square stools about the oaken tables laden with sweet viands, Ilyá took not the highest place, but a lesser, and put the sots from the imperial pot-house about him. And they began to eat and drink and make merry.

Thus was Ilyá reconciled to courteous Prince Vladímir.

DOBRÝNYA THE DRAGON-SLAYER, AND MARÍNA.

FROM far, very far in the open plain, and farther yet in the valley, fled the herd of beasts, of wild beasts and serpents: at their head ran the Skiper-beast, with woolly hide, crumpled horns, and little hoofs of steel. The Skiper-beast fled to the Dniepr river, and all the Dniepr's waters were troubled. Its fair steep banks quaked, the delicate tree-tops fell to the earth in concert, brothers, when they heard of that birth. — For in Holy Russia the Rich, young Dobrýnya[1] Nikítich was born that day.

When Dobrýnya grew to man's estate, three years he feasted, three years he served as steward, three more he stood as keeper at the gate. Yet no fair word did he win of Vladímir, or soft bread, but only a good steed.

In the tenth year, courteous Prince Vladímir made a great feast in royal Kíef town, whereat many heroes and bold warrior-maidens were assembled, eating and drinking merrily. Young Dobrýnya Nikítich sat at the end of the oaken board, and spoke:

"Fair Sun Vladímir of royal Kíef! I have

---
[1] Dobrýnya is partly historical. See Appendix.

served thee long in thy princely court: grant me leave now to wander about Kíef, through its narrow lanes."

"Fly not forth, young sparrow," answered Prince Vladímir, "young Dobrýnya, gallop not away."

But all the mighty Russian heroes said: "Go crave permission of the honorable widow, Afímya Alexándrevna, thy mother, to prowl about the narrow lanes of Kíef."

This Dobrýnya did, and his mother counselled him: "Walk through all the streets of Kíef town, roam the little alleys at thy will; only, go not to the vile Princess Marína Ignátievna, who dwelleth in a certain little lane. She is a witch, she hath murdered Prince on Prince, many Kings and Crown princes, nine Russian heroes, clear falcons all, and common folk without number. If thou goest to that Marína, thou wilt lose thy life, Dobrýnya."

The next day Dobrýnya rose right early, washed himself very white in spring water, took his stout bow, his quiver of fiery arrows, and set out. As he wandered through the streets and many narrow lanes, he shot small sparrows on the halls, blue doves upon the chambers, and so wandering, came at length to Marína's lane. Her palace was richly adorned. In her window sat a dark-blue dove and his mate cooing, yellow bill to bill, and mouth to mouth, with wing enfolding wing; and it pleased not Dobrýnya that they should sit thus. He strung a silken cord to his bow, and fitted thereto a flaming arrow, and shot at the dove and his mate. The cord sang on the stout bow, but his left foot slipped, his right hand trembled — the arrow struck not the dove and mate, but flew straight to the lofty palace, through the lattice window to Marínushka the vile, and slew Tugárin Dragon's Son her dear friend who was with her there.

Dobrýnya reflected: — "If I enter that palace I shall lose my head; if I enter not — my arrow." Then he sent his trusty servant, his page, for the arrow. "Thou miscreant, Marína! give back our burning arrow," quoth the page. But Marína said: "Nay, let him who shot the arrow come himself." Thereupon Dobrýnya entered with haste the spacious court, and with courtesy the new halls: fairly came he into the new chamber, and took his fiery arrow.

Marínka lay upon a couch; in her right hand was a fiery dragon; on her left, two little serpents. She took Dobrýnya by his white hand, by his silver ring, kissed his sugar mouth, and said:

"Ah, sweet Dobrýnya Nikítich, give me thy love!" Dobrýnya made answer: "Sweet Marínushka Ignátievna, I will not! Thou hast slain nine mighty Russian heroes, and art minded to slay me likewise." Then he turned from the new chamber, and went forth into the spacious court, and so home to his mother.

Up sprang Marínushka then, seized her dagger, and hacked Dobrýnya's footsteps, flung them into the oven painted with many devices, and conjured them with a powerful incantation: " Burn, ye footsteps of Dobrýnya, burn, in this oven of many hues; and may his spirit likewise burn within him for me! As I cut these footsteps, may Dobrýnya's dear little heart cut for me!"[1]

Then worse than a sharp knife cut Dobrýnya's heroic heart. That evening he ate nothing, at midnight he slumbered not, and waited only for the white dawn.

Early rang the matin bells, and very early he arose, girt on his sharp sword, and went to the cathedral to the service; and thence to Marína's dwelling.

When he came to the Princess, he bowed low before her; but she rose not, sat in discourteous wise, and returned not his salutation.

"Ah, sweet Marínushka, give me thy love!" he said.

"What need is there for thee, young Dobrýnya, to jest and make merry over me? Long since I sought thy love, and thou lovedst me not: — and now thou cravest it of me! Now thou art in my hands! If I will, I can turn thee into a magpie, a raven, a pig, or an aurochs with golden horns,

---

[1] The "charm of footsteps" practised by the ancient Germans is still employed in a slightly different form among the Burmese.

silver hoofs and velvet hide, or into a frog of the under world; — and from that last estate there is no return forever."

Then she transformed him into a brown aurochs, and sent him forth into the open plain, to drink swamp water and to eat marsh grass, to be chief over the nine brown aurochs who roamed there — the mighty heroes her bridegrooms.

And as Dobrýnya roamed there, a golden-horned aurochs, he espied a flock of geese, which belonged to Avdótya Ivánovna, his beloved aunt. All these did he trample under foot to the last gosling, not one did he leave. Then the goose-herds came and made complaint.

"Aï, young Avdótya Ivánovna! an aurochs with golden horns hath trampled under foot all our geese; not one hath he left us." After them followed the keepers of the swans, the shepherds and herdsmen, with the same complaint. Not a living creature of all their flocks and herds had the golden aurochs spared. Then Avdótya Ivánovna spoke:

"That aurochs of the golden horns is my well-beloved nephew, young Dobrýnya, whom Marína the Vile hath transformed." But when the guardians of the horses came and told how the aurochs had dispersed their charge over all the plain, sparing none, Avdótya rose in wrath. She turned herself into a magpie, and flew to Marína the Vile, perched in her little lattice window, and began to scold, and say : " Vile Princess Marínushka ! why hast thou transformed Dobrýnya into a golden-hornèd aurochs, and loosed him to roam the open plain ? Turn back Dobrýnya from his aurochs form, else will I turn thee into a long-tailed dog, and the children shall pursue thee ; — into a magpie, and thou shalt hover evermore above the open plain in semblance of a pie."

Then Marína perceived that there was no help, and so transformed herself into a gray swallow, flew to the open plain, and alighting upon the aurochs's golden horns chattered and said : " Swear to me, Dobrýnya Nikítich — for thou hast roamed the field and art weary, the bubbling marshes and art tired — swear now a great oath to take the golden crown with me, with Marínushka, and I will turn thee back from a golden-hornèd aurochs to thine own shape again."

" Ah, sweet Marínushka ! " Dobrýnya answered, " only turn me from this form, and I will take that great oath. I will wed thee, Marína, and will even give thee the little lessons wherewith a husband instructeth his wife."

Then Marína believed him, and turned him into a goodly youth as of old.

" Now I must wed thee about a bush, Marínushka," he said, " about a willow bush in the open plain." So three times about the willow bush they paced, and Dobrýnya called Marína his wife,[1] and set out with her for royal Kíef town.

When they were come to Marína's lofty palace, Dobrýnya commanded the servant:

"Aï, my trusty servant! prithee a cup of green wine; yet give me first a sharp sword."

Then Marína turned him into a little ermine, and began to frighten him; but the ermine escaped her snares. Then she turned him into a falcon, and began to alarm and to tease the falcon, which waved his wings, and besought the Princess Marína:

"I cannot fly as a falcon should, I can only wave my wings; grant me to drain a cup of green wine."

The young Princess thereupon transformed him into a goodly youth, and Dobrýnya shouted:

"Ho there, my trusty servant! a cup of green wine!"

But the trusty servant gave him very quickly a sharp sword. The cup of wine he quaffed not, but brandished his sword, and cut off Marína's turbulent head for her ungentle deeds.

In the morning he went to his warm steam bath, and thither came princes and nobles.

"Hail, Dobrýnya Nikítich, with thy bride!" they said.

"Hail, ye princes and nobles and all the Court of Vladímir! Last night I was wedded, brothers, and no longer alone, but now I am single and no

---

[1] See Appendix: *Dobrýnya the Dragon-slayer*.

longer wedded. I have cut off Marína's turbulent head for her ruthless deeds; for she had slain many Russian people, Princes and their heirs, Kings and Crown Princes, nine mighty Russian heroes, and of common folk an innumerable host!"

IVÁN GODINÓVICH.

In Kíef town dwelt a great and mighty hero, Iván Godinóvich,[1] nephew to Prince Vladímir. Long he roamed through many infidel lands; many great hosts did he assemble, frightened Tzars and slew warriors.

Upon a certain day, courteous Prince Vladímir made a great supper, whereat sat many honorable widows. Iván Godinóvich sat with eyes fixed upon the floor, eating nothing, drinking nothing, tasting not the white swan.

"Ho there, Ivánushka!" spoke Prince Vladímir. "Wherefore art thou sad? Is not thy seat to thy liking? Have I passed thee by with the cup of drunkenness? Hath the fool scoffed at thee, hath a black raven cawed at thee, or have the dogs barked?"

"None of these things have come to pass, Fair Sun Prince Vladímir," Ivánushka replied. "But all in Kíef town are wedded: I only sit alone."

"Why then dost thou not wed likewise, Iván Godinóvich?"

"Fain would I wed, lord, but that may not be.

---
[1] See Appendix.

Where I would take, there I am refused: and where they would give, I will not take."

Then spoke courteous Prince Vladímir: "Ho there, Iván! Sit thou on this folding-chair, and write a letter."

So Iván sat upon the folding-chair, and wrote a letter of wooing to Dmítry the rich merchant in Chérnigof town; and Vladímir the Prince set his hand to it. "'Tis not thou, Iván Godinóvich, who now goest a-wooing: — 'tis I, Prince Vladímir, who woo."

Then quickly did Iván array himself, and quickly, very, very quickly and with speed did he ride to Chérnigof town, one hundred and eighty versts by measurement: that space Iván compassed in two hours. When he came to the courtyard of Dmítry the Merchant, he leaped from his good steed and bound him to the oaken pillar. Then he entered the fair hall, prayed to the Saviour's picture, did reverence to Merchant Dmítry, and laid the letter upon the round table.

Guest[1] Dmítry broke the seal, looked upon it and read it.

"Foolish Iván! Senseless Iván!" quoth he. "Thou art not the first, Ivánushka! My Avdótya

---

[1] The ancient name for a merchant of the highest class. In the time of Iván the Terrible, according to the Code, a Guest received damages to the extent of 50 rubles for an insult, a common merchant 5 r., a boyárin 600 r. The comparative rank indicated had long prevailed, probably from Vladímir's day.

is now betrothed to Tzar Koschéi of a distant land. If I give her to a Tzar, she will be a Tzarítza, and all the nobles will bow before her in homage; but if I give her to thee, she will be a serf, and must sweep the cottage and clean the stable. But I have a dog in my courtyard; her will I give to thee."

Then was Iván grieved: he seized the letter and ran forth, mounted his good steed, and hastened with what speed he might, to Kíef, and told Prince Vladímir all that had passed.

When Prince Vladímir heard how Iván had been scorned, he was grieved for Ivánushka's sake, tore the black curls[1] from his head, and cast them upon the brick floor. "Take her not, Iván," he said.

Then was Iván wroth, and departed from the oaken tables, from the cloths richly patterned with drawn work; leave took he of none, but opened the doors very wide and shut them very hard, thrusting the door-posts aside.

"Ho there, Iván Godinóvich!" cried courteous Prince Vladímir then, "Take a hundred of my men, and a second hundred of the princely nobles, and yet a third hundred of thine own. Go in honor to woo, and if they give not the maid willingly, then take her by force."

In haste did the youths assemble, and prepare for their journey. They had but passed the swift

---

[1] Vladímir's hair is sometimes black, though generally golden.

Dniepr when a powdering of white snow fell, and upon this light, pure snow they beheld traces of three beasts. The first trace was of a brown aurochs, the second of a fierce lion, the third of a wild boar. Then Iván began to tell off the youths in companies. He sent a hundred men after the brown aurochs, commanding them to take him with care and without bloody wounds; another hundred sent he in pursuit of the fierce lion, and a third hundred after the wild boar, — these likewise must be taken heedfully and without disfiguring wounds, and borne to royal Kíef, to great Prince Vladímir.

But Iván himself went on alone to Chérnigof town, rode into the midst of Guest Dmítry's spacious court, and bound his good steed to the oaken pillar. Then he entered the fair chamber, and prayed before the Saviour's picture, but did no reverence to Dmítry the rich merchant. With Dmítry were sitting then, divers of the Tatar body-guard,[1] who had brought a garment, in value one hundred thousand rubles, from the Tzar Koschéi to his love Avdótya Dmítrievna. — The Tzar himself was but three versts from Chérnigof, and with him was a host of three thousand men.

"Give me thy daughter," spoke Iván Godinóvich.

"Thou shalt have the dog in my courtyard," Dmítry made answer as before.

---

[1] Uláni.

"I shall neither ask thee much nor long dispute," said Iván; and thereupon he rose from the hewn wall bench, pushed aside the silken hangings, and so came into the new hall where sat the White Swan weaving linen. "Hail, Avdótya the White Swan!" he said in greeting. Upon Avdótya's head were white swans, on her left shoulder black sables; on her right shoulder sat bright falcons; on the frame of her loom perched dark blue doves, and on her loom-bench, black ravens: and her face was like the first fair snows of autumn.

"And hail to thee, fair Iván Godinóvich," she answered; then left her delicate linen, took Iván by his white hands, kissed his sugar lips, and fondled him.

Then Iván delayed no longer, but led Avdótya forth to the fair hall. There she began to weep and to say: "Thou hast known, my father, how to feed me and give me drink, to cherish me until I had attained my growth: but one thing, my father, thou hast not known — how to give me in marriage without great bloodshed!"

To this the Chérnigovian made reply: "Wilt thou not eat bread and salt with me, Ivánushka Godinóvich?"[1]

"Thou hast not refreshed the guest at his coming," quoth Iván, "and at his going it shall not be permitted to thee."

---

[1] "Bread and salt" is the epic euphuism for hospitality.

Said Dmítry: "I have written a letter to Koschéi the Deathless, and have thereto set my hand, and he shall cut off thy turbulent head."

"When Koschéi cutteth off my head," quoth Iván, "then will be the fitting hour to boast, both for him and for thee."

Then he set Avdótya on his good steed, and rode forth upon the open plain. After they had forded many streams, night overtook them on the plain; and Iván pitched a pavilion of white damask linen for himself and his Avdótya.

Now when the news came to Koschéi, he went forth to the stable-yard, took a foal with nine chains, put on him heroic trappings, girded on his broad sword, took his sharp spear and his battle-mace, seized on the way his steel dagger, and rode forth over the plain until he came to Chérnigof. There he learned that Iván Godinóvich had in truth carried off Avdótya the White Swan, and he rode in pursuit.

When he espied the pavilion of white damask, he shouted in a piercing voice: "Dwelleth there any in this pavilion of fine damask? Let him who is alive therein, come forth!"

Iván heard this, and roused himself, good youth, from sleep, came forth, and washed himself with fresh spring water, dried himself upon a towel of fine damask, crossed himself as prescribed, did reverence as enjoined, and prayed to the most wondrous Saviour. Then he mounted his good steed, took his arms, and rode at Koschéi. The adversaries went apart about the space of three versts, and when they came together they greeted each other, and smote each other with their Tatar spears, but yet pierced one another not. Again they rode aside about three versts, came at each other, saluted courteously and brandished their battle-maces.

Iván's mace fell upon Koschéi's head, and Koschéi flew from his good steed. Ivánushka was cunning: he leaped over his good steed's mane to the earth, hurled himself upon Koschéi's black breast, undid the silken loops, unfastened the buttons of pure gold, and would have pierced his black breast, and taken out his restive heart with his liver. But he had forgotten his dagger of damascened steel, and shouted with a great voice: "Ho there, my White Swan Avdótya! Throw my steel dagger from the white pavilion: I must needs prick Koschéi's black breast, and draw forth his restive heart."

Avdótya obeyed his behest, and fetched the dagger. But when Koschéi espied her, he spoke this word:

"Bethink thee, Avdótya the White Swan! If thou livest with Iván thou wilt be a servant, and must bow in lowly reverence before all men: but I will make thee a Tzarítza. Many lands shall do homage to thee, and all nobles shall do reverence to thee. Do thou therefore seize Iván by his ruddy curls, and drag him from my breast."

And Avdótya listened to his counsel. She flung the dagger far out upon the plain, seized Iván by his ruddy curls, and dragged him aside; and so Koschéi got the upper hand. As he sat upon Iván's white breast he opened his garments, and would have taken out his restive heart, and his liver, with his dagger which he snatched from its sheath.

But Avdótya had compassion on Ivánushka, and said:

"Pierce not Iván's white breast, Koschéi, pluck not his restive heart therefrom. Let us rather bind him with this three-stranded cord to yon damp, ringbarked oak." And they did so.

— As Koschéi came forth from the white pavilion, very early the next morning, two dark blue doves alighted upon the damp oak; and he told Avdótya.

"Shoot me those dark blue doves," quoth the White Swan, "for I would fain eat of them."

Koschéi hearkened to her, fitted a sharp burning arrow to his bow, and conjured it:

"Fall not, my arrow, in the water or upon the damp earth; but fall, my shaft, upon the damp oak tree, and into the right eye of the blue dove thereon."

But Iván conjured in his turn: "O stout bow,

clear burning mother arrow! fall not to earth, strike not the dove; but bound back from this damp oak, and pierce Koschéi's black breast, drag forth his royal heart, to the discontent of old crones, and the cawing of black crows."

So the arrow did, and attained Koschéi's impetuous heart; and thus died Koschéi the Deathless.[1]

Then Avdótya bethought herself once more and wept. "Long is woman's hair," she said, "but short, in sooth, are her wits! I have deserted one shore, yet attained not unto the other. I will slay Iván, and go back to Chérnigof a maid."

Thereupon she took the sharp sword from where it lay upon damp mother earth. But Ivánushka began to entreat her: "Aï, Avdótya, my White Swan! unbind me now from the damp oak!"

"Wilt thou take me for thy wife, young Iván Godinóvich? If thou wilt swear it, I will sever the silken bonds upon thy white hands. But if thou wilt not swear it, I will give thee over to speedy death."

Then Iván spoke firmly as he lay upon the damp earth:

---

[1] Koschéi is merely one of the incarnations of the dark spirit. His "death" is generally concealed in some object remote from him, which it is necessary to destroy. He frequently figures in the *skázkas* (tales), and occasionally dies, as in this case; though always called the "Deathless." Specimens of these tales may be found in "Russian Folk-lore" (p. 85), by W. R. S. Ralston.

"Release me, and I will neither beat thee, nor impute to thee great blame. I will but read thee three lessons meet for a wife."

Yet Avdótya was afraid, and would still have cut off Iván's turbulent head, with her sharp sword. But her white hands trembled; and the sword fell not upon Iván's white throat, but upon the silken cords, and severed them.

Then the good youth rose up at liberty, placed Avdótya upon his good steed, and rode over the open plain.

"Alight now at the ford, Avdótya my White Swan," he said: "pull off my morocco boot and fetch me fresh water therein, for I would fain drink at this spot."

Avdótya answered him: "Thou carest not to drink, Ivánushka Godinóvich, but only to slay me!"

This seemed to Ivánushka a grief and a great evil; so he hewed off Avdótya's arms to the elbow, for her first wifely lesson: "I need not these," quoth he; "they have embraced Koschéi." For his second lesson he cut off her lips, saying: "These I need not: they have kissed Koschéi." And for the third lesson, he smote off her feet to the knee: "Of these I have no need," quoth he: "they bore thee from my white pavilion to drag Iván by his ruddy curls."

Last of all, he cut off her turbulent head.

Then he washed his sword in the Dniepr river, and rode to Kíef town, where all the mighty heroes came forth to meet him.

Alyósha Popóvich laughed in his face:

"Hail, Ivánushka!" said he. "Thou art wedded? But thou hast no companion with whom to dwell."

And Iván Godinóvich replied:

" I have wedded my sharp sword!"

DOBRÝNYA AND THE ADVENTURE OF THE PAVILION.

As young Dobrýnya Nikítich roamed the open plain on a day, he came to a damp oak, whereon sat a black raven. Dobrýnya drew his bow from its case, fitted to the cord a flaming arrow, and made ready to shoot the raven. But the bird addressed him in human language:

"Now aï, Dobrýnya Nikítich! Slay me not, and I will reveal all things to thee. The children in the streets have a proverb: 'In killing a graybeard there is no salvation, and none shall receive profit from shooting a raven.' With the blue plumes of a raven may no man solace himself, and my flesh thou canst not eat." Half the raven's wings were white; — and he said:

"Aï, Dobrýnya Nikítich! Go thou to the lofty mountain; for there be three wondrous marvels, three marvellous damsels. The first is a wonder of white whiteness, the second is redly beautiful, the third a black marvel of darkness."

Dobrýnya reflected then in haste, and replied to the raven: "What thou hast said of the old man and the raven is true." Then he put aside his dart, and thought: "Better is it that I should go to the lofty mountain, to yon steep hill, and view those three wondrous marvels, those three marvellous damsels."

So he turned his good steed in haste, quickly, quickly, very, very quickly, and with speed, and rode to that lofty mountain. And as he gazed about him, lo! there stood a pavilion of white linen. On the pavilion was a lock of damascened steel, and upon the lock this writing: "Whoso entereth this pavilion, shall not issue thence alive."

Dobrýnya's heroic heart burned within him when he read that, and he smote the lock with his fist, so that the lock fell upon the damp earth. Within the pavilion, he beheld tables set and viands thereon, and he entered. Much as the youth ate and drank, even more did he fling upon the ground, pour out and trample under foot.

Then the youth lay down to sleep, and as he slept and took his ease, he wist not of the peril hanging over him.

From afar in the open plain came Alyósha Popóvich riding, and gazed upon that sight. — More had been cast down, poured out and trampled under foot, than had been eaten. Then was Alyósha very wroth, and his heroic heart burned within him. He grasped his sharp-pointed spear, and would have pierced Dobrýnya's white breast; but he reflected:

"No honor shall I win, nor youthful praise, if I slay a sleeping man, who is no better than a dead one. Rather will I mount Dobrýnya's good steed, and fight and contend with this Dobrýnya on his own good steed."

So Alyósha mounted, and smote Dobrýnya with the butt end of his spear. Thereupon the hero awakened from his sleep, and sprang quickly forth in his fine white shirt without a girdle, and without his shoes, grasped his heroic mace, and they two began to fight. Dobrýnya leaped about on foot, but Alyósha rode Dobrýnya's good steed. All day they contended eating nothing, all day they fought drinking nothing. Two more days and nights they fought.

Then came a clap of thunder, and mother earth began to quiver. When Ilyá of Múrom the Old Cossáck heard that, he pondered: "'Tis Russian heroes in battle. Where contend they now, and fight?"

In haste he saddled his good steed, Cloudfall, with girth upon girth, saddlecloth on saddlecloth, felt on felt, and over all his little Cherkéssian saddle, with its girth of silk, saying to himself: "Not for dainty beauty is this, brothers, but for heroic strength." — They saw the good youth as he mounted, as he rode they saw him not nor knew whither his course was directed.

When Ilyá came to the lofty mountain, he beheld young Dobrýnya and bold Alyósha in combat.

Then he seized Dobrýnya in his right hand, bold Alyósha in his left, and shouted at the top of his voice: "Why contend ye, mighty Russian heroes?"

Alyósha answered: "Ah, thou Old Cossáck, Ilyá of Múrom! How could I refain from fighting? The tables were all laid in my pavilion, and viands set thereon; and this Dobrýnya Nikítich cast to the earth and trampled under foot as much as he ate and drank, so that I was ashamed for the youth."

"I thank thee, Alyósha," spoke Ilyá, "for defending thine own." And to Dobrýnya he said:

"And thou, Dobrýnya Nikítich, my cross-brother in arms, why contendest thou?"

"Ilyá of Múrom, my brother in arms, Old Cossáck! How was it possible not to fight? For this dog and robber had a lying inscription written: 'Whoso entereth this pavilion shall not issue thence alive,' and I desired to remain alive."

"I thank thee, Dobrýnya," quoth the Old Cossáck, "for that thou hast entered boldly into the dwelling of a stranger." And yet more said little Ilyá.

"Calm now your heroic hearts, and call each other brother in arms, and swear brotherhood, with exchanging of crosses." Then he flattered and persuaded them, and they began not again to fight and contend, but swore brotherhood on the cross: Dobrýnya called himself the elder brother, and Alyósha called himself the younger. And so they parted and came to Kíef town.

CHURÍLO PLENKÓVICH, THE FOP.

In royal Kíef town, courteous Prince Vladímir held a great feast. The day declined, the feast waxed merry, and Prince Vladímir solaced himself greatly. Then strange people thrust themselves into his presence, — one hundred young men, and a second hundred and yet a third of bold youths. All were beaten and wounded, their turbulent heads all bruised with cudgels and bound about with their girdles. They touched their foreheads to the earth, and made complaint:

"Our light, our lord, Prince Vladímir! As we rode upon the plain, beside Soróga river, across the royal fens, we found no living thing: neither fierce roving beast nor flying bird. We found but three hundred youths; their steeds were Latínsky,[1] their caftáns of damask, their surcoats of scarlet, their caps had golden crowns. They set snares of silk in thy pine forests for the black sables and the martens, drove the foxes and the white foreign hares from their burrows: they shot the aurochs and stag, and us they beat and wounded. And

---

[1] General name for any thing from Western Europe, where the *Latin faith* prevailed, in contradistinction to "Orthodox" Russia.

thou, lord, hast no booty and we no guerdon, and our wives and children are deprived of their protectors; — for we must wander through the world, for lack of food."

Vladímir, prince of royal Kíef town, ate, drank, and made merry, and heeded not their petition. And this host had not departed from the court when another host arrived, three hundred youths, five hundred youths, all fishermen, all beaten and wounded sore, their tempestuous heads bound with girdles, for the cudgel blows. They also did lowly reverence to bright Prince Vladímir, and made complaint, in like fashion to the first. They had traversed the lakes and rivers and royal ponds, and had taken nothing, but had espied five hundred youths catching white-fish, pikes, carps, and lesser fishes, so that the Prince could get nothing. They, receiving therefore no payment save a cudgelling from those bold youths, would be forced to roam the world for a livelihood.

To this complaint Vladímir paid no more heed than to the first, but continued to eat, drink, and make merry. This company had not quitted the courtyard when two more appeared, the royal falconers and hawkers, with their turbulent heads all broken and bound up. These made complaint that in all the open plains, royal fens and pleasure isles, they could espy neither hawk nor falcon, nor aught but a thousand men, who rode hither and thither, catching bright sparrow-hawks and white noble falcons. And these men, who had assaulted and wounded the royal falconers, were called Churílo's [1] body-guard.

While the falconers still stood in the royal presence, came merchants and gardeners, and told how Churílo's wild guards had plucked up all their garlic and onions, broken all their white cabbages, and insulted all the young damsels and the young men of Kíef.

This word touched Prince Vladímir, and he inquired of them: "Who is this Churílo?" Old Bermyág Vasílievich stepped forth.

"Lord, I have known Churílo this long while; he dwelleth not in Kíef, but in Little Kíef.[2] His palace covereth seven versts; about it standeth an iron fence; upon each paling thereof is a knob, and that knob is a pure, round pearl. In the midst of the courtyard stand halls, chambers of white oak, hung with gray beaver skins; and the ceilings thereof are hung with black sables, and the centre beam is covered with leather. The floor of his own bower, the space about the oven, is of pure silver, the hooks and hasps of damascened gold. His first gates are of carven oak, the second all crystal, the third of tin. All his thresholds are of precious fishes' teeth, and all his ovens of tiles."

---

[1] See Appendix.
[2] In modern times a place near Kíef has been known by the name of Churilóvshina.

When Vladímir heard that, he arrayed himself in haste, and commanded a journey. With him he took his Princess, his nobles and mighty heroes, Dobrýnya Nikítich, and old Bermyág Vasílievich, summoned five hundred men, and set out for Churílo Plenkóvich's court.

Old Plenkó came to meet them. For the Prince and Princess he opened his gates of carved work, for the princes and nobles those of crystal, for the common folk the tin. Then old Plenkó the silk-merchant led Vladímir and the Princess Apráxia to a richly patterned chamber, to another of crystal, and a third of lattice work, and so to the golden-domed tower where all was heavenly with sun and moon, stars innumerable and white dawns.

In the fair hall he seated them at tables richly decked, and assigned fitting places to the princes and nobles. Then the cunning cooks fetched sweet viands and mead, and all sorts of liquors from beyond the sea, to give mirth to the princes. Joyful was their converse, and cheerful the day.

Prince Vladímir pulled aside the little lattice window by which he sat with his princess; and as they gazed forth upon the open plain, they saw a hundred good youths come riding from afar, from mother Soróga river.

The youths' good steeds were all of one matched color, their bits alike of bronze, their caftáns all of scarlet cloth with streaming girdles. The shoes upon their feet were of green morocco, the tips awl-like, the heels sharp (under the heels small sparrows might hop and flutter, over the insteps, an egg might roll).

Then Prince Vladímir inquired of Plenkó whether it were his son thus riding, and the old silk-merchant made answer, smiling:

"Nay, these be Churílo's cooks, who make his green wine."

When that throng had entered the court, another of five hundred came riding from the plain, all mounted alike and apparelled.

Again Vladímir inquired of Plenkó whether this might be Churílo and his guard; and old Plenkó made answer that these were but Churílo's stewards who served his table. When this troop had entered, a third a thousand strong came from afar, and in their midst a goodly youth, fairer than they all. His locks were like a field of gold with silvery sheen, his neck like the white snows; his cheeks outdid the poppy in hue; like the clear falcon's gleamed his eyes, his brows were like black sables, his little feet were wondrous small: — their traces on fresh fallen snow could not be told from those of the white ermine or the hare. Beneath his mantle of rich sables, he was clad in green samite, with carven buttons of red gold, in fashion like to apples of Siberia.

Lightly rode that host; beneath them the soft grass bent not, the azure flowerets broke not.

From horse to horse sprang that fair youth, from the third horse and past the fourth, hurling high his spear to heaven, as it had been a swan's feather, and catching it hand over hand: as he leaped also, he snatched the good youths' shápkas from their heads, and placed them upon others.

"A misfortune hath come upon me for my sins!" cried Prince Vladímir. "Lo! I am far from home, and there rideth hither to me, a King from the horde, or some threatening ambassador, to sue for my fair niece Beauty.[1]

But old Plenkó poured him a cup of wine, saying: "Fear not, Prince Vladímir! 'Tis but my son Churílo with his guard. When he shall stand before thee, lord, this feast will be but half a feast, this banquet will seem but poor."

Then all began again to eat and drink and make merry, sitting without thought or care. In the court the white day had drawn to even, the fair red sun was sunk in the west, ere Churílo arrived. Yet before him was borne a canopy, that the sun might not scorch his white face.

Old Plenkó went forth upon the railed balcony behind the hall, and cried: "Aï, Churílo Plenkóvich! thou hast here in thy hall, a much-loved guest, Fair Sun Vladímir of royal Kíef. What

---

[1] Zabava or Zapava.

wilt thou now set before him, what gifts bestow upon him?"

Now Churílo was quick-witted and crafty. He took his golden keys, went to his iron-bound coffers, and drew thence great treasure of black sables, and a mantle of precious sables, soft and feathery beneath rich samite from beyond the sea, for Prince Vladímir, fine white damask, in value a hundred thousand rubles, for the Princess Apráxia. To each noble he gave little foxes of the cavern, to every merchant, marten skins, and to the common folk, much gold.

Vladímir accepted these gifts, and said:

"Though the complaints against Churílo were many, yet are his offerings still greater. And now I will not give judgment against him."

And to Churílo he said: "Young Churílo Plenkóvich, it is not fitting that thou shouldst dwell in the country. Wilt thou not come to Kíef, and serve me as seneschal and cupbearer?"

Though some buy off misfortune, Churílo purchased ill-luck at great cost. Yet he rebelled not, but ordered them to saddle his steed in haste, and all rode back to Kíef, so that all maids and wives gazed and marvelled as they passed through the streets.

Then that bright lord, Prince Vladímir, made a great feast for his new steward. Churílo laid the oaken tables, and as he shook back his golden curls, they fell apart as fair round pearls do roll asunder; and as young Princess Apráxia was carving the swan, she cut her right hand, and said:

"Marvel not at this, ye gentlewomen, for I gaze upon Churílo's beauty, upon his yellow curls, his golden ring, and my clear eyes are troubled! Fair my lord, Prince Vladímir, make Churílo thy groom of the chambers. Let him spread the downy feather-bed, place the high cushion, and sit by thy pillow to play upon his gúsly of maple-wood, and solace thee."

Then Vladímir told Churílo that thus it must be; for some buy off misfortune, but Churílo purchased his. So he performed the varied service of groom of the chambers, to the great solace of Prince Vladímir and his Princess, young Apráxia.

When Vladímir made a feast, he sent young Churílo to bid the princes and nobles, and from each guest he commanded him to take ten rubles for himself. And as the goodly youth passed through the streets upon his errand, shaking back his yellow curls like fair round pearls, nuns turned in their cells to gaze upon his beauty, young maids tore off their kokóshniks [1] in admiration.

Then the Princess Apráxia spoke to courteous Prince Vladímir: "Fair lord, this service befitteth Churílo not."

---

[1] A headdress, in shape like a coronet.

Vladímir perceived that misfortune was come upon him, and spoke this word then to Churílo:

"Dwell thou in a cell, Churílo Plenkóvich, or depart now to thine own house, for in my palace I have no longer need of thee."

Then Churílo bowed low in reverence, and went forth from the palace, from Kíef town, and came to the Púchai river, where he began again to dwell in mirth and pleasure.

ILYA AND THE BOON COMPANIONS.

From the city of Galich to Kíef town ran a broad road of forty fathoms: along that road fared a pilgrim, and the road bent beneath his weight. His smock was tattered with use, and a rag was his girdle. His cap weighed forty poods, his foot-gear was of bast, his crutch was nine fathoms, and he leaned upon a hooked staff.

The old man's beard was sprinkled with gray, his head was all white. That aged pilgrim entered Kíef town, and craved refreshment after his long journey, desiring to drink green wine in the royal pot-house.

He entered very softly, trod very lightly, said a prayer, crossing himself as enjoined and bowing on all sides as prescribed.

"Hail, ye vintner's men," quoth he. "Pour me a pail and a half of wine, to refresh me, a wandering pilgrim."

But the vintners made answer: "Nay, thou old dog, thou gray hound, we will not trust thee. We will not give thee the green wine without thy money."

But the pilgrim took from his neck an ancient

and wondrous cross, six poods and a half in weight, of purest antique gold. "Take this cross as surety," he said; but they dared not.

But the poor boon companions of the pot-house, the peasants and villagers gave each a kopék, and bought therewith a bucket and a half of green wine for the pilgrim. The old man grasped it with one hand, swallowed it in one breath, and said:

"I thank ye, boon companions, and peasants of the village! Ye have given the old man wine to drunkenness; but now it is late. Come ye therefore to me to-morrow right early, and I will give you all wine even to drunkenness, in return."

Then the aged man climbed upon the brick oven, and slept. Very early on the morrow, as the warm red sun arose, he descended to the cellars, burst open the doors with his foot, took a cask of forty under one arm, another of the same under the other, and rolled a third before him with his foot, into the green meadow, and so to the marketplace. Then he shouted with all his heroic might, in a piercing, thunderous voice:

"Ho, ye boon companions and ye peasants of the village! Come to the old man's feast! I will give ye all green wine even to drunkenness, without price."

When the vintners heard that, they assembled, eighty men in number, to take the green wine from the aged pilgrim, but could do nothing, and so went to petition Prínce Vladímir against him. They had told all their griefs, and Vladímir said:

"I will view this pilgrim, vintners, and I myself will requite you."

All the boon companions and village peasants had drunk their fill, when the old man said:

"Go now to your own homes, to your young wives and little children; but I will return to the royal pot-house, and sleep upon the oven of bricks."

This he did, and early on the morrow came trusty servants from the Prince, who said.

"Come to Prince Vladímir, thou wandering pilgrim."

But the old man answered: "In vain do ye disquiet me, brothers! Let the old man sleep." Then he descended from the oven, and went through Kíef, past the princely palace, and cried in a mighty voice:

"Hey, Prince Vladímir of royal Kíef! Receive here thy money for the green wine from the Cossáck of the Don, from Ilyá of Múrom. I go now to the open plain, to the heroic barriers, to the damp oak." And therewith he departed.

DIUK STEPÁNOVICH.

BEYOND the sea, the blue sea, from Glorious Volhýnia town, from Galícia the Fair, from Koréla the Perverse, from India the Rich, came young Lord Diuk[1] Stepánovich. Like a white gerfalcon fluttering, like a small white ermine coursing, like a small, clear goshawk flying, rode Lord Diuk forth. Like the bright falcon he sat his dapple-bay; his bow-case and his quiver beat his hips, and like a wild beast was his good steed Shaggy beneath him.

The young lord's casque and armor were of pure silver, in value three thousand rubles; his shirt of mail was of fair red gold, in value forty thousand. His good steed was worth five hundred rubles; — for at rivers he required no fords, but leaped a stream of five hundred versts, from shore to shore, at a bound. His stout bow was prized at three thousand; for its stem was of pure silver, the tips of red gold, the cord of white silk of Samarcand. Each burning arrow in his quiver was valued at ten rubles.

Lord Diuk rode a-hunting, beside the broad

---

[1] Dux — duke.˙ Little Russian, *duka*, a rich man. See Appendix.

blue Ocean-sea, and peaceful bays, shooting foxes, martens, blue-gray eagles, geese, white swans and small gray, downy ducks. By day he shot, by night gathered up his arrows. Where his arrows flew, a flame seemed to burn; where they fell and lay, rays streamed as from the bright, clear moon. Three hundred arrows he shot and three: the three hundred he found again, but not the three; and he marvelled thereat.

"I know the value of the three hundred, but of the three which are lost, I know not the value — for they are priceless. They were made of the reed tree, smoothed upon twelve sides and gilded, the shafts set with precious jacinth stones, so that they darted rays like the fair red sun. They were feathered with the plumes of the blue-gray eagle, fast set with sturgeon glue: — not the plumes of the eagle which flieth over the meadows, but of that eagle which hovereth over the blue sea, and reareth his young thereon, and alighteth upon the white Alátyr[1] stone. When he ruffleth his feathers the sea is tossed, the cocks crow in the hamlets; and as he plumeth himself, he droppeth his feathers. Ships came on a day with sailor guests, and gathered up three feathers, the eagle plumes, more precious than satin or cut velvet, and brought them as gifts to kings and princes and Diuk Stepánovich."

Then young Diuk mounted his good steed, and

---

[1] For some account of this curious stone, see Appendix.

rode towards home. On the broad highway he met one and thirty wandering psalm-singers, and shouted in piercing tones: "Are ye thieves, highwaymen, midnight prowlers or church robbers?"

The psalm-singers made answer: "Young Lord Diuk! we are no robbers; we go as pilgrims from Kíef the famous to Volhýnia town in broad India."

"Tell me, ye pilgrims, is the way long from Kíef to Volhýnia; to India the Rich?"

"Great is the way, Lord Diuk, from India to Kíef town. A whole year mayest thou journey on foot, and three months must thou ride."

Then said Diuk: "I thank ye, pilgrims;" and so rode back to Volhýnia.

It was the solemn Easter Even, and young Diuk went to vespers. 'Twas not the silken plume-grass waving, nor the white birch bending low, but the goodly youth, Diuk Stepánovich, bowing there before his mother, the most honorable widow Amálfya Timoféevna.

"Fair my lady mother! Must I live long thus at home, roaming the wide streets and solacing myself with childishness? 'Tis time for me to ride far, far across the open plain, to throw back my heroic shoulders, urge on Shaggy, my dapple-bay, and prove my youthful prowess and daring; to see people and to show myself. Many fair towns have I seen, but never have I been in Kíef the glorious, nor beheld Prince Vladímir and his fair

Princess Apráxia. Give me thy leave and blessing now, my lady-mother, to journey to Kíef town, to view it and them."

Amálfya Timoféevna made answer: "Aï, my dear child! Thou hast never been on the open plain, nor heard the roar of wild beast, the shriek and yell of Tatar; thou hast essayed no heroic quests. Thou wilt not be able to bring back thy head in safety from the plain. — And go not to Kíef, my fair child, thou lordly young scion, Diuk Stepánovich! There dwell evil people, who will squeeze thee as though thou wert a fine, juicy apple. — I will not give thee my blessing to go to Kíef, to courteous Prince Vladímir. Moreover, there stand three great barriers on the straight road. The first is the clashing mountains. Each second time they clash, — each second time they part: thou mayest not pass these, Diuk, and remain alive. The second barrier is the pecking birds: they will tear thee from thy good steed, Diuk, and them thou mayest not escape. And the third barrier is the Dragon of the Mountain with twelve tails. He will devour thee: — thou canst not escape."

But young Lord Diuk heeded not his mother's words. He went to the stall and curried his good steed with a fine comb of fishes' teeth. Winged Shaggy's mane swept the damp earth, on the left side; his flowing tail wiped out traces of hoofs as he passed over. On him Diuk put his braided bit, his metal-bound Cherkéssian saddle, with felt on felt, saddle-cloth on saddle-cloth beneath; and one of these was striped of red gold, pure silver, and bronze of Kazan, more precious than either of the first. These he made fast with twelve stout girths, and a thirteenth — not for beauty or for youthful vanity, but for heroic strength, that the heroic steed might not leap from under the saddle, and overturn the good youth in the open plain. The girths were all of the silk of Samarcand which teareth not, weareth not; the buckles of fair gold, the tongues thereof of silver, which corrodeth not; the stirrups of damascened steel from beyond the sea, which cannot be destroyed.

When Diuk had caparisoned his heroic steed, and plaited fair jewels in his mane, he went off a little from him and gazed upon him. "Art thou a horse, my good steed, or a wild beast? For under the trappings the good horse cannot be seen."

Then the horse answered him with human voice: "Tear not my sides with thy spurs, Diuk Stepánovich; lash me not with thy silken whip, tighten not my plaited bridle: but cling thou to my sacred mane; bind handfuls of damp mother earth under thy two arms, that thou mayest not fear to ride with me; for I shall leap from mountain to mountain, lakes and rivers I shall clear at a bound; and so shall I serve thee well."

Then Diuk took off his armor, and put on garments fitting for a journey, took his stout bow and a quiver full of burning arrows on his hip, and touched the earth with his brow in reverence before his mother.

His mother instructed him: " Aï, my dear child! when thou shalt come to famous Kíef town and to Prince Vladímir the Fair Sun, and he shall make a banquet and an honorable feast for thee, then boast not of thy orphan possessions, of thy wealth, or of me, thy mother." Therewith she gave him her leave and blessing, and kissed him. And he mounted and rode.

They saw the good youth as he mounted, but saw him not as he rode — 'twas but a pillar of dust afar in the plain, — a little darkening of the heavens, and he was gone.

And as he rode, he came to the first barrier, the clashing rocks; but his good dapple-bay sprang between, and they crushed him not. And at the second barrier likewise, his good steed leaped past ere the pecking birds of prey could spread their wings; and past the third barrier, the dragon of the mountain, ere he could uncoil his tails, faithful Shaggy bore him.

So the good youth came forth in safety, and rode farther over the open plain until he came to a damp, ring-barked oak, whereon sat a black raven cawing, and spoke this word: " Aï, thou cawing raven, thou bird of omen! I will bend my stout bow, I will lay a fiery arrow to the silken cord, I will scatter thy feathers over the open plain; I will spill thy blood on the damp oak, and give thee over to vain death."

Then spoke the raven with human tongue: "Shed not my hot blood, young Lord Diuk, but ride onward over the open plain, and thou shalt find an adversary, — one befitting thy stature."

Diuk rejoiced greatly that he should prove his heroic might, and so rode on, and came upon the traces of a horse. A hero had passed that way, and damp mother earth was furrowed with horse's hoof-marks like to a mighty grating. After that the bold youth came to where the hero had pitched a pavilion of white linen; and beside it stood a white, heroic steed, before whom was spread fine white Turkish wheat.

The bold youth reflected, and began to weep. "Now may I not pursue my way," he said, "and to enter that pavilion the courage faileth me. The hero will kill me in that white pavilion, and my head will fall. — But I will place my good steed beside this steed at the white wheat; if the horses eat the wheat in peace together, then will I enter the tent, and the hero shall not touch me. But if the horses begin to fight, I will go my way, for so I may."

When he beheld the good steeds feed in peace,

side by side, he entered the linen pavilion, crossed himself as enjoined, did reverence as prescribed; and behold! in one corner, slumbered a hero and snored until the threshold rang. Then he saw by the heroic inscription that this was the Old Cossáck of the Don, Ilyá of Múrom the Son of Iván. He essayed to wake the hero, shouting with all his might:

"Rouse thee, Old Cossáck, Ilyá of Múrom! 'Tis time to fare to glorious Kíef town, to royal Prince Vladímir, to matins on Easter morn." But the hero slept on, and woke not. At Diuk's third shout, the warrior woke from his deep sleep, and spoke:

"Aï, good youth! tell me thy land and horde, and how thou art called." And Diuk told him all this.

"And why hast thou wakened me from my deep heroic sleep? Wilt thou fight the accursed Tatars in the plain? Or wilt thou come with me thyself, good youth, to the plain, and prove thy youthful might and valor — which of us shall bear away his head, and which joyful news?"

Then Diuk wept and humbled himself before him. "Why should I go to the open plain with thee, Ilyá of Múrom, thou Old Cossáck? For thy death is not decreed in battle. Nay, there is but one sun in heaven, and one moon — and but one Cossáck of the Don in Holy Russia, Ilyá of Múrom, son of Iván."

This speech pleased Ilyá: he sprang to his nimble feet, caught Diuk by his white hands, his golden ring, kissed him on his sugar mouth, and swore brotherhood with him, exchanging crosses. Then they sat down to eat, drink, and make merry. And when they had had their fill, Ilyá said: "Go now, young Lord Diuk, to royal Kíef town, and if any there shall offend thee, send me word of it, and I will defend thee. But make no boasts."

So Diuk rode forth; and when he was come to Kíef, he leaped the walls, past the three-cornered towers, and came to the royal palace of white stone. In the spacious court he sprang from his good steed, struck the butt of his far-reaching lance into the earth, and flung his good steed's bridle over the point.

The Princess Apráxia was there, looking out. "Lo! the washerwoman," quoth Diuk, and bowed. "And where is courteous Prince Vladímir, the Fair Sun?"

Then was Princess Apráxia very wroth, and the serving-men made answer: "Royal Vladímir is at the Easter mass."

So Diuk, that good youth, vaulted quickly into his saddle, and rode to the cathedral church. There he dismounted, and left Shaggy, his little dapple-bay, unbound and without orders. In the cathedral, he took his stand in the place of the ambassadors, — the left porch. While the mass was sung, he prayed not so much as gazed about: — he gazed at the church and gulped, at Prince Vladímir and shook his head, at the Princess Apráxia and dropped his hand.

When the Easter mass was at an end, Prince Vladímir sent to bid the strange and goodly youth to his honorable feast. "Eh, brothers!" Diuk made answer to the messengers: "Ye have had spring weather. I have ridden far over swamps and mosses, and my flowered garments are bemired." Nevertheless he followed them, and bowed before Prince Vladímir until his yellow curls swept the damp earth.

As they came from the cathedral, they found a great throng of people gathered about Diuk's Shaggy, marvelling much at the good steed's rich trappings. Diuk followed Prince Vladímir to his princely dwelling, and the good steed came after his master.

Now great rains had fallen on the black earth with which the way was covered, and the road was heavy with mud to the knee. Diuk looked upon his little shoes of green morocco, and then upon Prince Vladímir, and shook his head. But Prince Vladímir heeded not, and began to inquire of him his name and country. This Diuk told him, and how he was come to view royal Kíef of which he had heard great marvels, to greet the Fair Sun Vladímir, and to pray to God in his temples.

Then Vladímir took him by his white hands, kissed him on his sweet mouth, and led him to the palace. When Diuk beheld the palace, he shook his head, and said to his good steed: " They will starve thee here, good Shaggy ; they will give thee frozen oats to eat ; and at home thou wouldst not touch the finest of white wheat."

And when Diuk beheld the banquet-hall, with its tables of oak, and cloths patterned with drawn-work, he shook his head yet more. — As they sat about the board, Vladímir inquired of Diuk if it were far from India to Kíef town.

" I set out after vespers on Holy Saturday," Diuk made answer, " and lo ! I was in Kíef at early mass on Easter Day ! "

" And are such steeds as thine dear in thy country ? "

" We have them for a ruble, and for two rubles, and for six rubles ; but my good steed is priceless."

Then spoke up Vladímir's heroes and nobles.

" Nay, lord, that may not be ! For by the straight road it is a three-months journey, and by the way about six months, and that when a man hath relays, and springeth from horse to horse, from saddle to saddle, tarrying not."

But Vladímir said nothing.

Then all began to make great brags, some of one thing and some of another ; and Diuk alone sat sad and silent, eating not nor drinking nor carving the white swan. And courteous Prince Vladímir spoke:

"Aï, thou bold and goodly youth! is the feast not to thy liking? Or art thou poor, perchance, with nothing whereof thou mayest vaunt thyself?"

"Fair Sun Vladímir, Prince of royal Kíef," said Diuk, "I have far greater possessions than thou. My father left me a little lad and rich, and I am not used to eat black bread." Yet courteous Prince Vladímir was not affronted by his speech.

Then green wine was brought, and liquors, and kalachí[1] of fine wheaten flour. Diuk drank but the half of his wine — the other half he poured under the table. The top crust of the cakes he laid upon the table, the middle he ate, and cast the under crust to the dogs beneath the board.

Seeing this, Vladímir's princes and nobles sprang to their nimble feet, and cried: "What discourteous churl is this? He is not Lord Diuk Stepánovich; never before this day hath he quaffed noble liquors, or tasted wheaten cakes; he knoweth not royal courtesy. He is a herdsman, the fugitive serf of some noble, who hath murdered his master or a merchant, stolen his flowered garments, and driven off his good steed! He is come hither that thou mightest make an honorable feast for him, royal Vladímir, and give him golden treasure, as is thy usage. He mocketh thee, Prince Vladí-

---

[1] Wheaten rolls or cakes.

mir; he is not noble, for he looked upon his shoes as he walked; and his mantle of sables, he never earned."

"I want not thy treasure," quoth Diuk. "I possess inexhaustible store of golden treasure, and bread and salt in abundance. I heard great marvels of glorious Kíef town, and so came hither. But things are not with you as they are with us in India."

"Why didst thou gaze about thee at mass, noble Diuk," said Prince Vladímir then, "in place of praying God?"

"I gazed, royal Vladímir," Diuk made reply, "because thy churches here are not the tenth part of the churches with us. Thy raiment is like the raiment of the very poorest among us, and the Princess Apráxia, likewise, is apparelled like our poorer women. Thy churches are of wood with domes of aspen wood: ours are of stone with roofs of purest gold. Our meanest huts exceed thy fairest palace of white stone. Thy streets are foul: ours are cleaned, tawny yellow sand is strewn upon them, with rugs spread thereon. The steps of thy palace are of black stone, with railings of turned wood fastened with wooden pegs which catch the garments: our steps are of ivory spread with silken rugs, and the railings are carved of pure gold. The floor of thy banquet-hall is of pine planks, and uneven, the walls and ceiling unpainted, the tables of oak, the cloths patterned with drawn threads. But the floors of our halls are of ash, the walls and ceilings all painted, the tables of gold and ivory; our cloths are of silk, and at their corners hang tassels of gold. Over my mother's gate are seventy ikóns,[1] and you have not even ten. From our churches to the palace, pavements of arrow-wood are laid, spread with fine crimson cloth."

"Why dost thou throw away my wine and cakes?" asked courteous Prince Vladímir. And Diuk replied:

— " I cannot eat thy wheaten cakes. The upper crust tasteth of pine, and the lower crust of clay. For your ovens here are of brick, your oven-brooms of pine. But my mother's ovens in India the Rich are of glazed tiles, and her oven-brooms are of silk dipped in honey-dew. He who hath eaten one of my lady mother's cakes longeth for another; when he hath eaten that, his soul burneth for a third; and having devoured the third, the fourth will not depart from his mind. — Thy wines and sweet liquors I cannot drink, for they are musty and ill-flavored. But in India the Rich, my mother's sweet mead and old liquors are kept in silver casks of forty buckets hooped with gold, and hung by brazen chains in caverns forty fathoms deep. From these vaulted caverns, pipes run to

---

[1] Pictures of saints.

the fresh air of the open plain; and when tempestuous breezes blow, they enter the caverns, and the silver casks rock in their chains, and murmur like swans at play upon the bosom of quiet bays. Our fair liquors never grow musty. Having drunk one cup, the soul burneth evermore for another, and the merit of those liquors no words can equal. The store of my lady mother's flowered garments is never exhausted; for the sewing-women are ever at work, — when one throng quitteth the court, another throng arriveth. My mother's under-garments are of precious stones, the upper of gold brocade; her cap is of fair round pearls, with jewels of great price in the front; and I wear a different dress each day. Our horses are fed only on fine Turkish wheat, and sport upon the plain. And we have twelve deep vaults strewn full of gold and silver and fair pearls. One vault alone would purchase royal Kíef, and even Chérnigof beside."

Then spake royal Vladímir in displeasure:

"I would that Churílo Plenkóvich the Fop were here; for he would know how to answer thee as thou deservest."

Thereupon the oaken doors of the banquet-hall were opened wide, and Churílo entered, clad in a fine white blouse without a girdle; he crossed himself, and bowed to all save to Diuk Stepánovich.

Then said Diuk: "The fame of Churílo's beauty was not false, — for his neck is like the driven snow, his face red as the poppy. But the fame of Churílo's courtesy was false,—he knoweth not how to do homage nor to salute."

Quoth Churílo: "Dost thou boast, thou nobleman's serf, of thy wealth and possessions? Lay a wager, now, with me, a great wager of thirty thousand rubles. For three years we shall go about Kíef; each day we shall wear fresh apparel;— each day ride a horse of different color. And he that hath the fairest shall be adjudged the victor."

"Thou dwellest here in Kíef, Churílo Fop," said Diuk; "and thy presses are full to overflowing with raiment, while I have but my travelling garb; and it is well worn."

Nevertheless, Diuk made that great wager, for three years and three days. Then he sat down at the oaken table, in a folding-chair, wrote in haste a scroll to his mother, and went forth with it to the court, where stood his dapple-bay. He laid the scroll in the saddle-bags beneath the rich Cherkéssian saddle, and spoke: "Speed home, my Shaggy, to India the Rich; and when thou comest to my lady mother's palace, neigh loudly."

So the good bay flew swiftly to India the Rich. And when the honorable widow Amálfya Timoféevna beheld the empty saddle, she wept sore; for she thought her dear child had lain down his bold head upon the open plain, in Holy Mother Russia.

But when the grooms unsaddled good Shaggy, they found the scroll, and gave it to Diuk's lady mother, who rejoiced greatly that her son still lived.

"Alas! the foolish child hath boasted," she said, when she had read the scroll: "yet I must save his honor and his head."

Then she took her golden keys, and packed up changes of raiment for three years and three days, — three changes for each day, — and bound them on the good steed's back. Over all she put an old and much-worn garment.

"Spring forth, good steed, to thy young lord!" she cried: "and apprise him of thy coming with a neigh."

— Then Churílo Fop and young Lord Diuk began to ride about Kíef town with new garments and horses every day. Churílo had great herds of horses driven in from Chérnigof; but Diuk anointed his Shaggy each morning with dew, and so changed the color of his hair. Three years they rode thus through Kíef. The last day was Easter, and they went to mass, and stood in the porch on either hand.

The raiment of Churílo Fop was rayed with gold and silver; his clasps were figures of stately youths, his loops in semblance of fair maidens. Beneath the high heels of his slippers of green morocco, nightingales might fly — from their awl-sharp tips curving to the instep, eggs might roll. His black murman[1] cap drooped soft and downy, so that his clear eyes might not be seen in front nor his white neck behind. His mantle was of black sables from over the sea.

But young Lord Diuk went all unadorned through Kíef town that day;—save that the points of his foot-gear, woven of the seven silks, and the insteps thereof, were studded thick with precious stones, in value above all that city save only the settings of the Virgin and the Saints.— For over all, concealing utterly his egg-shell raiment, he had put that worn garment sent by his lady mother.

Churílo took his stand upon Vladímir's right, and fingered his carven clasps:— when he touched the clasps, the fair maids poured green wine and gave to the comely youths; when he pulled the loops, the good youths plucked their little gúslys solacing the maidens fair.

Then spake Prince Vladímir: "In sooth the young Lord Diuk hath forfeited his wager! For such devices, Diuk, thou surely canst not show to us, how fair soever thy garb may be."

"I care not for the thirty thousand of coin," quoth Diuk, "but for my own good fame I have a care. The gold I now bestow upon thy town of Kíef." And therewith he cast aside his mean garment, and his apparel beneath gleamed fair, so that

---

[1] Norman. There is a game called "the murman cap," for a description of which see "Songs of the Russian People" (W. R. S. Ralston).

all the people fell to the earth in wonder at its beauty. In the front of his cap sat the fair red sun; on its back, the radiant moon; on his crest a flame seemed ever burning.

Then he touched his clasps in semblance of small singing birds — they straightway hopped and twittered. He pulled his loops — dragons and fierce lion-beasts were they, that crawled and leaped, and hissed and roared. Then all the folk were terrified, and fell to the damp earth, and with them Churílo the Fop. Lord Diuk alone stood firm.

"Thou hast won, good youth," spake Vladímir; and besought him: "spare me at least a remnant of my people. Call back thy beasts and birds."

This Diuk did, and all Kíef gave him thanks for having outshone Churílo in foppery. And with the thirty thousand, Churílo's wager, he bought green wine, and gave to all the people freely.

But Churílo Plenkóvich was out of measure wroth, and said: "Aï, young Lord Diuk Stepánovich! let us make yet another great wager. Let us prove now whose horse shall leap the Dniepr river (for Mother Dniepr is three versts in breadth), and our turbulent heads shall be the stakes. He whose horse leapeth not over shall yield his turbulent head to be hewn off by the other."

"I have but my poor travelling nag," young Diuk made answer. Yet did he accept the challenge; and going forth to his good steed in the stall, he wept.

"Aï, my Shaggy, my good dapple-bay! Knowest thou not of my great misfortune? If thou leap not fairly over Mother Dniepr river, they will cut off my tempestuous head:—and the breadth of Mother Dniepr is three versts. But if thou canst not leap the Dniepr flood, then will I go seek my cross-brother, Ilyá of Múrom, the Old Cossáck. He will aid us."

Good Shaggy replied in human speech: "Weep not, pathetic master mine! Not over Mother Dniepr's flood alone will I leap, but yet three versts upon the further shore will I bear thee on my outstretched pinions. If I yield not to my elder brothers, much less will I give way before the younger. For my eldest brother is with Ilyá of Múrom, my second with Dobrýnya Nikítich: I am the third, and Churílo's steed is but the fourth of us."

Then Diuk saddled his good steed with his own hands, and rode far out over the open plain, with Churílo Fop to Mother Dniepr river. Many mighty heroes, princes, nobles, and of the common folk of Kíef not a few, went also to view that contest.

"Do thou leap first," said Churílo Fop.

"Nay," quoth Diuk; "leap thou the first. And when we leap together in India, then will I take the lead."

So Churílo made ready to leap. His good steed reared upon his hind legs on the bank, and essayed the flight, but floundered in mid-stream.

Then Diuk essayed. His good steed bore him in safety past the flood, and turning leaped back whence he came. As he flew, Diuk grasped Churílo by his yellow curls, and dragged him to the shore, and so to Prince Vladímir's presence, where he would have cut off his turbulent head.

But all the old women, young wives, and lovely maids of Kíef began to beseech Diuk urgently that he would spare the life of Churílo the handsome Fop; and royal Vladímir spoke also in his behalf.

Then Diuk gave Churílo a mighty kick: "Go, Fop, bewept of women, since Prince Vladímir entreateth; go sit among the women, and dally with the maids. But come thou never more into the company of heroes, weak dangler after women, and beloved of ancient crones!"

But Churílo spoke with malice: "Fair lord, Prince Vladímir, if this child boasteth with reason, let us send talesmen to the splendid Indian land, to take lists of all his cattle and possessions."

"Whom shall we send?" said courteous Prince Vladímir.

"Let Alyósha Popóvich go."

"Nay! Alyósha shall not go to my India," quoth Diuk: "for he hath pope's eyes, greedy eyes, and pope's pilfering hands. He will never return."

Then he sat down in a folding-chair at the oaken table, and wrote a billet with haste. And, having fastened it to an arrow, he shot it, bidding it fly forth to Old Cossáck Ilyá in the open plain, and crave his aid.

Then Ilyá sent Dobrýnya to inquire what aid Lord Diuk required; and if Dobrýnya might not render it, then would he come himself.

"Ho, Dobrýnya Nikítich! Thou shalt go to my India," said Diuk then; "but not Alyósha with his greedy pope's eyes and thieving fingers."

So Vladímir appointed Dobrýnya and two more to make the lists. If Diuk had the greater possessions, then should Vladímir become his vassal, and contrariwise: if Diuk's brags were not established, then should he serve Vladímir loyally so long as he lived.

"Take paper for three years and for three days," quoth Diuk, "for six scribes may not write the tale of my possessions in twenty years. And of a surety, ye shall do homage to my serving-maids, mistaking them for my lady mother."

Then the talesmen set out, and with them went three great carts of paper. When, after long wanderings, they came to India the Rich, they climbed a lofty mountain, and beheld the land glowing before them. And one said: "Of a surety, Lord Diuk hath sent warning to his native land, that they should set on fire great India the Rich, for lo! it burneth!"

But when they drew near they saw that it was but the golden roofs of the dwellings flaming, and the temples' precious domes which glowed, and the ways strewn with tawny-yellow sand and spread with fair cloth of scarlet. Diuk's palace of white stone had three and thirty towers which flowed together at one point; their domes all were sheathed with green copper, more precious than red gold. About the palace lay a garden of seventy versts, set with all manner of pleasant fruit-trees and of shrubs, walled about with a lofty railing of carven pillars of gold, surmounted by knobs of copper, and the gates were of fair brass. In the court, maids richly apparelled walked with the serving-men, or played at chess.

Within, the palace was reared upon three hundred pillars of silver, four hundred of gold, and others innumerable of precious copper and of iron. In all Kíef was nothing like it, and all Kíef town would not suffice to purchase that palace alone; and through the town flowed a river of gold.

The talesmen feared to enter; but when at length they did so, and came to the first tower, they found an aged woman of motherly aspect: her garments were of pure silver, with but small admixture of silk, and they bowed to the earth before her.

"Hail, most honorable widow, Amálfya Timoféevna, mother to Lord Diuk Stepánovich!" they said.

"I am not the Lord Diuk's mother," said the woman. "I am his cowherd."

Then the talesmen were sore vexed and shamed, that they should have done reverence to Diuk's cowherd because of her rich array, and inquired no further that day, but went and pitched a tent without the town, and there abode that night.

The next day they came again to the lordly palace, and essayed the second tower. There they found an aged woman of reverend mien, clad in silver and gold; and to her they did homage. But she refused it, saying, "I am the Lord Diuk's washerwoman.

And in like manner, to their exceeding shame and great amaze, they bowed before Diuk's cook, his chamber-women, his baker of cakes, his nurse, and others, — all women of stately mien and venerable aspect, and more richly arrayed than the Princess Apráxia on festal days.

At length the nurse told them that the honorable widow was gone to the long mass, and that they might know her as she came thence by these signs: Before her would come a host with shovels, and then a host of sweepers, to make all clean, and sprinkle orange-tawny sand, and others still spreading cloth of scarlet. Then would follow the most honorable widow, Amálfya Timoféevna, supported on either hand by scores of maidens.

"Ye must not salute all the women in rich raiment like this of mine, whom you shall meet," spoke the nurse; "for of such there are very many in this town, and ye would never make an end."

So they went forth to meet the honorable lady, and when she came, attended as had been described to them, they were dazzled, and bowed to the earth. The red sun glowed upon her brow, the bright moon and thick-clustering stars gleamed fair behind, and her attire was rich beyond compare.

The lady returned their greeting courteously, and inquired why they were come thither.

"Lord Diuk sent us," they made answer, "to take rate of his cattle and goods."

"That ye cannot do," quoth she; "yet come first and eat bread and salt with me, and feast: then will I show you what ye list."

— At that feast were white swans, and great abundance of all choice viands, green wine and sweet liquors, and cakes of fine wheaten flour, such as Diuk had spoken of in Kíef, for which their souls burned. After they had eaten and drunken all they would, the honorable widow showed them first, Diuk's horses; and they would have counted them — but could not. Then she showed them Diuk's foot-gear; this also they would have reckoned — and could not. After that, she led them to the deep vaults with vents to the open plain, where swung the gold-hooped casks of silver in their chains of brass, and murmured like white swans in sweet converse on the bosom of tranquil bays; and to the treasury of trappings for the horses. Three years they sat and reckoned what might be the value of the Lord Diuk's saddle of state, incrusted with jewels, and of exceeding rich workmanship — and could not so much as begin to compute it.

Then they sent word to Kíef, to royal Vladímir: " Sell Kíef for paper, and Chérnigof for ink, and then, mayhap, we may make a beginning of reckoning Diuk's great possessions."

When courteous Prince Vladímir heard that, he spoke: " I pray thee, Lord Diuk, be my guest in the lofty palace, taste of my bread and salt, and carve the white swan; and trade thou evermore in Kíef without tax."

" Nay, Prince Vladímir," young Diuk made answer; " the Fair Sun gave forth no warmth in the morning, and at eventide he will give no heat. No courtesy hast thou used with the youth when he came, and thou shalt have no profit of him now."

A little space thereafter, went Prince Vladímir and Churílo Fop, and all the princes, nobles, and scribes, to Volhýnia town in India the Rich, to view and compute Diuk's possessions. When they came to Diuk's dwelling, they marvelled greatly, for such a palace even royal Vladímir himself had never yet beheld, — and they feared to enter.

So young Lord Diuk took the Fair Sun by the hand, and led him in. One half the floor was of crystal; beneath flowed limpid water, and in the water swam fishes of many hues, and sported. When they lashed the water with their tails, the crystal floor resounded. Prince Vladímir held back, fearing to tread thereon, but Diuk led him still forward, for so they must needs go; and at the golden tables they feasted on viands such as they had never so much as heard of, and drank liquors which they had never seen, no whit worse than Lord Diuk had bragged.

Then Prince Vladímir inquired for his talesmen, and they were led to him; and lo! they were all withered up like shavings, for grief that they could not compute the value of so much as one saddle.

But Vladímir looked on the saddle, and said: "Of a truth, he who wrought that may alone compute its worth."

So Prince Vladímir acknowledged himself vassal to Lord Diuk, as they had agreed; but Diuk said:

"I need thy service not. Go home, and look to it that henceforth the unknown man and stranger suffer no offence in thy house."

VASÍLY THE DRUNKARD AND TZAR BÁTYG.

FROM beneath the cross Levanídof,[1] from beneath the birch so white, issued forth two aurochs, and three aurochs, and roamed past Kíef town.

By Kíef they beheld a wondrous marvel, a marvellous wonder: a damsel came forth, weeping bitterly, and bearing in her hands the book of the Holy Gospel. And as she read, she wept in twofold measure.

Then the aurochs went to their mother: "Hail, mother aurochs!" said they; "we have been to Kíef town, and beheld a marvel:" and they told her of the damsel.

"Foolish aurochs are ye, little children!" quoth mother aurochs. "That was no damsel weeping sore, but the city wall lamenting, for she hath foreseen ill fortune for Kíef. Tzar Bátyg[2] is come with his son, his son-in-law, and with his learned scribe. His son's host numbereth forty thousand; the host of his son-in-law, forty thousand; and the learned scribe's no less."

— Bátyg marched to Kíef town, pitched his

---

[1] Or Levantínof, in one version: the cross of the East.
[2] See Appendix.

white pavilions, and demanded of Prince Vladímir an adversary in single combat.

Now, it chanced by evil fortune, that the best of the heroes were not in Kíef town. Ilyá had been despatched to the Latínsky land to buy heroic steeds, Dobrýnya to the Cherkéssian country for saddles, and Alyósha to the Sorochínsky land for wheat.

But there dwelt in Kíef in those days, a hero and good youth, Vasíly Ignátievich by name, who abode in the imperial pot-house. He had squandered in drink his wife's dowry and all his possessions.

"Ho there, ye my princes and nobles!" quoth Prince Vladímir; "summon Vasíly Ignátievich hither to me."

Then the nobles went to the royal pot-house, and sought out Vasíly, and addressed to him these words:

"Ho there, little Vasíly the Drunkard! Why dost thou lie there naked on the oven, without a thread? Nothing knowest thou, nor carest. Tzar Bátyg hath come upon us, and is now before Kíef. The dog hath written to our Prince, and maketh boast. — 'I will burn and rase Kíef town, I will dissolve God's churches in smoke, I will take captive the Prince and his Princess.' And us, the princes and nobles, he will seethe in a kettle."

Then Vasíly slipped down from the oven, barred

up the pot-house, making all very fast, tore from the princes and nobles all their fair apparel, wrenched out a door-post, and belabored the men upon their naked ribs, pursuing them even to the royal court.

When Vladímir looked on them he smiled, and said : " Ho, my princes and nobles ; have ye drunk or gamed ? "

" Little father ! Prince Vladímir," they made answer, " we have neither drunk nor gamed, but Vasíly the Drunkard hath done us this dishonor."

" Ah, ye stupid nobles and senseless ! " quoth Vladímir, " ye have not appeased the youth, but irritated him."

Then Vladímir went himself to the royal pot-house, prayed before the wondrous picture, saluted on all four sides, with a special reverence to Vasíly, and spoke to him in the words of the princes and nobles.

" Fetch me a little cup of drunkenness, little father, Prince Vladímir ! " quoth Vasíly, " the cup from which drinketh Ilyá of Múrom."

— Now Ilyá's cup held six buckets and a half; but he drained it dry.

" Fetch yet another cup for health, little father ; the one from which drinketh Dobrýnya Nikítich."

And that cup, of four buckets and a half, Vasíly drained also ; and yet a third, the cup of Alyósha, of two buckets and a half.

Then Vasíly said: "Now I may sit my horse, and wield my sword of ninety poods."

Thereupon he went forth upon the city wall, and from the angle tower thereon he shot an arrow which slew three of Bátyg's best heads — his son, his son-in-law, and his cunning scribe.

Tzar Bátyg had fleet horses and good, and he sent swift messengers to Kíef town, demanding that the offender be delivered up to him forthwith. But Kíef town is not small; a falcon may not fly about it in a summer's day, nor a little bird soar across — and the guilty man could not be found.

Vasíly mounted his good steed, and clad in warlike array, with his Tatar spear, his sword of ninety poods, his stout bow, and gilded arrows, sallied forth before the face of Bátyg.

"Hail, Tzar Bátyg!" he said. "Wilt thou receive me as thy comrade? We will take Kíef together, we will burn and destroy it, and God's temples we will turn to dust."

Tzar Bátyg was beguiled with his speech; and when Vasíly asked for forty thousand men to take Kíef, he gave them gladly. Then Vasíly rode forth into the open plain with this host, made a turn to the right, unsheathed his sword of ninety poods, and cut down and slew them to the last man.

Then he returned again to the face of Bátyg.

"Forgive this my first fault," he said; "I have

lost that host of forty thousand. But I have spied out Kíef town and viewed it, where the gates are open and unbarred."

So Tzar Bátyg gave him another band of forty thousand, and forty forties of black sables, besides gold and silver without measure.

Again Vasíly rode to the open plain; and having cut down and slain his host, he returned to Bátyg craving pardon and yet another troop.

Tzar Bátyg gave them, and rich presents likewise; but when Vasíly had slain these men also, Bátyg took a spyglass and viewed the glorious open plain, and beheld the evil deed.

Then he assembled his good steeds, and returned to his own country, and swore an oath never more to lay siege to Kíef town, for in Kíef was no lack of heroes.

And from that day forth they began to sing the Song of Vasíly, which shall be sung for evermore.

ILYÁ AND IDOL.

Mighty Iváuiusho arrayed himself and set out for Jerusalem, to pray to the Lord, to bathe in Jordan, to kiss the cypress tree, and to visit the grave of the Lord.

Mighty Iváuiusho's foot-gear was of the seven silks, his hooked staff weighed forty poods; into his foot-gear precious stones were woven. On summer days his course was lighted by the fair red sun; in winter, by a precious jewel.

As he returned from Jerusalem he passed Tzargrád, and found that the accursed Idol was come thither, that the holy ikóns had been shattered and trodden in the mire, and horses were fed in the temple of God. Then mighty Iváuiusho caught a Tatar by the breast, dragged him forth into the open plain, and began to inquire of him:

"Tell me now, thou faithless Tatar! Conceal nothing: what manner of man is yon accursed Idol? Is he great of stature?"

Said the Tatar: "Our Idol is three fathoms, well measured, in height, and three in breadth; his head is like a beer-kettle, his eyes like drinking-cups. His nose is an ell long from its root, and he cheweth the cud like an aurochs."

Ivániusho caught the accursed Tatar by the hand, and hurled him upon the open plain; and the bones of the Tatar flew asunder. Then Ivániusho pursued his journey, and met Ilyá of Múrom in the way.

"Hail, Ilyá of Múrom, thou Old Cossáck!" said Ivániusho; and they greeted each other there.

"Whence wanderest thou, mighty Ivániusho?" inquired Ilyá. "Whither lieth thy road?"

Then Ivániusho told him how he had been to Jerusalem, and had passed Tzargrád; and Ilyá began to inquire of him:

"Is all in Tzargrád as of old? Is all as it was wont to be?"

"Nay," said Ivániusho; and he told Ilyá of the conquest, and how God's temples were defiled.

"A fool art thou, stout and mighty Ivániusho!" cried the Old Cossáck. "Thy strength is as twice my strength, but thy boldness and daring are not as the half of mine. For thy first speech I could have pitied thee, but for this last, I could have chastised thee upon thy naked body! Why hast thou not delivered Tzar Constantine?[1] But now,

---

[1] In some variants, Idólishe (the Idol or Idolater) attacks Prince Vladímir, and the scene is laid in Kíef. This version has been chosen as an interesting instance of the adaptation of a *bylína* to different localities. He came to Kíef, the minstrel explained, as a punishment for the Princess Apráxia's sin against Kasyán Mikáilovich.

undo quickly thy foot-gear of the seven silks from thy feet, and put on my morocco shoes, for I will go sadly as a wandering psalm-singer." — And it grieved him to give his good horse to the pilgrim. — " Ride softly as water floweth," he said ; " remain in some place of easy access, and wait for me, for I shall soon return. And give hither thy staff of forty poods."

Then Ilyá strode on quickly, and each stride was a verst and a half in length : — and when he came to Tzargrád, he shouted with full might :

" Ho there, Tzar Constantine ! Give gold, give saving alms to a wandering psalm-singer."

Tzar Constantine rejoiced, and at the singer's shout, the forty towers rocked, the liquor on the tables splashed over, damp mother earth quivered, and the palace of white stone heaved from corner to corner. At the third shout the accursed Idol was greatly terrified, and spoke to Tzar Constantine.

" Your Russian psalm-singers are loud-voiced fellows," quoth Idol. " Receive this pilgrim, feed him, give him drink and gold at thy pleasure."

Constantine went forth upon the railed balcony, and bade the pilgrim enter. And when the pilgrim had eaten and drunk, the Idol took him to himself to question :

" Tell me truly, thou Russian pilgrim, and conceal nothing. What manner of heroes have ye in Russia ? And your Old Cossáck, Ilyá of Múrom,

— is he great of stature? Can he devour much bread, drink much green wine?"

And that Russian pilgrim made answer: "Yea, thou accursed Idol. We have Ilyá of Múrom in Kíef, and his stature differeth not from mine by so much as a hair's breadth. We have been brothers in arms. His beard is gray but handsome. Of bread he eateth three consecrated loaves, and his drink is two cups of green wine."

"A fine hero, in sooth, for Kíef!" quoth Idol. "If I had but that hero in this place, I would set him on the palm of one hand, and with the other I would press him until he became a pancake. And I would blow him away into the open plain! For lo! I am Idol, three fathoms in height, and my breadth is three fathoms well told. I can put a loaf in one cheek, and the same in the other, and a white swan is but a mouthful for me. I eat seven poods of bread and three oxen at a meal, with wine in due proportion, — a cask of forty buckets."

"The pope of Rostóf had a greedy cow," said Ilyá. "She ate and ate, and drank until she burst."

This speech pleased not Idol the Accursed. He seized his poniard from the oaken table, and hurled it at Ilyá of Múrom, that wandering psalm-singer. But Ilyá was nimble of foot, and leaped quickly aside upon the oven, and turning, caught the weapon in its flight, upon his staff. The poniard glanced off, struck the white oak door; the door flew from its fastenings; the poniard bounded into the ante-room, slew twelve Tatars, and wounded yet another twelve. Ilyá snatched his little cap of nine poods from his head, and flung it at Idol the Accursed, and Idol flew through the wall into the open plain. Then Ilyá sprang into the great courtyard, waved his staff, slew all the accursed Tatars, cleared the city of Tzargrád, and delivered Tzar Constantine.

DOBRÝNYA AND THE DRAGON.

YOUNG Dobrýnya took his stout, death-dealing bow, his fiery little arrows, and went a-hunting, and came to the Blue Sea.

At the first bay he found no geese, swans, nor small gray ducks; neither did he find them at the second bay, nor at the third. Then Dobrýnya's restive heart grew hot within him; he turned about quickly and went to his home, to his mother, sat down upon the square hewn bench, and dropped his eyes upon the oaken floor. Therewith came his mother to him, and said:

"Aï, young Dobrýnushka Nikítich! Thou art returned in no merry mood."

"Aï, my mother!" quoth Dobrýnya; "give me thy leave and blessing to go to the Púchai river."

"Young Dobrýnya," his mother made answer, "I will give neither leave nor blessing. None who hath gone to the Púchai stream hath ever returned thence."

"Aï, little mother," said Dobrýnya, "if thou give thy leave I will go; and if thou give it not, — I will go."

So his mother consented. He threw off his

flowered raiment, and put on garments meet for a journey, and on his head a wide-brimmed hat from the Grecian land. Then he saddled and bridled a good steed which no man had ever ridden, took his stout bow, his fiery arrows, his sharp sword and far-reaching spear, and his battle-mace.

And as he rode forth, accompanied by his little page, his mother laid her commands upon him.

" If thou wilt go to the Púchai river, young Dobrýnya, immeasurable heats shall overcome thee : yet, bathe thou not in Mother Púchai flood ; for she is fierce and angry. From her first stream fire flasheth ; from her second, sparks shower ; from her third, smoke poureth in a pillar."

— They saw the good youth mounting, they saw him not as he rode, — there seemed but a wreath of mist far out on the open plain.

When he was come to Mother Púchai river, intolerable heat overpowered him, and he heeded not his mother's behest. He took from his head his cap from the Grecian land, put off his travelling garb, his shirt, his foot-gear of the seven silks, and began to bathe in the Púchai.

" My mother said this was a wild and angry stream," quoth he ; " but 'tis gentle — peaceful as a pool of rain-water." He dived like a duck beneath the first stream, and through the second likewise. — And lo ! there was no wind, but the clouds sailed on ; there were no clouds, yet the rain dropped down; no rain was there, yet the lightning flashed; no lightning, yet sparks showered fast. No thick darkness was it that obscured the sky, nor gloomy clouds descending, but a fierce Dragon flying down upon Dobrýnya, the savage Dragon of the Cavern, with her twelve tails.

"Aha! young Dobrýnya Nikítich!" quoth the Dragon. "Now will I devour Dobrýnushka whole! I will take dear little Dobrýnya in my tail, and bear him into captivity."

"Ho, thou accursed Dragon!" said Dobrýnya. "When thou shalt have captured Dobrýnya, then will be the fitting time to boast; but thou hast not yet Dobrýnya in thy claws!" Then he dived swiftly beneath the first stream, and out through the second. But his young page had been overhasty, and had driven away Dobrýnya's good steed; he had carried off the stout bow, the sharp sword, far-reaching spear, and war-mace. The cap alone was left, the wide-brimmed cap from the Grecian land.

Dobrýnya seized his cap, filled it with sand from the river-bank, and with it smote the cursed worm, and hewed off three of her tails — the best of all.

Then the Dragon of the Cavern besought Dobrýnya:

"Aï, thou young Dobrýnya Nikítich! Give me not over to fruitless death, shed not my innocent blood! I will not fly in Holy Russia, I will imprison no more heroes, nor strangle young maidens, nor orphan little children. I will be to thee a submissive Dragon; and thou, Dobrýnya, shalt be my elder brother, and I will be thy younger sister."

Dobrýnya was taken with her wiles, and loosed her at will, and returned to his home, to his mother, to the banquet-hall, where he sat himself down upon the four-square bench.

But the wily Dragon raised herself upon her wings over royal Kíef town, caught up Beauty, niece to Prince Vladímir, and bore her off to a cavern in the hills.

At that time Royal Vladímir made an honorable feast for many princes, nobles, bold warrior-maidens, mighty heroes, and wandering good youths. And Dobrýnya prayed his mother's leave and blessing to go to that honorable feast.

"Nay," she made answer: "abide thou in thine own dwelling, Dobrýnya, with thy mother; drink green wine until thou art full drunken, and lavish golden treasure at thy will. But go not to this feast." But when her son would have gone in any case, she gave both leave and blessing, and Dobrýnya arrayed himself as was meet.

On his little feet he put shoes of green morocco, with lofty heels and pointed toes. About their sharp beaks, an egg might roll, under the heel might sparrows fly. His garments were of flowered stuffs, his mantle of black sables from beyond the sea.

He saddled his good steed, and rode forth to the spacious court. When he was come thither he bound his steed in the centre, to the ring of gold in the carven pillar, and entered the banquet-hall. There he crossed his eyes as it is written, he did reverence as prescribed, to two, to three, to four sides, and to the Prince and Princess in particular. Then they led him to the great place of honor at the oaken board, with its savory viands and honeyed drinks, and poured him a cup of green wine, a second of beer, a third of sweet mead : — the measure of that cup was a bucket and a half, and the weight thereof, a pood and a half. This Dobrýnya took in one hand, and drained at one draught.

Royal Vladímir, as he paced the banquet-hall, stroking his curls, looked on the heroes, and spoke this word: " Aï, ye stout and mighty heroes! I will lay upon you a great service. Ye must go to the Túgy mountains, to the fierce Dragon that hath carried off our royal niece, Beauty the Fair."

Then the great hid behind the lesser, and they, in turn, behind the small, and from the least in rank, no answer came. From the middle table spoke Semyón, lord of Karamýchetzka : " Little father ! Vladímir of royal Kíef ! But yesterday in the open plain, I beheld Dobrýnya beside the Púchai river in conflict with that Dragon. And the Dragon beguiled him, — calling him her elder

EPIC SONGS OF RUSSIA. 193

brother, herself his younger sister. Send Dobrýnya, therefore, to the Túgy mountains, for the Princess Beauty."

So Vladímir laid his commands on Dobrýnya, and Dobrýnya mourned and was sad. He sprang to his nimble feet, in his place within the granite palace, and stamped upon the oaken floor. The tables rocked, the liquor quivered in the glasses, and the heroes were thrown from their seats with the shock. Dobrýnya rushed forth into the courtyard, loosed his good steed from the golden ring, mounted and rode to his own dwelling. When he had spread fine Turkish wheat before the horse, in the midst of his own courtyard, he entered his mother's dwelling, sat on the wall-bench, and hung his turbulent head.

"Why art thou sad, Dobrýnya?" his mother inquired of him. "Was thy seat at meat not to thy liking, or unbefitting thy rank? Did the cup pass thee by? Did some drunken boor spit in thine eye, or did the fair damsels scoff at thee?"

"Mine was the place of honor at meat," Dobrýnya answered, "the greatest place, not the least; no fool offended, no damsel scoffed. But Prince Vladímir hath laid upon me a great service. I must go to the Túgy mountains, and free his niece from the fierce Dragon of the Cave."

"Grieve not, Dobrýnya," spoke his mother, the honorable widow, Afímya Alexándrevna. "Lie down to sleep early this evening; to-morrow will be wise, for the morning is wiser than the evening." Her son heeded her; and the next morning, rising early, he washed himself very white, and arrayed himself for the journey.

"Be not sad," spoke his mother: "thy father went to the glorious Túgy mountains and slew an accursed serpent, and now thou must needs go thither likewise. Take not thy swift, stout bow, nor thy war-club, thy far-reaching spear, nor yet thy sharp sword. I will give thee a little whip of the seven silks, which thou must brandish; and I will give thee a magic kerchief. Thy right hand will droop, the light will fade from thine eyes, and the Dragon will begin to drag thee away, and to hurl thee down, and the little dragons to bite thy horse's fetlocks as he trampleth on them. But take thy magic kerchief, lift it to thy white face and wipe thy clear eyes, and thou shalt be stronger than before.— Then draw this whip, braided of the seven silks, from thy pocket, and beat thy good steed between the ears and on his hind legs. With that thy brown will begin to prance, and will shake off the Dragon's brood from his feet, and crush them to the last one. And brandish this silken whip; so shalt thou bend the Dragon to earth and subdue it like a Christian beast; and thou shalt sever its twelve tails, and give it over to speedy death."

So Dobrýnya mounted his good steed, and rode to the Túgy mountains and the Dragon's cavern. Twelve days he rode, and ate nothing but a wheaten roll. On the thirteenth day he came to the glorious hills, but the Dragon was not in her cave, and the Prince's royal niece he could not see. Then he began to trample on the little dragons, and they coiled about his horse's fetlocks so that the good brown could no longer leap. He drew from his pocket the little whip of the silks of Samarcand, and beat the good steed between the ears and on his hind legs; the good brown began to prance thereat, shook off all the dragon brood, and crushed them to the very last.

Dobrýnya gazed out over the open plain, and lo! the accursed serpent came flying towards him. When she espied him, she let fall from her claws upon the damp earth, the soft, thick grass, the dead body of a hero, and flew straight at Dobrýnya.

"Aï, little Dobrýnya Nikítich! Why hast thou broken thine oath, and crushed all my little dragons?"

"And aï, thou accursed Dragon!" quoth Dobrýnya, "what devils bore thee over Kíef, that thou shouldest seize young Beauty Putyátichna? Yield her now without battle or bloodshed."

"Without battle and bloodshed I will not yield the Prince's niece."

So they waged mighty battle all that day until

the evening; and the snake began greatly to prevail. Yet Dobrýnya, recalling his mother's counsel, wiped his clear eyes and his white face upon the kerchief, and his strength was greater than before. The next day they contended until the evening, and again the third day, so that Dobrýnya would have fled before the serpent. But a voice from heaven warned him that if he would fight yet three hours longer, he should overcome the beast.

He fought on, but might not endure the Dragon's blood, so great was the flood thereof. Then he would have left the Dragon, but the voice spoke yet again from heaven: "Tarry yet three hours by the serpent, Dobrýnya. Take thy far-reaching spear, smite upon the damp earth, and conjure thy spear: 'Yawn, damp mother earth, in all four quarters, yawn! Suck up the Dragon's blood!'"

When he had done this, and had fought the three hours, he overcame the beast. Recalling his mother's behest, he drew forth his whip of the silks of Samarcand, hewed off the twelve tails, cut the sinuous body into small pieces, and strewed them over the open plain.

After that, he entered the Dragon's deep den, and released the Russian prisoners, — Tzars, Kings and Princes by forties, and of lesser folk many thousands, — and bade them go where they would. But young Beauty, the Princess, he could not find, until he came to the farthest den. There she lay chained with hands outstretched. He released her straight, and led her forth to the white world. Then he mounted his good steed, and setting Beauty upon his right hip, rode out over the plain.

Said Beauty: "For thy great service I would fain now call thee little father, but that I may not do; for thy great deed, I would call thee my own brother, yet now I may not; gladly would I call thee friend and lover, but that thou lovest me not, Dobrýnushka."

To her Dobrýnya made answer: "Aï, Beauty Putyátichna! Thou art of princely birth, and I am but of peasant stock:[1] it is not possible for thee to call me friend and lover."

As they thus rode over the plain, they came upon the traces of a horse, great clods of earth cast up, so that one might sink in the hollows, even to the knee. Dobrýnya followed and found Alyósha Popóvich in the way.

"Ho there, Alyósha Popóvich!" cried he; "take the Princess Beauty, and bear her in honor to Vladímir, our Fair Sun Prince in royal Kíef, and thy head shall answer to me for her." And this Alyósha performed.

When he had thus sent away Beauty, Dobrýnya followed again after the tracks, and came upon a hero in the open plain, riding, in woman's garb, upon a fair and goodly horse.

---

[1] This agrees with Vladímir's uncle, Dobrýnya, in history.

"Eh!" quoth Dobrýnya; "this is no hero, but a bold damsel-errant, some maid or wife, forsooth!" Therewith he rode after the warrior-maiden, and smote her upon her turbulent head with his mace of damascened steel. But the warlike virgin sat her good steed firmly, wavering not nor glancing back. — Dobrýnya sat his good steed in terror, and departed from that bold polyánitza: "Plainly," quoth he, "Dobrýnya's valor is as of yore, but his strength is not the strength of other days."

Now there stood near by in the plain, a damp oak, six fathoms in girth. This Dobrýnya smote with his mace, and shivered into atoms; and he marvelled greatly.

"Of a truth," he said, "Dobrýnya's might is as of old, but his courage is not the courage of earlier days!"

Then he again rode in pursuit of the bold warrior-maid, and smote her honorably upon her tempestuous head. — She wavered not, glanced not behind. But Dobrýnya was sore amazed, and tested his might upon a damp oak of twelve fathoms, — and shivered it in splinters. Thereupon, Dobrýnya waxed wroth, as he sat his good steed, and rode after the bold virgin-warrior a third time, and smote her with his mace.

Thereat she turned and spoke: "Methought the Russian gnats were biting, but lo! 'tis the Russian hero tapping!"

Then she seized Dobrýnya by his yellow curls, twisted him from his good horse, and dropped him into her deep leather pouch, and rode her way over the open plain.

At length her good steed spoke: "Aï, thou young Nastásya, Mikúla's [1] daughter, thou bold warrior-maid! Two heroes I cannot carry. In might that knight is thine equal, and the courage of that knight is as twice thine."

Quoth young Nastásya Mikúlichna: "If the hero be very aged, I will cut off his head; if he be young and well pleasing in my sight, I will call him friend and lover; if he please me not, I will set him on one of my palms, and press him with the other, and make a pancake of him."

Then she drew him forth from the leather pouch, and liked him well. "Hail, dearest Dobrýnya Nikítich!" quoth she.

"How knowest thou me, bold virgin knight? for thee I know not."

"I have been in Kíef town, and have seen thee, Dobrýnushka; but thou couldst by no means know me. I am daughter to the Polish King, young Nastásya Mikúlichna, and I roam the open plain, seeking an adversary. If thou wilt take me for thy wife, Dobrýnya, I will grant thee thy life. And thou must take a great oath; if thou swear it not, I will make of thee an oat-cake."

---

[1] Mikúla the Villager's Son; and father to Stavr's wife, according to one singer.

"Leave me but my life, young Nastásya, and I will take that great oath, and I will take also the golden crown with thee."

So they took the oath, and set out for Kíef town, to courteous Prince Vladímir. Dobrýnya's mother came to meet them, inquiring: "Whom hast thou there, Dobrýnya Nikítich?"

"Ah, Afímya Alexándrevna, thou honorable widow my mother! I bring my enemy, young Nastásya Mikúlichna; I am to take the golden crown with her."

Then they went to Prince Vladímir, and entered his banquet-hall, where Dobrýnya did reverence to all, and in especial, to the Prince and Princess.

"Hail, Fair Sun Vladímir of royal Kíef!"

"Hail, Dobrýnya Nikítich! Whom hast thou there?"

Thereupon Dobrýnya told him all; Nastásya was received into the Christian faith, and they took the golden crowns. Courteous Vladímir made them a great feast for three days; and thereafter they lived happily for a space.

EPIC SONGS OF RUSSIA. 201

IVÁN THE MERCHANT'S SON AND HIS HORSE.

IN royal Kíef town, glorious Prince Vladímir held a mighty feast, for his princely nobles, stout Russian heroes, and rich merchants. The day was half spent, the feast half over, and all were making brags. Prince Vladímir waxed merry, and paced the banquet-hall.

"Ho, all ye princely nobles, and Russian heroes all," he cried at length: "I too can boast. I have three hundred stallions, and three of exceeding merit: one is an iron-gray, the second's mane hangeth all to one side, the third is coal-black. Him Ilyá of Múrom captured from the Dragon's Son, Tugárin. He can gallop from Kíef to Chérnigof, between mass and matins, and the distance is three hundred versts and thereto thirty versts and three. Is there in all Kíef town a man whose horse can do the like?" All hid, and made no answer. Then Iván Merchant's Son stepped forth, and cried in piercing tones:

"Lord, courteous Prince Vladímir, such a horse have I. And I will lay a great wager;—not a hundred rubles, nor yet a thousand,—but my turbulent head shall be the stake,—that he will run against thy horse from Kíef to Chérnigof, between mass and matins, as thou hast said."

"What devil wilt thou ride, then, Iván?" quoth Vladímir.

With that all the princely nobles and ship-merchants staked a hundred thousand rubles for the Prince; but none laid any stake for Iván, save only the ruler of Chérnigof.

Then with speed did they write out the strong contracts, and set their white hands thereto, that they might be binding and effectual.

And, when Iván Merchant's Son had quaffed a cup of green wine, of a bucket and a half, he saluted all and went forth.

When he came to the stall of white oak where stood his shaggy brown steed of three years, he fell down before the horse's left hoof, and wept in floods. "Help me, good my steed," quoth he; and told him of the great wager.

Thereto his shaggy brown made answer in human Russian tongue: "Hey, courteous master mine! Thou hast no cause to grieve. I fear not that iron-gray. If I run for thy wager, I shall outstrip him. But do thou water me for three dawns with mead, and feed me with Sorochínsky wheat. And when the three days are past, a stern messenger shall come to thee from the Prince, bidding thee ride against him. Then saddle me not, Iván, but take me by my silken bridle, and lead me to the royal court. Don thy mantle of sables, — thy mantle of three thousand rubles, with its embossed clasps of five hundred rubles. When thou leadest me to the court, I shall rear up and paw thy mantle, and nip the black sables, and prance in all directions. Then shall the Prince and his nobles marvel. But care thou not, for it shall go well with thee. I will redeem thy turbulent head, and put courteous Prince Vladímir and my elder brother to shame."

All came to pass as the shaggy brown had foretold. When he began to pluck at Iván's mantle, and to trample on the black sables, all the princely nobles and rich merchants assembled in the spacious royal courtyard stood and marvelled.

"Foolish art thou, Iván Merchant's Son!" they cried. "Thy good steed will spoil thy mantle. Prince Vladímir gave it thee, and he will pardon a great wrong rather than this."

But sweet Iván made answer: "The foolish are ye. For if I live I shall win another mantle, and if I die I shall have enjoyed this."

Then, as the shaggy brown danced about the court, he began to roar like an aurochs, and to hiss like a dragon. The three hundred stallions were affrighted, and fled the royal court; the iron-gray broke two legs, the long-maned steed his neck; the captive black fled, neighing, with tail uplifted, to the Golden Horde, leaping the Dniepr stream in his flight.

All who saw it were terrified, and Iván cried: "Is it not time, Prince Vladímir, for us to set out for Chérnigof town?"

Prince Vladímir called to his stable-men to collect the three hundred stallions, and pick out the choicest, the three. But the men made complaint that all the three hundred lay dead, by reason of that terrible cry of Iván's steed, and there was none left whereon the prince might ride.

Then said sweet Iván Merchant's Son: "Delay not, Prince Vladímir, but count out to me that great wager of a hundred thousand rubles."

This Vladímir did with sorrow, and said: "Yield me thy steed, Sweet Iván Merchant's Son; for I have none whereon to ride."

Quoth sweet Iván: "My steed was bought in the Great Horde, from under his mother, for five hundred rubles, and before he came to me he cost a thousand. Shall I give such a steed to Prince Vladímir?"

Nevertheless, he yielded him; and Vladímir commanded that the horse should be led to the stable, and fed with fine wheat, and watered with sweet mead.

But the stable-men came running in dire haste, making great complaint, that the steed would neither eat nor drink, but hissed and shrieked like a dragon, and struck dead all the horses.

Then was Prince Vladímir very wroth: he

wrapped himself in his mantle of sables, and spoke this word: " Ho there, thou Iván Merchant's Son! Lead that horse from my court forthwith. The devil take thee and thy steed!"

Thus was the great race ridden.

ILYÁ OF MÚROM AND FALCON THE HUNTER.

ON the road to Kíef town of courteous Prince Vladímir, stood a great barrier and strong — a force of seven mighty heroes, bold warriors all, and lesser knights.

The first was Ilyá of Múrom, our Old Cossáck of the Don; the second Dobrýnya Nikítich, the third Alyósha Popóvich, the fourth Churílo Plenkóvich, the fifth Mikáilo the Rover, the sixth and seventh the Agrikánof brothers. They pitched their pavilions, and slept until the white dawn.

The barrier was strong: no horseman galloped past nor wayfarer journeyed by, no wild beast crouched, no bird soared overhead; and if, by chance, a bird flew by, it dropped its feathers there.

There, late at even, passed young Falcon the Hunter.[1] He asked no leave at the barrier, but leaped across, and roamed the open plain.

The next morning, right early, at dawn of day, our Cossáck of the Don went out to the white court to refresh himself, and espied the traces of

---

[1] See Appendix: *Ilyá of Múrom.*

a horse's hoofs, the marks of a heroic ride and a black steed.

Then Ilyá entered again the white pavilion, and spoke these words: " Comrades, brothers, ye heroes stout and mighty! What sort of a barrier is this of yours — what manner of stern fortress? But now I beheld the traces of a horse's gallop, of a heroic ride. Arm ye then, friends, for a sally into the open plain to seek the rash intruder." Then he began to hold a great council:

" It will not do, children, to send Váska Longskirt, for he will get entangled in his skirts in the encounter; nor Gríshka the Noble, — for men of noble descent are boastful, and he will vaunt himself in the combat. Nor may Alyósha go against the unbidden visitor, for Alyósha is of popish descent, and popes' eyes are covetous, popes' hands pilferous; Alyósha will see the braggart's great store of gold and silver, and will covet them. Dobrýnya Nikítich must go: if the knight be Russian, then shall Dobrýnya swear brotherhood with him, but if he be an infidel knight, he shall challenge him to single combat."

Dobrýnya sprang to his nimble feet, saddled and mounted his good steed, and rode forth to Father Sakátar river, by the blue sea. As he looked along the straight road, he beheld a knight riding before him, with youthful valor. The horse under the hero was like a wild beast; at each leap he compassed a verst, and the tracks he left were as large as a ram or a full-grown sheep. From that good steed's mouth flames flashed, from his nostrils sparks showered abroad, from his ears smoke curled in rings.

The helmet on the hero's head glowed like fire, and his horse's bridle darted rays; stars sprinkled from his stirrups, on his saddle stood the dawn, the morning dawn. At his left stirrup sprang a greyhound, and a dragon of the hills was also chained thereto. On his right stirrup perched a blue-gray eaglet, who sang and whistled without ceasing, caressing and diverting the hero. From shoulder to shoulder hopped a falcon clear, plucking his long locks from ear to ear.

The knight sat his good steed well, and diverted himself in noble wise, hurling his steel mace to the clouds, and catching it as it fell, in his white hands, without permitting it to touch the damp earth. As he thus played, he conjured his mace: " Lightly as I now whirl this mace aloft, even so lightly will I twirl Ilyá of Múrom."

Then Dobrýnya shouted: " Ho, thou Falcon the Hunter! Turnest thou not back before our barrier?"

Cried Falcon, " 'Tis not for thee to pursue me in the open plain! high time is it that thou wert in the village herding the swine."

At that heroic cry, the peaceful bays were troubled, the waters grew choked with sand. Dobrýnya's charger sank to his knees, and Dobrýnya fell to the damp earth, where he lay as in a heavy sleep for the space of about three hours. When he awoke from that swoon, he mounted his good steed, and, returning to the barrier, told Ilyá of Múrom all.

Said the old man: " There is none to take my place, the place of this turbulent old head."

Then saddled he his good charger Cloudfall, both quickly and stoutly, and sprang upon his back without touching the stirrups. On his saddle-strap hung his war-club, and its weight was ninety poods. On his hip rested his sharp sword, in his hand he held his silken whip. Thus armed he rode in pursuit of the knight to the Sorochínsky mountains, and looking through the circle of his young fist, he descried a black spot in the plain, and rode towards it.

" Thief! dog! braggart! " he shouted in piercing tones. " Why hast thou passed our barrier, doing no reverence to me, asking no leave ? " When the braggart hunter heard that, he turned and rode at Ilyá; and Ilyá's heart died within him. — 'Twas not two threatening clouds which clashed, nor yet two mountains moved together, but two stout heroes who rode against each other.

First they fought with their maces, until these snapped short at the hilt, — and wounded one another not. Then they fought with their sharp swords, until these brake, — and wounded one another not; and so likewise with their sharp spears: and when these were shattered they lighted down from their good steeds, and fought hand to hand. All day they fought till even, till midnight, till the white dawn: — and so they did the second day, and likewise the third, and sank to their knees in the earth.

Then Ilyá waved his right hand, and his left foot slipped from under him. — 'Twas not a gray duck fluttering, but Ilyá falling to the damp earth like a stack of hay.

Falcon the Hunter planted himself upon Ilyá's white breast, snatched out his dagger of damascened steel, and would have pierced that white breast, closed Ilyá's clear eyes, and struck off his turbulent head, and plucked out his heart with his liver; but his arm was stiffened from the shoulder down, and he could not move it.

"O Lord!" said Ilyá: "It is written on my right hand that I shall not die in battle." And to Falcon he said: "O brave, good youth! tell me, from what land art thou, from what horde? Who are thy father and mother?"

Then the hunter began to curse: "Full time is it, thou old dog, that thou shouldest shave thy head, and go to a monastery!"

Ilyá's heroic heart grew hot at that, and his

young blood boiled. He smote Falcon upon his black breast, and hurled him higher than the standing wood, yet lower than the flying clouds. When Falcon descended again to the damp earth, Ilyá leaped to his nimble feet, and sat upon the hunter's breast.

"Tell me now, good youth, thy land, thy horde, thy father's name."

"Sat I on thy white breast," the hunter answered, "so would I not inquire of thee thy name and country. But I would pierce thy white breast, and scan thy restive heart, and scatter thy white body over the plain, to be torn of the gray wolf, and picked by the black crows."

Then Ilyá inquired no further of him, but drew forth his dagger. The youth perceived that misfortune was close at hand, and answered:

"I come from the blue sea, from the palaces of gray stone, from mighty Zlatigórka; and my father I do not know. When I rode forth upon the open plain, my mother enjoined me to greet the Old Cossáck, Ilyá of Múrom, if I should chance to meet him, but without approaching; to dismount from my good horse and do reverence to him, touching my forehead to the ground."

Then the old man felt compassion; for he knew now that this was his own Falcon, by that fierce Zlatigórka whom he had overcome in single combat, and to whom he had given his golden ring with an inscription, and set with a rich jewel. He took Falcon by his white hands, kissed his sugar lips, and called him his son, weeping greatly as he looked upon him. Then he blessed him with a great blessing.

"Ride, my child, my dear son, whither thou wilt, over the open plain, but shed no blood without cause, waste no strength in vain. And go now to the blue sea, to thy mother, and greet her lowly from me, from the Old Cossáck Ilyá of Múrom. For shouldst thou fall into the hands of our Russian heroes, thou shouldst hardly escape thence alive."

The secret of his birth overwhelmed the good youth as a great misfortune, and he rode straightway to the blue sea, to the palaces of gray stone, to his mother.

When he came to the fair porch, he shouted with a great voice: "Ho there, thou bold and evil warrior-maid! Come forth to meet the good youth!"

So Zlatigórka came forth to meet him, bowing low, and saluting him. But Falcon met her with his sharp sword, and greeted her so that she fell there upon the fair porch. For he liked it not that he should be the son of a peasant, and of dishonor.

"I go now," quoth he, "to give that old dog over likewise to speedy death, for so dishonored I will not live."

Therewith he wheeled his good charger about, and rode to the pavilion of white linen. There he fitted a burning shaft to his stout bow, and sent it at Ilyá's breast as he lay buried in sleep. But it glanced aside from the wondrous golden cross, three poods in weight, which Ilyá wore, and roused him from his slumber. He leaped forth from the tent all unclothed as he was, seized Falcon by his yellow curls, flung him upon the damp earth, cut out his little heart, and scattered his four quarters over the plain.

So Falcon's praise is sung, and Ilyá's glory is not diminished; and forever shall Ilyá be celebrated in song.

SWEET MIKÁILO IVÁNOVICH THE ROVER.

FAIR Sun Vladímir made a great and notable feast to his nobles and heroes. And when all had eaten and drunk their fill, Prince Vladímir paced the banquet-hall, waved his right hand, and distributed service to his knights, to Ilyá of Múrom, Dobrýnya Nikítich, and sweet Mikáilo Ivánovich.[1] He poured out a cup of green wine, and gave to each sweet mead, saying:

"Taste now a cup of green wine, and serve me, your Prince, with perfect loyalty. Do thou, Old Cossáck, Ilyá of Múrom, the chiefest of our Russian heroes, render a great service. Go thou to the Golden Horde, slay all infidels, both great and small, sparing none. Thou, young Dobrýnya, must go to the glorious blue sea, and conquer it, and add territory to Holy Russia. Sweet Mikáilo the Rover shall be intrusted with a great mission — he shall go to the black halls in Podólia the crafty, and collect the gifts and tribute for the years that are past, and for this year — for twelve years and for half a year."

So these three heroes rode forth to the Levanídof

---

[1] See Appendix.

oak, and swore brotherhood. Ilyá was the eldest brother, Mikáilo the next, and young Dobrýnya the youngest. Then they made a covenant, that he who should first return should await the other two at that oak. With that they parted, riding different ways.

When Mikáilo was come to the famous black horde, he demanded the gifts and tribute due, — twelve swans, twelve white falcons, and a writing of submission.

But the men of Podólia assembled, and would not surrender the gifts and tribute. Then Mikáilo the Rover waxed very wroth, threw back his heroic shoulders, and began to kill and to destroy, so that the men of Podólia yielded and fetched the tribute.

So Mikáilo departed thence, and wandered by the blue sea, past warm and peaceful bays, shooting swans and geese. As he turned to leave the precipitous shore, he gazed out upon the quiet bay, and beheld a white swan floating there. Through her feathers she was all gold, and her head was covered with red gold, studded with fair round pearls.

Then Mikáilo drew from his bow-case his stout bow, from his quiver a burning arrow, grasped his bow in his left hand, the arrow in his right, and laid the arrow to the silken cord. As he drew the stout bow to his ear, with the burning arrow of seven ells, the cord twanged, the horns of the great bow creaked, and he would have let fly. But the white swan besought him:

"Aï, Mikáilo Ivánovich the Rover, shoot not the white swan, else shalt thou have no luck for evermore!"

Then the swan rose over the blue sea upon her white wings, flew to the shore, and turned into a beauteous maiden. Mikáilo went to her, took her by her little white hands, by her golden ring, and would fain have kissed her upon her sugar mouth.

But the fair maid said: "Kiss me not, Mikáilo Rover, for I am of infidel race, Márya, Princess of Podólia, and unbaptized. If thou wilt take me to glorious Holy Russia, to famous Kíef town the royal, I will go to mother church of God, and receive the Christian faith. Then will we take the golden crowns, and then also shalt thou kiss me if thou wilt." So they set out.

Ilyá of Múrom was come first to the Levanídof oak, and had brought with him gold in bulk like to a rick of hay. Next came young Dobrýnya, and his gold was likewise like unto a hay-rick. The last to come was sweet Mikáilo the Rover, and not one copper coin brought he, but only sweet Márya, the White Swan of Podólia. Then spoke his brothers in arms:

"Hast thou been led astray by woman's wiles, Mikáilo Rover, that thou bringest hither no treasure? With what face wilt thou present thyself in

Kíef?" But Mikáilo answered them that he would go straightway to Kíef with his White Swan, and without red gold.

When they were come to Kíef town, Ilyá and Dobrýnya flung down their vast heaps of treasure, but Mikáilo led sweet Márya by the hand.

"How may I reward thee for this thy service?" quoth Vladímir of royal Kíef. "Shall I give thee villages with their hamlets, cities with their suburbs, or countless golden treasure?"

"None of these do I require," said Mikáilo; "for whatsoever thou mightest bestow upon me, that should I squander in drink. Better will it be to give me an ukase with thy royal red seal, that I may go to all the pot-houses and drinking-houses, and drink green wine without payment, — that money be never required of me." Then Prince Vladímir gave Mikáilo that ukase with his fair seal gladly, and said:

"I sent them forth to find brides, but these two youths understood me not, — they coveted gold and silver. In our Holy Russian land, a race of young heroes is more precious than either silver or gold."

Then spoke sweet Mikáilo the Rover to Máriushka the White Swan: "Let us wed."

"Nay, not so, Mikáilo Rover," she replied, "but under one condition. Let us take a great and solemn oath that when either one of us shall die, the other shall go, living, into the grave with the dead, and there abide for the space of three months."

This oath they took, and were married in God's church. Then they began to live, and take their pleasure; and sweet Mikáilo went about from pot-house to pot-house, drinking green wine, — here a cup, there half a bucket, and again a bucket and a half.

— Again spoke Prince Vladímir to Mikáilo the Rover: "Lo! Bukár, king of the land beyond the sea, hath sent to demand tribute and gifts for twelve years, and if I give them not, he will come and destroy our royal Kíef."

Quoth Mikáilo: "Write thou a scroll to that king beyond the sea: write that thou hast de-spatched the gifts and tribute by Mikáilo Ivánovich the Rover. But I will go without tribute."

So he went to Tzar Bukár in the kingdom beyond the sea, and saluted him. And Bukár inquired:

"Whence comest thou, good youth, from what land or horde?"

"From Kíef town I come, young Mikáilo Ivánovich the Rover. I bring thee gifts and tribute for twelve years from that Fair Sun, Prince Vladímir."

"Where are these gifts and tribute?"

"All were sent in copper coin, and the carts broke down upon the road; the men are even now mending them."

"How divert ye yourselves with such joy in Russia?" asked Tzar Bukár.

"We play with ashen checkers upon boards of oak."

"Let us play at ashen checkers," quoth Bukár.

So they began to play. Tzar Bukár staked the gifts and tribute, and Mikáilo Rover staked his good steed and his turbulent head — and lost. Then they played another bout, and again Tzar Bukár staked the tribute, adding the good steed and the turbulent head. Mikáilo staked Márya the White Swan and his own mother — and won. Then Bukár waxed wroth, and staked the half of his kingdom, and Mikáilo staked the tribute. As Mikáilo won this game, the oaken doors were opened wide, and Ilyá of Múrom the Old Cossáck strode in and spoke:

"My brother in arms, thou knowest not the evil fortune that hath befallen thee. Thou sittest here gaming and taking thy pleasure, while Márya the White Swan, thy young wife, lieth dead in Kíef town."

When sweet Mikáilo heard that, he sprang up, and hurled the chess-board full at the oaken door, so that the door and its framework flew outward.

"Take thou half the goods and kingdom of Tzar Bukár in this land beyond the sea, my brother in arms," said he, "and rule thou whilst I go home to Kíef." Then quickly, quickly, very, very quickly, with speed, he rode to Kíef town, to his palace of white stone. There he hired craftsmen, and they made him a spacious coffin of oak, wherein two might stand, or sit, or lie.

When this was done, he made provision of food and green wine for three months. And he fashioned for himself three pair of pincers and three rods of iron, and took his seat in the coffin with the dead body.

"Why take ye the rods and pincers?" asked Vladímir.

"That the dragons of the under-world may not crawl into the coffin and gnaw my white body."

They drew the White Swan's body to the grave on a sledge, with sweet Mikáilo alive beside it.

Then they lowered the coffin into the deep mound, and also his good steed with his rich trappings, and covered them with ruddy yellow sand. Three months did Mikáilo the Rover sit therein.

After that, a Dragon of the under-world crawled to the white oak coffin with her brood, pressed upon it, and the hoops began to burst asunder. Mikáilo sprang to his nimble feet. A second and yet a third time did the Dragon press, and thereupon the coffin yawned widely.

When that beast espied sweet Mikáilo, she rejoiced that she should have a living man to satisfy her hunger, as well as the dead body.

But Mikáilo seized the Dragon with his iron

EPIC SONGS OF RUSSIA.   221

pincers, and began to smite her with the iron rods, and to cry: "Aï, thou Dragon of the under-world! Fetch me the waters of life and death[1] to revive my young wife."

"Loose me, sweet Mikáilo Rover," the Dragon made answer, "and I will fly to the blue sea, and fetch thee those waters, to revive thy Russian beauty, in three years."

But he ceased not to belabor her stoutly, and without mercy; and she promised to fetch the waters in two years. Yet ceased he not until she had sworn to fetch them within three hours.

Then said he: "Give me as hostage, one of thy little Dragons." And when she gave it, he set his heel upon the little serpent, and crushed it to dust.

"Why hast thou destroyed my child?" the Dragon asked.

"Fetch me the waters," answered Mikáilo, "and I will revive thy child together with my young wife."

Then she made haste and fetched the waters, and sweet Mikáilo essayed them first upon the little dragon; — the first time he sprinkled it, the dragon flew together, at the second sprinkling it moved, at the third, it crawled forth from the coffin.

Then he sprinkled his Russian beauty, Márya

---

[1] These waters figure in several of the popular tales translated by W. R. S. Ralston in "Russian Folk-lore."

the White Swan. First her blood played, then she moved, and at last sat upright in the coffin, and spoke: "Long have I slept, and suddenly arisen."

— It was on Sunday, when the nobles, princes, and mighty heroes were coming from the mass. Mikáilo shouted with full strength of his head, so that damp mother earth quaked, the waters were troubled with sand, Prince Vladímir's lofty palace rocked to and fro with the shout, and the nobles and heroes spoke among themselves: "Is not this a marvel, brothers, on land and sea?"

But Ilyá of Múrom made answer: "No marvel is it, nor monster issuing from the waters, or from some distant land. But the hero within the bosom of the earth is wearied of the dead body. Take, therefore, implements of iron, remove the yellow sands, and reach the coffin of white oak."

So they delved, and sweet Mikáilo the Rover came forth, leading his young wife by the sleeve.

Great fame of this heroic young woman went abroad throughout all lands and hordes. Never had such a beauty dwelt under the fair red sun. At the fame of her beauty came forty Tzars, Kings and Princes to the Sorochínsky mountains, and wrote a cartel in haste: "If the Fair Sun Prince Vladímir yield not that young heroic woman without conflict or great battle, and in good will, then will we destroy all Kíef town."

Thereupon came Prince Vladímir to Mikáilo: "Sweet Mikáilo Rover," he said, "destroy not my whole kingdom, I pray thee, for the sake of one woman. Deliver up thy young heroic wife, without conflict or great battle."

"Nay, Fair Sun Prince Vladímir," sweet Mikáilo made answer. "Deliver up thine own fair Princess Apráxia. But my wife I will not give with my own good will."

Then he disguised himself in woman's apparel, laid on his good steed his great battle-sword, his sharp blade, and rode forth to the Sorochínsky mountains. When he was come near to those Tzars and Kings, he pitched a tent of fair linen, shook down fine white Turkish wheat before his good steed, and lay down to sleep.

The Tzars and Princes sent an ambassador to inquire who had adventured so near them, and Mikáilo made answer:

"Márya the White Swan hath come to wed with the forty Tzars, Kings and Princes."

Then all those royal suitors donned their richest raiment, mounted their best steeds, and rode to the pavilion of linen.

"Foolish are ye, ye forty Tzars, Kings and Princes," quoth sweet Mikáilo. "I cannot marry all. Grant me therefore to shoot arrows, and he who first returneth with one shall have me."

To this they all agreed, and Mikáilo shot forty

arrows, — some into the brushwood, some into the water: — and was it a light task to find them?

When the first Tzar fetched an arrow, Mikáilo struck off his head, and hid it in the pavilion, and so he did likewise with the second and the third, until all were slain, and not one of the forty royal suitors was left alive.

Then sweet Mikáilo rode back to Kíef town, and his brothers in arms met him there, but not his young heroic wife. Mikáilo inquired of them where she was, and they replied: "Tzar Vakraméy Vakraméevich came hither, and carried off thy young wife to the Volhýnian land."

Forthwith rode sweet Mikáilo in pursuit, eating not, drinking not, dismounting not from his good steed. When he came to Volhýnia town, Márya espied him, and came forth to greet him with a kovsh[1] of the liquor of forgetfulness.

"Aï, sweet Mikáilo Rover," said she: "I can neither eat nor drink nor live without thee. But woman's hair is long, her wits are short. Whither they lead us, there we must needs go, and Prince Vladímir gave me against my will. But now drain a bowl of the liquor of health, and thou shalt be yet stronger than of yore, Rover." So Mikáilo

---

[1] A kind of boat-shaped bowl with a long handle — a sort of ladle for kvass or beer. It is still used to ladle out kvass among the peasantry, in monasteries, and so forth.

drained that bowl of the wine of oblivion, and fell unconscious there.

Then the White Swan went to Vakraméy Vakraméevich, and spoke this word: "Aï, Tzar Vakraméy, do what thou wilt with this man who is as dead."

But he spat in her eye: "One tree doth not make a dark forest, nor is one man a host on the open plain!"

Nevertheless she was distrustful, and took Mikáilo by his yellow curls, dragged him forth upon the open plain, swung him about her head, and flung him over her shoulder.

"Where stood sweet Rover Mikáilo, there henceforth let a white stone stand," she said. "Let it fly over the earth for the space of three years, and after that let it sink through the damp earth!" And sweet Mikáilo was turned into a stone straightway.

His brothers in arms, remembering sweet Mikáilo, grew weary with longing for him, and said: "Let us go, brothers, to the Volhýnian land, to inquire whether our brother be slain or captive there." So they put on the weeds of wandering psalm-singers, threw pouches over their shoulders, took staves of forty poods, and set out.

As they journeyed to the Volhýnian land, an aged man came to meet them in the way, and said: "Take me with you as your comrade." And they did so, and came to the land of Volhýnia, to Tzar Vakraméy.

There they beat upon the earth with their staves, and begged alms. The White Swan looked forth from the little lattice window, and perceived that the psalm-singers were come from Kíef town, and that the third was a strange man, and said: "Aï, Tzar Vakraméy! summon these pilgrims into thy palace, feed them well, and give them wine until they are well drunken, and gold at thy desire."

So Tzar Vakraméy called them in; and the Russian heroes inquired of Márya the White Swan, where their brother in arms might be, sweet Rover Mikáilo.

"I grieve sore for sweet Mikáilo the Rover," she made answer; "but I know not where he is."

Then she gave them great alms, and much food and drink, so that they were intoxicated, and lay upon the floor. But the aged man ate not, drank not; and when Márya the White Swan sent twelve knights to kill the psalm-singers, that aged pilgrim brandished his staff, and slew them all, leaving not one alive.

When Tzar Vakraméy saw that his whole kingdom could not stand against that one pilgrim, he pondered what might chance when the other two should wake. So he went in haste to his deep vaults, took gold, silver, and fair round pearls, and gave to those psalm-singers; and the next morning they set out for Kíef town.

As they journeyed, they came to a stone; and the aged pilgrim said: "I must leave you, brothers. Let us divide our possessions on this stone." Then he began to part the alms into four lots, whereat Ilyá could not restrain his restive heart, but spoke: "For whom is that fourth lot, thou stranger pilgrim?"

Said the wandering psalm-singer, the stranger: "It shall belong to him who shall raise this stone, and cast it over his shoulder, so that, falling upon the damp earth, it shall burst asunder."

Ilyá of Múrom sprang forward, grasped the stone, and raised it to his knees,— and sank to his knees in the damp earth. "Is this the devil or God's might, that is in this stone?" quoth he.

Then Dobrýnya essayed to lift it, and could not so much as make a space for the air to pass beneath it. But the aged psalm-singer put his little hand beneath the stone, raised it to his shoulder, and as he flung it, he conjured it: "Break, stone! and let sweet Mikáilo the Rover appear in thy stead!"

Out sprang Mikáilo, crying, "Fy, fee, brothers! how long I have slept!"

Then spoke the aged pilgrim: "Mikáilo, when thou art come to Kíef town, burn a candle to Saint Mikóla. And fare ye well now, ye mighty Russian heroes! pray to Mikóla of Mozháisk, and he will raise you from the blue sea!" Therewith he vanished, leaving the money with them, and they saw not whither he went.

Rover Mikáilo took leave straightway of his brothers in arms, and returned to the land of Volhýnia, and entered the spacious court of Tzar Vakraméy's palace, and shouted in a heroic voice.

White Swan Márya heard that cry, and spoke to Tzar Vakraméy: "My former husband is come," then ran out to Mikáilo with a bowl of wine.

"Aï, sweet Mikáilo Rover!" she said, "without my hero I cannot live. It was not I, but Tzar Vakraméy, who imprisoned thee within that white and burning stone. But take now this bowl of wine in one hand, and empty it at a draught, and we will go to Kíef town to courteous Prince Vladímir."

Now Mikáilo was susceptible to wine and woman's charms. He took the bowl, and quaffed the liquor, and where he drank, there he fell down in a stupor.

Then Márya the White Swan seized him by his yellow curls, and dragged him to a deep dungeon, and there made him fast to the wall with nails through his hands and feet. Yet a fifth nail for his heroic heart was lacking, and Márya ran to the bazaar to buy one.

While she was gone, Anna the Fair, sister to Tzar Vakraméy, took a little serving-maid, and went to view the Russian hero; and as she looked, she loved. Mikáilo's stupor was already passed, and he began to entreat her to set him free.

"Take me for thy wife," she made answer, "and I will save thee from vain death."

And he swore to her, "If thou wilt but save me, I will sever the turbulent head of Márya the White Swan, and take the golden crown with thee."

Then she drew out the spikes with her fingernails, took in haste a Tatar chosen for his stature, hair and beauty, and fastened him to the wall in Mikáilo's stead, took sweet Mikáilo under her cloak of black sables, and led him across the spacious court. Tzar Vakraméy espied her, and inquired:

"What hast thou there beneath thy cloak?"

"I took a little maid with me," she answered, "to view the Russian hero, and she is frightened. I have her beneath my cloak, and am leading her to mine own chamber, to comfort her."

Márya the Swan returned with her nail, and perceived not that it was a Tatar in the dungeon, and not her husband.

When fair Anna had brought sweet Mikáilo to her lofty tower, she dressed his bleeding wounds with herbs for three months, and healed them, then asked: "Hast thou thy strength as of yore?"

And sweet Mikáilo made answer: "If I had but my suit of chain mail, my great battle-sword, and my good steed, I should not fear your Tzar Vakraméy."

"There was once a hero among us in past years," quoth Anna the Fair, "and to this day none in our kingdom can wear his armor, nor wield his brand, nor guide his good steed."

Then Mikáilo told her what she must do; and she lay as though ailing, and sent word to Tzar Vakraméy that some one should be sent to heal her. When the leech came she said:

"I slept, and dreamed that if I might but don a coat of mail, and ride a heroic steed over the open plain, it would be well with me once more."

So the good steed of that hero of past years was led forth; and Rover Mikáilo arrayed himself in woman's garb, laid the coat of mail upon the horse, grasped the bridle, and led him forth behind the city wall. There he put on the coat of mail, armed himself, and mounting leaped the wall, and came to Tzar Vakraméy's palace.

When White Swan Márya saw him, she said to Tzar Vakraméy: "Lo! my former husband is alive again: pour him a cup of green wine, and mingle the herb of sleep therein."

This Vakraméy did; and when Márya presented it to Rover Mikáilo, beseeching him to drink it, and return with her to Kíef, he would have done her bidding. But Anna the Fair thrust herself out of the lattice window to the girdle, and shrieked in a piercing voice : " Drink not, sweet Rover Mikáilo! Remember thine oath. If thou drink that wine, thou hast lost thyself forever."

Thereupon he dashed aside the cup, drew his sword of damascened steel, and cut off the head of Márya the White Swan.

Vakraméy also he would have slain, but that his sister begged for his life. So he left Vakraméy in possession of his kingdom, took the Princess Anna the Most Fair, and went to Kíef town, to courteous Prince Vladímir. There they were married, and lived in happiness. And sweet Mikáilo Ivánovich the Rover built a church to Saint Mikóla of Mozháisk.

NIGHTINGALE BUDÍMIROVICH THE SAILOR HERO.

LOFTY are the heights of heaven, and deep the Ocean-sea, broad are the steppes o'er all the South, fathomless the Dniepr's reefs. Swamps and mosses lie over the sea, and frosts afar in the North. Barren are the shores about the White sea, and dark the forests that hem in Smolénsk. Lofty hills stand about Chigúnsk; wide stand the gates, and sarafáns[1] are fair on the Móshy river; round Opskof town spread the open plains.

From beneath the oak, oak, the damp oak, the willow-bush, from the white curling bush, the crimson elm, and the jacinth stone, flowed Mother Vólga river: past Kazán, Ryazán, and Ástrakhan she flowed, and fell through her seventy mouths into the blue sea, the Turkish sea!

'Twas not the storm-clouds gathering, nor blue clouds rolling up, but thirty dark-red ships and three, sailing from out the glorious sea. From Kadól's Isle in the land of Ledenétz they ran, o'er the many-bayed sea, with green curving lines of shore, towards Mother Dniepr river.

---

[1] A long, sleeveless tunic for women.

One ship, the fairest, sailed before, as flies the falcon clear, and proudly she bore her head on high. Like a dragon fierce her prow was fashioned, her sides like the aurochs of Litvá.[1] In place of ears were two sharp spears, — little white ermines hung thereon. Her brows were rare black sables from Siberia, from Yakútsk, and her eyes fair jacinth stones; rare gems, self-luminous, were they, not for beauty, but for guidance in the dark autumn nights. Her mane was two red foxes, her tail, two white sea-bears. The sails and pennons on that dark-red ship were of the silk of Samarcand; the cables and cordage likewise of that silk, that weareth not, teareth not; and the masts of gold, and the anchors from Siberia, of damascened steel. For oh! my brothers, our ship was fair adorned!

— Amid the ship stood a green tiled bower, its ceiling hung with black cut velvet, its walls with sables black. Its covering was foxes and martins, long and downy, from Siberian caves.

In that green tiled bower, on carven seats of precious fishes' teeth, sat Nightingale Budímirovich:[2] on his right sat his lady mother, young Ulyána Vasílievna, on his left his body-guard of three hundred youths, none better. Shoes of green morocco were on their feet, and golden buckles with silver tongues; their garments were of fine scarlet cloth; on their heads were Norman caps.

---
[1] Lithuania.   [2] See Appendix.

On his sounding gúsly played Nightingale, and solaced his lady mother. String after string he touched, and blended his voice therewith in tones from Nóvgorod and Jerusalem, in ditties from over the sea blue and glorious, from Kadól's Isle and the green-bayed shore.

Then quickly he went forth, and began to pace the ship, to shake back his yellow curls, and speak this word:

"Brothers, and brave guards of mine! Hearken to your chief, and do the deed commanded: take rods of iron, sound the reefs, scan the blue sea, that we run not into the shallows, but sail securely past."

So they sounded the depths, and ran in safety past the perilous reefs. But Nightingale still paced the deck, shook back his curls, and gave further command to his good youths:—

"Listen to your chieftain, and do the thing commanded: climb now the mast, and from the topmost yard look toward famous Kíef town, and see if it be far."

They answered from the yard:

"Aï, young Nightingale Budímirovich! Kíef town standeth close at hand."

Then he gave commandment that they should run into the harbor, and cast out steel anchors upon the steep shores, and throw out three landing stages; one of red gold for Nightingale himself, one of silver for his good body-guard, and one of bronze for his lady mother, the honorable widow, Ulyána Vasílievna.

Then young Nightingale took his golden keys, and from his treasure-chests, iron bound, he drew great store of treasure: forty forties of black sables, fox and martin skins without number, countless geese and swans, fine damask on which the red gold corrodeth not, the fair silver breaketh not. Not dear was the red gold, the pure silver upon that damask fair; that which was beyond price was the pattern from beyond the sea, of Nightingale's own devising. All these things he laid on a dish of gold, and went to Prince Vladímir's palace of white stone, to the banquet-hall. There he crossed himself as prescribed, did reverence as enjoined, to all, to two, to three, to four sides, and to the royal Prince in particular, greeting him and his Princess.

"Hail, thou bold and goodly youth!" spoke Vladímir then. "I know neither thy name nor country, whether thou be a Tzar or Tzarévich, a King or Crown Prince, or a fierce Cossáck from the peaceful Don."

"None of these am I," quoth the youth; "but young Nightingale Budímir's son, from the blue sea, from the Isle of Kadól in the land of Ledenétz." Then he offered his gifts to Vladímir and his Princess. The Princess was greatly pleased thereat, accepting and praising them all; and in particular the damask, the like of which for richness, and cunningness of device, was not in Kíef nor ever had been. And the Princess Apráxia entreated Vladímir that he would give Nightingale sweet viands, green wine, and sweet mead.

So Vladímir feasted him, and spake in pleasure:

"Aï, young Nightingale, what guerdon shall I bestow upon thee in return for all these great gifts? Wilt thou have cities with their villages, or golden treasure?"

And Nightingale made answer, as he paced the banquet-hall: "None of these do I need, for I have all these things at my desire. But grant me now a little plat, whereon to build three golden-crownéd towers, within the green garden of fair Love, where they bake pepper-cakes and little tarts; where pancakes are sold, and children barter wares."

"As thou knowest, so do," answered courteous Prince Vladímir: "build where thou wilt, in my green royal gardens."

"Thanks, royal Vladímir, for thy princely gift," quoth Nightingale, and went straightway to his men.

"Brothers, my brave, stout guards, do now the thing commanded: put off your caftáns of scarlet cloth, and your fair green shoes; don raiment fit for labor, of elkskin, and heavy foot-gear. Take sharp steel axes, go to Love's garden, root up the oaks and elms, hew oaken beams, and build me there this night, three golden-crownéd towers, with roofs o'erlapping and rich halls, so that I may dwell there at to-morrow's dawn."

Then late, right late at even, his good youths labored like woodpeckers tapping trees, and at midnight the palace was complete. Three-towered it stood, with golden domes which merged, three latticed halls, and in the midst a guest-chamber. Full richly were the towers adorned. In the heavens stood a sun — and in the towers a sun; in heaven a moon — a moon in the towers likewise; stars and dawns in heaven and in the towers, and all beauty under heaven.

— Early chimed the bells for matins, when Love the Fair awoke from sleep, washed herself very white, and gazed from her latticed casement upon her garden green. And lo! a marvel presented itself to her — three gold-domed towers stood in her garden fair.

"Ho there, nurses and handmaidens mine!" Love cried, "come hither and view this marvel. But yestere'en that hillock was bare, and now 'tis fully crowned."

"Prithee, dear Love," they answered, "look thyself! For thy fate hath come to thy court."

Then Love put her shoes in haste upon her naked feet, flung her robe upon one shoulder, and ran out to walk in her garden fair. When she came to the first, the grated tower, she heard a clashing and a clinking, and listened there: 'twas Nightingale's brave body-guard telling over his countless treasures of gold. As she listened at the second tower of glass, she caught a whispering — the honorable young widow Ulyána Vasílievna praying God for her dear son. And at the third tower of red gold was again clashing and great noise; for fair young Nightingale sat therein, on a stool of precious fishes' teeth,[1] playing on his harp, and singing. String after string he plucked, accompanying his voice in songs from Nóvgorod and Jerusalem, and all the little ballads from beyond the blue Turkish sea, and Kadól's Isle, with its many bays and green incurving shores.

The maiden rejoiced greatly, and was likewise greatly terrified, and listened all that day until the eventide. Then she entered the lofty tower, prayed God, and bowed to Nightingale. Nightingale returned her greeting, and she spoke:

"Young Nightingale Budímir's son! thou art unwedded; take me, a fair maid, to wife."

To this Nightingale made answer: "Thou art pleasing to me, maiden, in all things save this one; — that I like not, — thou hast wooed a husband for thyself. This should not be, fair damsel. Bet-

---

[1] Walrus-tusk.

ter were it for thee to be at home, drawing water, milking the cows, feeding the calves."

Upon that, with great shame she turned and ran to her home.

Then young Nightingale Budímirovich donned with speed his richest apparel, and went to Prince Vladímir of royal Kíef, in state, to woo, seated himself in the great place, and spoke this word:

"Aï, thou Prince of royal Kíef town! Thou hast a much-loved niece, young Love. Give her to me now for my wife."

So Prince Vladímir betrothed the fair maiden, his niece, and the young people went to God's church to take the golden crowns.

Then in haste did young Nightingale remove from Love's garden his golden-crownéd towers, made all things as they were at the first, and betook himself to his dark-red ship with his lady mother, his good body-guard, and his fair young wife, and sailed away to his own land. There he dwelt thenceforth, and his wife, in joy and peace.

DANÍLO THE HUNTSMAN AND HIS WIFE.

IN Kíef town the Fair Sun Prince Vladímir held a feast, great, honorable, and merry. And when the throng of princely nobles and mighty heroes had eaten half their fill, and were half drunken with wine, they began to boast among themselves. One vaunted his wealth, another his foreign merchandise, another his style of living or his estates, his prowess or his young wife.

Then spoke our father Prince Vladímir:

"Aï, all ye my princely nobles, and heroes mighty! ye are all married, while I alone go unwed. Know ye not where I may find a bride with whom to hold sweet converse, of whom I may make boast in banquet-hall and bower, to whom ye may pay homage?"

Putyátin Putyátovich made answer: "Prince Vladímir, little father! take to thyself the bride of Danílo the Huntsman. For I have journeyed much in foreign lands, have viewed many princesses, and proved their understandings. One was fair of face, but lacked wit; the wit of another exceeded her beauty. Yet never found I so fair a woman, and so fitting, as the bride of Danílo the

Huntsman, Vasilísa Mikúlichna. She is fair of face, and of good understanding: she knoweth well how to read and write the Russian tongue, and is learned likewise in the legends of saints and in church-singing. None is more meet to be our Princess and our mother."

This word displeased Vladímir greatly, and he said: "Where was it ever seen or heard that a woman should be taken from a living husband?" And he commanded that Putyátin should be executed.

But the man was crafty, and slipped aside: "Ho, little father, Prince Vladímir," he cried; "wait! hang me not in haste; command me to speak yet a word." So Vladímir commanded him.

"Let us send Danílo on some distant service, from which there is no return, to the Island of Buyán.[1] Command him to slay the fierce beast with blue feathers and bristly hide, and to take out its heart. — Let us send him afar on the open plain, to the Levanídof meadow, to the thundering spring: command him to take the white-throated bird, and fetch it hither to thy royal banquet, to slay the fierce lion, and bear him hither."

Prince Vladímir liked this counsel well; but Ilyá of Múrom, the Old Cossáck, spoke up, and said: "Little father, Prince Vladímir! if thou slay

---

[1] See Appendix: *Alátyr Stone.*

the bright falcon, yet shalt thou not capture the white swan!"

But this speech angered Prince Vladímir, and he set Ilyá in a deep dungeon.

Then he called Danílo, and commanded him to go upon this quest. And Danílo went forth from the richly spread tables of oak, the sweet viands and honeyed drinks, mounted his good steed in the spacious court, and rode homeward.

His young wife Vasilísa in her lofty castle watched him as he came, and saw that he went not merrily: his turbulent head drooped low, his clear eyes were bent upon damp mother earth. When she had inquired of him whether Prince Vladímir had duly honored him with cup and seat at the feast, he answered that he had had the highest seat at the board, and the cup had come to him first of all.

"But woman's intrigues have wrought my ruin," he said. "Fetch me now my little quiver with a hundred and fifty darts." Nevertheless she gave him the great quiver with full three hundred, whereat he reproved her: "Thou art ill-taught. Why art thou thus disobedient? Fearest thou me not?"

But Vasilísa was not angry, and said: "My hope, my heart's friend, young Danílo the Huntsman! a spare dart may prove of service to thee."

So the good youth journeyed to the Isle of

Buyán. When he espied the fierce beast, he grasped his stout bow firmly, fitted a gilded arrow to the silken cord, slew the beast, and took out his heart and liver. Then he sat down to eat bread, and carve the white swan. And as he looked toward Kíef town, he beheld not white snows gleaming nor black clouds gathering fast, but a Russian host flashing black and white against Danílo. Then shed he burning tears, and said: "Of a truth, I am greatly out of favor with Prince Vladímir! and my service he requireth not."

With that Danílo seized his sharp sword, and cut down the Russian host to a man. And after a little space, he looked again towards Kíef town: — 'twas not two fierce beasts coursing o'er the open plain, nor yet two damp oaks quivering; but two great heroes riding, Nikíta, Danílo's own brother, and Dobrýnya, his brother in arms.

When Danílo saw that, he wept bitterly, and spoke: "Of a truth, the Lord is wroth with me, and Prince Vladímir greatly displeased: for when was it ever heard or seen that brother should be sent to contend against brother?"

Thereupon he caught up his sharp spear, thrust the butt-end into the damp earth, and fell upon the point; and as it pierced his white breast, Danílo closed his clear eyes forever.

When the heroes came to him, they wept sore,

and turned back, and told Prince Vladímir: "Bold Danílo is dead."

Then Vladímir collected a great following, seated himself in a golden chariot, and went to Danílo's dwelling. When he was come thither, he entered the lofty tower, and kissed Vasilísa's sugar mouth.

But Vasilísa said: "Little father, Prince Vladímir, kiss not my red mouth, without my friend Danílo."

But Vladímir commanded her: "Don thy fairest apparel, thy wedding robes."

This she did, then took a sharp knife, and said:

"Grant me now, Prince Vladímir, to look upon my dear friend, and to take leave of his white body."

So Vladímir permitted her, and sent with her two heroes. And, when she went to look, lo! they were making the coffin.

"Make it wide, ye master carpenters," quoth Vasilísa, "that his heroic bones may have space to turn!"

And to the two heroes she said:

"Go now, ye heroes, and say to Prince Vladímir, that he must not leave my body upon the open plain, but must lay it with the body of my dear friend Danílo the Huntsman."

Upon that, she took her sharp knife, pierced her white breast, and closed her clear eyes.

The two heroes wept, and returning, told all to Prince Vladímir.

Then Vladímir released Ilyá of Múrom from the dungeon, and kissed him on the temple. "Well hast thou spoken, thou Old Cossáck, Ilyá of Múrom!" he said, and graciously bestowed upon him a mantle of sables. But to Putyátin he gave a kettle of pitch.[1]

---

[1] It is difficult to determine the epoch of this *bylína*. Possibly, in some version of the song which has not come down to us, Vladímir is represented as courting Danílo's wife during the lifetime of the Princess Apráxia. This would answer to the historical Vladímir before his baptism.

ILYÁ AND THE ADVENTURE OF THE THREE ROADS.

THE old man rode over the open plain. From youth to old age he had ridden, and he marvelled at himself. " Oh age, old age! " he cried : " oh deep old age of three hundred years! Thou hast overtaken the Cossáck in the open plain, thou hast caught me like a black raven, thou hast alighted upon my turbulent head. — And youth, thou youth, my early youth! Thou hast flown away, youth, over the open plain, like the falcon clear! "

In the open plain the light snows gleamed not white, little clouds darkled not, the blades of the steppe grass waved not. — But over the open plain still rode the Old Cossáck of the Don, on his heroic steed. The horse under him was fiery as a wild beast, and Ilyá as he sat was like the falcon bright. No ferriage asked the Cossáck, for good Cloudfall leaped lake and river, wide morass, and floating swamp.

As he rode, he came to a place where three ways met; and there stood a burning white stone, Alátyr,[1] whereon was written: " Whoso rideth to

---
[1] See Appendix.

the right shall gain great wealth, whoso goeth to the left a wife, he that fareth straight on, his death."

The Old Cossáck halted, marvelled, and shook his gray head in thought.

"Wherefore should I, an old man, crave wealth? I have countless store of golden treasure. And why should the old man win a wife? There is no joy in an ugly wife, and a fair one is taken for the envy of other men. A young wife is coveted of others; an old wife would lie on the oven, and eat kisél,[1] she would sit by the oven, and order the old husband about. Nay; but I will ride that way where I may win death."

Then the good youth, the Old Cossáck, rode on. Hardly had he passed Koréla the Accursed, not yet had he attained to India the Rich, when he entered a gloomy forest. There stood a band of forty thousand robbers, and they coveted Ilyá's good steed.

"In all our lives," said they, "we have beheld no such horse. Halt then, good youth, halt, thou Russian hero!" And they would have robbed him; but Ilyá said:

"Ho, ye robber horde! Ye may not kill the old man, nor rob him. I have no treasure with me, save five hundred rubles. The cross on my breast is worth but five hundred, my cloak of sables three thousand; my cap of forty poods, and my sandals

---

[1] A sourish porridge, or pudding.

of the seven silks, five hundred each; my fine
caftán of orange-tawny taffeta is valued at but
little, my braided bridle rimmed with precious
stones, but a thousand rubles. My Cherkéssian
saddle bordered with eagle's feathers — that eagle
which flew not over lofty mountains, but over the
blue sea — is priceless. Between my Cloudfall's
eyes, and under his ears, are jewels fair, clear
jacinth stones, — not for youthful vanity, but be-
cause of the autumn nights. Wheresoever my
good steed goeth, he can see thirty versts on all
sides, thirty versts well told; for they gleam like
the bright moon. — And my good steed Cloudfall
is worth nothing at all."

The robbers jeered as they answered: "Thou
art old and garrulous, Cossáck! Since we have
roamed this white world, never saw we such a fool.
The aged fool hath told the truth as though we
had demanded it! Seize the old fellow, children!"
And they would have dragged the Old Cossáck
from his horse.

But young Ilyá of Múrom drew a fiery dart
from his quiver, and sped it forth from his stout
bow, and struck the damp mother of oaks. The
ringbarked oak was shivered in fragments, and
the earth was ploughed up round about.

The robbers were greatly terrified thereat, and
lay senseless for the space of five hours. Then
they entreated him:

"Good youth, great Russian hero! Enter thou into comradeship with us. Take what thou wilt of golden treasure, flowered garments, horses and herds."

Ilyá laughed: "Eh, brothers, mine enemies," quoth he, "I have no wish to feed your sheep."

Then he turned back to the white and burning stone Alátyr, erased the old inscription, and wrote anew:

"I have ridden this road, and have not been slain." So ended the adventure of the first road.

Again Ilyá of Múrom the Old Cossáck sallied forth into the open plain. He rode three hundred versts, and lo! before him in a green meadow, stood a marvel of marvels, a wonder of wonders. Too small was it to be called a city, too large to be a village. It was, in truth, but a fair palace of white stone, with golden roofs, lofty walls, and three-cornered towers.

When Ilyá came to that palace, there issued forth from it forty damsels, and with them came also the Princess Zeníra the Most Fair. The beautiful Princess took the old man by his white hands, by his golden ring, kissed his sugar mouth, and bade him enter the palace of white stone to feast with her.

"Long have I journeyed in Holy Russia, but such a marvel I have never yet beheld," said Ilyá. Then she led him in. The good youth crossed himself as prescribed, made salutation as enjoined, to all sides, and lowest of all to the fair Princess, who placed him at the table of white oak, and fetched him sugar viands and sweet mead.

"Eat not to satiety, good youth," said she, "and drink not to drunkenness, for there is more to come."

But Ilyá said: "I have journeyed three hundred versts, and my hunger is great," and ate and drank his fill.

Then Zeníra the Fair led him to a rich warm chamber, to a bed of yew wood and ivory, with soft cushions of down.

"Lie thou next yon brick wall, thou bold and goodly youth," spake the Princess.

"Nay," said Ilyá, "I will lie upon the outer edge, for I often rise in the night to visit my good steed."

Thereupon he seized her by her white breast, and flung her upon the bed of yew wood, against the wall.

Now that bed of yew was false; it turned, and the fair Princess was hurled down into her dungeons, forty fathoms deep.

Then the good old youth went forth into the spacious courtyard, and spoke to the nurses, women and faithful servitors: "Give me the golden keys which undo the dungeon doors. Show me the way to those deep vaults."

So they showed him; and he found the way choked with yellow sand, and barred with vast logs of wood.

He had no need of the golden keys; he tore the locks asunder with his hands, forced the doors back with his heels, until they flew from their frames. Then from the dungeons forty Tzars and Tzaréviches, forty Kings and Princes, their heirs, together with Dobrýnya Nikítich, Alyósha Popóvich, and many more, an innumerable host, sprang to their nimble feet, and came forth.

All bowed before the Old Cossáck, and thanked him for showing them once more the white world.

"Go hence, ye Tzars, to your empires," spake Ilyá, "ye Kings, to your kingdoms, to your wives and children, and pray God for the Old Cossáck, for Ilyá of Múrom."

But when the fair Princess came forth, Ilyá took her by her white hands, bound her to three untamed horses, and drove them apart, so that they scattered over the open plain, here a hand, there a foot, and everywhere her white body. All her estates and treasure he divided among those bold and goodly youths, the strong and mighty heroes; and her palace of white stone he gave over to the flames.

Again the Old Cossáck returned to the white stone, crossed out the old inscription, and wrote a new one:

"This legend is falsely written; I have ridden that way, yet am I still unwed!"

"I will go now," quoth he, "where wealth is to be won."

Then the old man rode over the plain; three hours, three hundred versts he rode, and came at length to a green meadow where deep pits were dug, and to a gloomy forest where was a vault filled with treasure, fair gold, pure silver, and fine seed-pearls; and on the vault was an inscription: "This treasure shall fall to Ilyá of Múrom."

Ilyá reflected; and having hired wise and cunning craftsmen, he built on that spot a monastery and a cathedral church. And he instituted there church singing, and the sound of bells. "Let him whose that treasure was come for it now," quoth Ilyá of Múrom, and returned to famous Kíef town, to courteous Prince Vladímir the Fair Sun.

Vladímir inquired of him: "Where hast thou tarried so long, thou bold and goodly youth, thou Old Cossáck, Ilyá of Múrom?"

And Ilyá related his Adventure of the Three Ways, and all that he had done, to Fair Sun Prince Vladímir.

EPIC SONGS OF RUSSIA. 253

DOBRÝNYA AND ALYÓSHA.

FROM beneath white curling beeches, and Levanídof the wonder-working cross, from beneath the holy relics of Borís, and white Alátyr stone, rose, rose and flowed, flowed and rolled, swift Mother Vólga river.

Broad and far ran Mother Vólga past Kazán, and broader yet by Ástrakhan; many a river did our Mother Vólga flood receive into her bosom, and yet more brooks did she ingulf. A vast sweep she gave at Dalínsky, along the lofty mountains of Sorochínsky and Smolénsk's gloomy forests; in a bed of three thousand versts she ran, and fell into the Caspian Sea, through seventy mouths: — and broad is her flood at Nóvgorod. And this, brothers, is no fable, no play of words: neither is it Dobrýnya's tale, which shall straightway find beginning.

— Dobrýnya went to royal Kíef town, where courteous Prince Vladímir had made an honorable feast to his princes, nobles, heroes, and warrior-maids.

The long day drew towards evening, the honorable feast waxed merry, the fair sun sank to the west. And the feast grew ever merrier, and the heroes began to boast of many things, — the wise man of his father and mother, the foolish of his young wife. Vladímir the Prince grew warm as he paced the banquet-hall, and he went forth upon the fair round porch to gaze off on the open plain.

Far, afar over the open plain, the clear falcon flew not, nor fled the small white hare ; the little ermine galloped not, weaving the prints of his small pretty paws. But from the verge of the plain a bold and goodly youth emerged, — little Ilyá, the glorious, of Múrom, — rode straight to Prince Vladímir's court, and entered the banquet-hall.

He crossed himself, and did reverence as enjoined, to all four sides, and seated himself at the oaken board in the great corner of honor, on the bench of precious fishes' teeth.[1] Already had the guests tasted bread and salt, and now were carving the white swan, when Vladímir came into the hall, stroked his black curls, and spoke:

"Ho, ye princes, nobles, strong and mighty heroes all, and all ye bold warrior-maids ! stand for the Christian faith, for me, your Prince Vladímir, and for my Princess Apráxia, for widows, orphans, and unhappy women ! Whom shall we send to defend the mighty barrier, and wage battle with the Discourteous Knight ? For he hath writ-

---

[1] Walrus-tusks.

ten me a challenge to single combat, and is now flying hither in form of a raven. Whom shall we send to fight that raven, and to collect tribute of the Golden Horde which hath been due us these twelve years and a half, to visit the disobedient hordes, and clear the straight roads to the stern King Etmanýla Etmanýlovich, to beat back the white-eyed Finns, to exterminate the Circassians of Pyatigórsk, the Kalmýks and Tatars?"

All at the feast held their peace, each hiding behind some lesser man. Then glorious Ilyá of Múrom, that bold and goodly youth, stepped forward, and stood firm upon his nimble feet, and bowed low until his white face touched his feet.

"Foolish are ye, Russian heroes, to hold your peace thus, uttering no word! Not long is it, brothers, since I returned from the open plain. I have dwelt upon the Sorochínsky road, at the heroic ditch of defence, contending in single combat and waging battle these twelve years. Thither flew the Discourteous Knight in form of a black raven, but would not show himself to my eyes; else would I have slain that dog of a churl with my stout bow. But if I go, there will be none to defend the barrier. Let us therefore send young Dobrýnya Nikítich."

Then Dobrýnya drained a cup of green wine which Prince Vladímir himself brought him, but tarried not long at the feast, going thence in uncheerful mood. When he came to his mother he wept bitterly.

"Fair my lady mother," he lamented, "why didst thou bear me in an unpropitious hour, without genius, strength, great beauty, or tall stature, great wealth, or curling hair? Rather shouldest thou, fair and honorable widow, Afímya Alexándrovna, my mother, have wrapped my turbulent head in a sleeve of white linen, and cast me like a white pebble into the black Turkish sea. Then I should have lain at the bottom of the sea like a precious stone; the stormy winds would not have blown upon me, and I should not have roamed through Holy Russia, shedding innocent blood, causing tears to fathers and mothers, and making little children orphans."

Then his mother made answer: "Gladly would I have borne thee with the genius and fortune of Ilyá of Múrom, the strength of Hero Svyatogór, the mincing gait of Churílo Plenkóvich, the beauty of Ósip Most Fair,[1] the daring of Alyósha Popóvich, the wealth of Sadkó the merchant of Nóvgorod, the fame of Volgá Busláevich, the curls of the Tzar Kudryánisha.[2] But to Dobrýnya God gave courtesy alone; and other gifts were not bestowed upon thee."

---

[1] The biblical Joseph figures under this name in the religious songs.

[2] Curly, literally; but said to be in reality a corruption of the Emperor Hadrian's name.

He said to her: "Fair and good my mother, thy youth hath neither good steed nor heroic trappings."

"Go through the first unused stable, Dobrýnya," his mother answered him, "and in the second choose for thyself a good, well-broken steed. And if none there shall please thee, descend into the deep vault where standeth a good heroic steed bound with twelve silver chains, with twelve fine bits of silk, — not of our silk, but of the silk of Samarcand, which weareth not nor teareth. There lie also heroic trappings and all caparisons meet for a youth."

Dobrýnya inquired no further. He sprang to his nimble feet, ran to the first stable, found there no horse that pleased him, and in the second none likewise, and so descended to the deep vault. There he beheld a goodly steed, and fell down before his right fore-foot.

"Thou good heroic steed," he cried, "thou hast served my father and grandfather; serve now also Dobrýnya on his heroic quests." Then he unchained and loosed the horse, and saddled him, girding him with twelve girths of the silk of Samarcand, the indestructible, and a thirteenth for heroic strength, lest the good steed should spring from under the saddle and throw the good youth upon the open plain.

After that he arrayed himself. Under the heels

of his shoes of green morocco, studded with golden pins, sparrows might fly; from their awl-like beaks an egg might roll; his cap was gilded, — not for youthful grace, but for heroic might. Next he put on a coat of mail, not heavy (in weight but ninety poods), and set his foot in the stirrup of damascened steel. — More lightly than a hare he sprang — more sharply than a little ermine turned, seated himself in the Cherkéssian saddle, and came to the palace of white stone, to his mother, and said: " Give me thy leave to ride upon this heroic quest."

So his fair, good mother laid the cross of blessing on him, and led to his left stirrup his beloved wife, young Nastásya Mikúlichna, and having bade him farewell, went into the palace and wept bitter tears, wiped them away with a fair linen cloth, and said : " The warm and fair red sun which made my midsummer hath set behind the gloomy forests and lofty hills, behind mosses and wide lakes: and now the bright moon alone lighteth me: young Nastásya, my son's bride, alone tarrieth with me."

Young Nastásya, as she stood by his stirrup, began to inquire of him: " Aï, my dearest Dobrýnya Nikítich! when may I expect thee from the open field? Tell me when I may await thee from yonder lands."

" I will tell thee, fair Nastásya. Three years shalt thou wait for Dobrýnya; if in that time I am not here, then wait yet another three. And when that space of six years is past, and I am not returned from the open field, wait for me three years more, and yet three years. And if after twelve years I come not, then shall I not be among the living. Then live a widow, or marry, at thy pleasure. Choose a prince, a noble, or a mighty Russian hero. But wed not with my brother in arms, Alyósha Popóvich, that scoffer at women. For a brother in arms is worse than an own brother. Therefore, marry a robber or a brigand if thou list, but not Alyósha, the scorner of maidens: for he loveth to mock at women, young widows, and fair maids."

— They saw the good youth as he mounted, they saw him not as he rode: from the court he departed not by the gates, he traversed the plain not by the highway. His steed's first leap was over the city walls, the second compassed three versts, and of the third leap no trace could be found evermore.

— Year followed year as the falcon flieth. Three years Nastásya waited, and Dobrýnya came not.

But Alyósha Popóvich was cunning. He rode forth into the open plain, and after that turned back and came to Nastásya.

"Lo, Nastásya Mikúlichna!" quoth he: "as I roamed the open plain but yesterday, I saw Dobrýnushka dead. He lieth with his head in a willow bush, his nimble feet amid the plume-grass tall; in his yellow curls small wood birds have woven their nests; Polish ravens have plucked out his clear eyes; silken grass springeth through his white breast, and amid it azure flowerets blossom. His weapons are scattered, his good steed roameth the plain, and his wife still liveth a widow. Therefore, lady, wed now with me."

"Nay, Alyósha Popóvich," Nastásya answered, "thou hast not been on the open plain; thou hast but wandered with the dogs in the outskirts of the town."

— Day followed after day, as the rain doth fall, week grew on week as groweth the grass, and like the river, year flowed after year. Six full years passed. Alyósha came again to the palace of white stone, did reverence and crossed himself as enjoined, seated himself upon the wall-bench, and began to woo young Nastásya for his bride.

"Now marry me, a goodly youth, Nastásya! Dobrýnya will never more return from the open plain."

"Aï, bold Alyósha Popóvich! I have kept a man's oath, and now will I keep a woman's. If in twelve years Dobrýnya return not, then I shall be free to live a widow or to wed. But thee, Alyósha, I may never wed."

Then Alyósha was not merry, and said: "Thou

mayest turn and strive thy uttermost, but none other wilt thou get for a husband; and so shalt thou wed with me."

Thereupon he went forth from the palace of white stone; and time passed on until the full term of years was accomplished.

Again he came to woo with Fair Sun Prince Vladímir, and sat upon the wall-bench as before.

"Marry me now, young Nastásya Mikúlichna," said he.

"I will not marry thee," she answered.

The Fair Sun Prince Vladímir spoke: "Young Nastásya Mikúlichna, if thou wed not bold Alyósha Popóvich, I will shut thee up in a nunnery; I will give thee in marriage to Murza the Tatar in the Lithuanian land; I will make thee my cowherd."

But she still made answer: "Nay, I will not wed bold Alyósha."

Then they said: "If thou wilt not do this freely, we will take thee by force." Thereupon they took her by her white hands, led her to the cathedral, and betrothed her to bold Alyósha. After that, Fair Sun Vladímir took their hands and led them to his palace, where he made for Alyósha a great banquet, and an honorable feast, and bade to it many of all degrees. And the honorable widow Afímya Alexándrevna wailed: "Now hath my bright moon set also!"

— Now Dobrýnya had gone to the Golden Horde,

and had fought for royal Kíef and his native land all those years, wandering far through many countries. When Nastásya married Alyósha, he was far away upon the open plain, beyond the glorious blue sea. As the good youth sat in his tent, diverting himself with chess, upon a board of gold, he knew not of the misfortune which had befallen him. Then flew thither a dove and his mate, perched upon a damp oak, and began to coo:

"There is feasting to-day in Kíef town, for Dobrýnya's young wife is wedded to Alyósha Popóvich."

When Dobrýnya heard that, he sprang to his nimble feet, and flung his golden board upon the damp earth, whereat mother earth quaked. Then he saddled his good steed with haste, fell down before his right fore-foot, and besought him:

"Aï, my good steed Fly-alone! Thou hast borne me hither in three years. Now bear me home in three hours to royal Kíef town."

Then he mounted his good steed, and quickly, quickly, very, very quickly, with speed, rode Dobrýnya from beyond the blue sea. Good Fly-alone left the earth; higher than the standing wood he soared, yet lower than the flying clouds. He leaped the lakes and rivers, dashed through the dusky forests, galloped round the dark blue sea, — afar in the open plain, 'twas not the first light snow descending, nor a white hare coursing fleet, nor snowy partridge fluttering, but a bold and goodly youth swift riding. Straight to Kíef town he rode; not through the gates, but over the city walls, past the angled towers, he entered, and took his way to the honorable widow's dwelling. He asked no leave of the porters at the gate, nor of the keepers at the doors. Thrusting them aside, he broke open the portals, and entered unbidden, unannounced, and boldly, the honorable widow's dwelling. "Hail, honorable widow, Afímya Alexándrevna!" he said when he had crossed himself and done reverence as was the usage.

The porters and door-keepers, entering, made complaint of the bold youth, and the widow said:

"Why, bold and goodly youth, hast thou entered the orphaned dwelling unannounced? Were my dear child living, young Dobrýnya Nikítich, he would have cut off thy turbulent head for thine unmannerly ways. Were he but alive, all the drunken boors would not come to jeer at this unprotected dwelling. But twelve years have passed since my fair red sun set forever."

"Mournest thou not in vain?" said Dobrýnya. "But yesterday I parted from Dobrýnya, and not a week hath passed over since we exchanged crosses. He went to Tzargrád, and I came to Kíef. He bade me, his own brother, inquire for his dear wife, young Nastásya. Where is she?"

"Go forth, thou pot-house boor, and mock not a poor old woman! Though I already totter with extreme old age, yet will I myself put thee out by force."

"Aï, my fair lady mother," answered young Dobrýnya. "Knowest thou not thy beloved son, young Dobrýnya Nikítich?"

"Young Dobrýnya had shoes of morocco upon his feet, but thine, thou sot, are torn and patched. Dobrýnya's face was white and red, — thine is dark and dust-begrimed. His eyes were clear as the sea falcon's, but thine are troubled. Young Dobrýnya had yellow locks, curling in three tiers upon his head, — thine hang upon thy shoulders. Upon his curls rested a fair new cap, and his raiment was flowered; but thy garments are rent and pieced."

"My garments have become worn in these twelve years past, fair my lady mother; my shoes are rubbed through on my stirrups, my white face the fierce heats have discolored, and my cap hath been soaked with frequent rains."

"If thou be indeed young Dobrýnya, my son, thou hast a birthmark upon thy right breast."

Then Dobrýnya showed her the mark. His mother heeded not her age, but ran and caught him by his white hands, and kissed his sugar mouth, calling him her beloved son.

"Where now is my young wife?" he asked.

"Where is Nastásya, that she cometh not to meet me, returning from the open plain?"

"The clear falcon hath flown into my court, but the white swan hath fluttered forth from it," his mother answered, and told him all Alyósha's treachery, and how it was now the third day of the wedding feast.

"Fetch quickly my minstrel's [1] garment, which lieth upon the table in the new chamber, and my little gúsly of maple-wood, from the peg in the cellar."

Then he arrayed himself in haste, and strung his harp, and took his way to the palace of white stone, where the wedding guests were making merry.

The gate-keepers had been strictly charged to admit no one, but when Dobrýnya gave them gold they permitted him to go in to the feast.

When he was come to the banquet-hall, he crossed himself, and did reverence on all sides, and in particular to the Prince and Princess, and to young Nastásya Mikúlichna.

"Fair Sun, Prince of royal Kíef," he said, "is there not a little place and small for the little jester, where he may play upon his harp?"

"Aï, little minstrel!" said Prince Vladímir, "all the places are filled; but there is yet a small place upon the earthen oven — the minstrel's place."

---

[1] *Skomorók*, buffoon, *jongleur*, minstrel, jester.

Dobrýnya was agile of foot: lightly he sprang upon the oven, and tuned his harp. One string he tuned to Kíef, one to Tzargrád, and the third to Jerusalem; and the tones he sang were from over the sea; but the theme was Dobrýnya's adventures, and the men of Kíef town.

"Ho, little minstrel," quoth Prince Vladímir, "thy place is not upon the oven. Come hither. Three places are thine to choose: the first is beside me, the second over against me, and the third is where thou wilt."

Then Dobrýnya seated himself opposite bold Alyósha and the young Princess Nastásya, and said to Vladímir:

"Fair Sun, grant me to pour out a cup of green wine, in measure a bucket and a half, in weight a pood and a half, and bear to whom I will."

"Thy song was great," said Prince Vladímir, "and the solace thereof was sweet. Pour the green wine without measure, take golden treasure without stint!"

So Dobrýnya poured a great cup of wine, dropped therein his marriage ring, and gave to Nastásya.

"Drink to the bottom, young Princess Nastásya, and thou shalt see good: and if thou drink not to the bottom, thou shalt not see good."

Then Nastásya took the cup in one hand, and drained it at a draught, and lo! she beheld the ring with which she had wedded Dobrýnya.

"Fair Sun Prince Vladímir," she said, "not he that sitteth beside me is my husband, but he that sitteth over against me, that little minstrel, young Dobrýnya Nikítich."

Thereupon she rose to her nimble feet, put her little white hands upon the oaken board, and vaulted over, fell upon Dobrýnya's white breast, and kissed his sugar mouth.

"The proverb saith — 'A man goeth to the forest for wood, and his wife doth wed straightway!' Take thy silken whip, therefore, Dobrýnya, and beat me."

But Dobrýnya answered, "I marvel not at thee, woman; as 'tis said, 'a woman's hair is long, but her wits are short.' But at Prince Vladímir, the Fair Sun, I do marvel, — that he should woo the wife of a living husband for another man, and should compel her to wed when she would not willingly. And yet more do I marvel at my brother in arms, bold Alyósha Popóvich. Yester-e'en was but a week that Alyósha saw me in the open plain; and now the younger brother hath taken away the elder brother's wife."

Then he seized Alyósha by the yellow curls, dragged him over the oaken table, hurled him upon the brick floor, and began to beat him with his little cudgel of ninety poods; and when he was done, he flung Alyósha under the wall-bench. Quoth he, "'Any man may marry,' saith the prov-

erb, 'but not with every man doth it go well!'"
Then the guests were all terrified and fled.

And Dobrýnya took his young wife by her white hands, and led her to his palace of white stone. Thenceforward he rode upon no quest, but dwelt in Kíef town; but Alyósha went, with shame and grief, to a strange and distant land.

And Dobrýnya's fame, and the fame of that feast, have been sung since that day, and shall be so forever, and forevermore.

ILYÁ OF MÚROM AND TZAR KÁLIN.

AT courteous Prince Vladímir's palace in royal Kíef town, an honorable feast was assembled of many princes, all the nobles, the mighty heroes and their bold body-guards, and all the merchant-traders.

The Fair Sun made good cheer; to one he gave cities, to another towns, to this man villages, to that one hamlets. And to Ilyá he gave a cloak of marten skins, with a collar of sables. But the cloak came not into honor with Ilyá, nor into praise. He bare that cloak of marten skins to the kitchen, dragged it about the brick floor by one sleeve, and began to say to it:

"I will drag about that serpent, Tzar Kálin, by his yellow curls, as I drag this cloak of marten skins. As I pour green wine upon this cloak, even so will I pour out his hot heart, with its seething blood."

But a black-visaged maid bore this saying to the Fair Sun Prince Vladímir. "Ilyá hath been in my kitchen," she said; "he hath dragged his mantle of marten about, and hath said that even so he would also drag Vladímir by his yellow curls.

And he hath poured green wine upon the mantle, and declared that even so he would pour out Prince Vladímir's burning heart with his own white hands."

Then was Prince Vladímir very wroth, and shouted in his thundering voice:

"Ye mighty heroes! lead Ilyá to our dungeon, and set an iron grating there; pile trunks of oak trees on all sides, and heap over all yellow sand."

The heroes went and told Ilyá all, and besought him to help them in this strait, else would Prince Vladímir overwhelm them with his displeasure. So Ilyá mounted his good steed, and rode willingly with them to the dungeon. There he dismounted from his good Cloudfall, took off the Cherkéssian saddle and plaited bridle, and let his brown horse wander free at God's good will.

Then he descended into the dungeon, and the heroes made all fast as Prince Vladímir had commanded.

When the Princess Apráxia heard of that, she dug a deep passage, and carried sugar viands and mead to Ilyá of Múrom the Old Cossáck. There Ilyá sat for the space of three years. And it came to the ears of the Dragon Tzar Kálin.

Then Kálin the Tzar assembled a great host from the Golden Horde, to ride against Kíef town, to take the Princess Apráxia for his wife. Each of the forty Tzars and Tzaréviches, the forty Kings and Princes, had a company of forty thousand men. They stood along swift-flowing Mother Dniepr, and about Kíef town on all sides, a hundred versts well told.

That dog Tzar Kálin seated himself on his faldstool, and wrote in haste a cartel, with a swan-quill pen, and pure gold in place of ink, upon crimson velvet. Then he chose his best and favorite runner, gave him the cartel, and commanded him in these words:

"Go thou to Kíef town; enter not by the white oak gates, but leap the city wall; bind not thy horse, but enter straight the palace of white stone; open the door wide, but close it not again; do no reverence to Vladímir, neither take thou thy cap from thy head. But take thy stand over against him, fling this cartel upon the golden table, and say to Prince Vladímir: 'Take this cartel, and look what is written there. Clean all thine arrow-straight streets, remove the wondrous crosses from God's temples, and build horse-stalls in the churches; for our good steeds shall be stabled there. And clean out all thy palaces of white stone, for our host is great. And brew sweet intoxicating liquors; let cask stand upon cask in close array. For Kálin the Tzar and his great host shall stand in thy city of Kíef; and he shall wed the Princess Apráxia.'"

All this was done as Kálin had commanded;

and when Prince Vladímir had read the cartel he wrote a submissive letter in reply: " Thou hound and Tzar Kálin! Grant me a truce of three months to clean the streets and palaces, and to brew the sweet liquors."

And Kálin granted the truce.

Prince Vladímir began to pace to and fro with bitterness; he dropped burning tears from his clear eyes, and wiped them away with a silken kerchief, and said:

" Ilyá of Múrom the Old Cossáck is no more; there is none to fight for our faith and fatherland, for the church of God and the city of Kíef; there is none to defend Prince Vladímir."

Then spake the Princess: " Little father! command thy trusty servants to go to the deep dungeon and see whether Ilyá be not yet alive."

" Thou foolish princess!" Vladímir made answer. " If I take thy turbulent head from thy shoulders, will it grow again? How can the bold good youth be living after these three years?"

Nevertheless he went himself to the dungeon, and found Ilyá with sweet viands, cushions of down, and warm coverlets, reading the Holy Gospel. He bowed to the earth before Ilyá, and besought him to defend them all, not for his own sake, but for pity of the widows and orphans. Then he took the Old Cossáck by his little white hands, by his golden ring, led him to his own table, and gave him to eat and drink of the best.

So Ilyá saddled his good steed, and sallied forth. They saw the good youth as he mounted, they saw him not as he rode. There was but a smoke-wreath on the open plain, and springs of water burst forth where good Cloudfall's hoofs beat the earth. He leaped to the crest of a lofty mountain, and the Old Cossáck gazed upon all sides, hoping to descry the absent Russian heroes.

In the east he espied white pavilions, for Alyósha Popóvich was come to the oak Nevída, to the cross Levanídof, to the white stone Alátyr. He had pitched a snowy tent, shaken out fine wheat for his good steed, planted a staff of twenty fathoms, and on it hung a golden tassel, — not for beauty and splendor, but as a heroic signal, that the accursed Tátars might know that Alyósha Popóvich stood on guard in the open plain.

From afar, very far, came also Dobrýnya Nikítich to the oak, the cross, the stone, pitched his pavilion, and displayed two tassels; and so the other heroes did likewise. Then came Ilyá, placed three golden tassels on his staff, flung the silken reins on his steed's neck that the good beast might gather up a little of the wheat, and entered the white pavilion, where twelve heroes of Holy Russia were sitting at meat.

All rose and kissed, and bade him welcome

heartily. Then they sat down again to eat and drink, and Ilyá announced his errand.

But his godfather, Samson Samóilovich, made answer: "Nay, my beloved godson! but we will not saddle our horses to defend Kíef town, Vladímir, and his Princess. For lo! he hath many princely nobles, to whom he giveth meat and drink and guerdon, while we have nothing from Prince Vladímir."

"It will be the worse for thee," quoth Ilyá; and so they wrangled.

Meanwhile Vladímir wrapped himself in his mantle furred with marten, and paced to and fro in Kíef town. For the truce was nearly expired, and the heroes were not come. As he thus walked the streets, his nephew, young Yermák Timoféevich,[1] sprang forth from the royal pothouse, and entreated Vladímir that he might have a heroic steed, a coat of chain mail of ninety poods, and a mace of equal weight, so that he might ride against the hostile host.

"Thou art but a braggart child," quoth Vladímir, "and hast never taken a mace in thy hand."

"If thou grant not the horse, uncle, I will go on foot."

So Vladímir yielded, and bade Yermák choose what horse he would from the stable, where he

---

[1] Yermák Timoféevich conquered Siberia during the reign of Ivan the Terrible.

should also find what armor he required. Thither went the youth in all haste; but the chain mail was so rusty, that he flung it down upon the brick floor, whereupon all the rust flew from it.

Then Yermák saddled a good horse, and rode to the barrier by the Nevída oak, and found the twelve heroes playing checkers upon a board of gold, and Ilya asleep upon a couch of fishes' teeth, beneath a coverlet of sables.

Yermák was vexed, and shouted with all his strength: "Ho there, thou Old Cossáck, Ilyá Múrometz! Yonder in Kíef there is bread to eat in plenty, but no one to defend the town."

Then said the Old Cossáck: "Climb into the damp oak, oak, young Yermák, and reckon yon host by the standards."

Yermák climbed the damp oak, viewed the vast host, and saw that it was sallying forth: damp mother earth trembled and bent under the weight thereof.

— The gray wolf could not skirt that force in a long spring day; the black raven could not fly about it in the longest day of summer, nor would the longest light of autumn suffice for the gray bird to fly over it.

Then Yermák leaped quickly from the damp oak, sprang upon his good steed, and rode straightway against that host. The heroes sat on in the white pavilion. Ilyá slept three days and nights.

During that space, young Yermák contended alone with the Tatars, pausing not to eat nor to drink, nor to let his good steed rest.

"Mount the damp oak, Dobrýnya," spoke Ilyá when he awoke. "Perchance young Yermák hath fallen thence."

From the tree-top Dobrýnya beheld the vast host, and something more: not the black raven flying, not the bright falcon soaring, but that bold and goodly youth Yermák galloping against those infidels. This he told to Ilyá.

"Rise, ye Russian heroes!" shouted the Old Cossáck then. "Mount your good steeds, and sally forth against that host. And take iron grappling-hooks, catch them in young Yermák's shoulders, and persuade him: 'Thou hast breakfasted to-day, now let us dine.' For the young lad will perish, and will never attain to herohood."

So Alyósha went forth with stout grappling-irons; but thrice did young Yermák break away from them, and Alyósha returned to the pavilion. And so it fared also with Dobrýnya. Then Ilyá went himself. He sat his charger like a century-old oak, wavering not, and caught hold of Yermák. "Calm thy heroic heart," he said, "we will labor now."

As the clear falcon swoopeth down upon the geese and swans, and small gray migratory ducks, so swooped the Holy Russian hero upon that Tatar horde, and began to trample the host under his horse's hoofs, and to lay them low, as a mower cutteth down the grass.

Then Cloudfall conjured him with human tongue: "Aï, thou mighty Russian hero! Boldly hast thou attacked this vast host, but thou mayest not overcome it. For that hound, Tzar Kálin hath many great heroes and bold warrior-maids; and moreover, he hath dug three great trenches in the open plain. If thou ride against that horde, we shall fall into those trenches. Out of the first I may leap and bear thee, and likewise out of the second. But out of the third I may not bear thee, and though I leap forth, thou wilt remain in the ditch. For I watched them dig the trenches whilst thou wert sleeping, and so watching had no time to eat my wheat."

This discourse pleased not the Old Cossáck. He grasped his silken whip in his white hands, and beat the horse upon his flanks. "Thou treacherous hound!" quoth he. "I feed and water thee, and yet thou wilt abandon me in the deep ditches of the open plain!"

So he heeded not good Cloudfall's warning, but rode on, destroying the host with his spear and his horse's hoofs; and his strength was not diminished.

When he fell into the first trench, his good steed bore him out in safety. Again he rode, and came to the second ditch; and from that also he escaped. From the third, heroic Cloudfall leaped nimbly (but bore not Ilyá with him), and fled far afield.

Then the accursed Tatars fell upon the Old Cossáck, fettered his nimble feet, bound his white hands, and led him to where Tzar Kálin sat in his linen pavilion.

"Aï, thou Old Cossáck, Ilya of Múrom!" quoth Tzar Kálin. "How should a young puppy prevail alone against my great host?"

And to his guards he said:

"Unbind Ilyá's white hands, unfetter his nimble feet." And it was done.

"Now sit thou at one table with me, Ilyá; eat my sweet viands, drink my mead, put on my flowered apparel. Marry my daughter, and serve not Prince Vladímir, but be vassal to me, the Tzar Kálin."

"Had I my sharp sword by me, thou dog, Kálin the Tzar, it should woo thy neck!" Ilyá answered. "None of these things will I do. But I will uphold the temples of God, the Princess Apráxia and Prince Vladímir, and the city of Kíef."

Then he heard a voice from heaven say, "Lift up thy hands, Ilyá." So he lifted them, and smote off Tzar Kálin's turbulent head, and going forth from the pavilion, he began to destroy the Tatars; and none opposed him. But he perceived that the task was not small, and so seized a Tatar by the heels, and began to beat the Tatars with a Tatar. "This Tatar is stout," quoth Ilyá, "he breaketh not; he is tough, and teareth not."

When he was come to the open plain, he flung the Tatar far from him, and blew a heroic blast on his aurochs horn; for his clear eyes were dimmed, his hot heart burned, and he could distinguish neither the white day nor the black night. His heroic steed heard that ringing blast, and galloped to his master from afar.

Then Ilyá mounted him, and rode forthwith to a lofty mountain, and gazed to the eastward, where the heroic steeds stood beside the white pavilions. He lighted down from off his horse, fitted a fiery arrow to his stout bow, and conjured it: "Fly, little dart aflame, to yonder white pavilion! Tear off the roof, pierce the white breast of my brother in arms, make a small scratch — not large. For he sleepeth, and taketh his ease, while I stand here alone, and can do but little."

The shaft sped straight to the white breast of Samson Samóilovich, and roused that glorious hero of Holy Russia from his heavy sleep. When he opened his eyes, and beheld that the roof of his tent was gone, and a little dart had flown into his breast, he sprang quickly to his nimble feet.

"Ho there, my mighty heroes of Holy Russia!" he shouted. "Saddle now your good steeds in haste, and mount with speed. An unwelcome messenger is come from my brother in arms, — a little dart. — Had it not been for the cross of six poods upon my breast, my turbulent head had been torn away."

Right quickly then did those Holy Russian heroes saddle their chargers, and ride towards Kíef town, and Ilyá went down from the lofty mountain to meet the twelve. And all thirteen heroes rode against the Tatar horde.

For five hours these good youths mowed down young and old, leaving not so much as a single soul to continue the race. And when they were come together again in one place, they began to boast, and to say: "If there were a ladder to heaven, we would climb it, and destroy all the heavenly host!" Then they began again to slay the Tatars: when lo! two, yea even three, rose up in place of every man they killed.

Then those mighty Russian heroes began to turn their arms against each other, to pierce and hew each other, so that of all those Russian warriors there was left alive only young Yermák Timoféevich.[1]

---

[1] In a version of this bylína obtained in 1840 from an old Siberian Cossack, by Mey the poet, the heroes do not kill each other. They become frightened at the ever-increasing horde of enemies, and "flee to the mountains of stone, to the dusky caverns. And as each hero reaches the mountains, he turns to stone." As this part of the Siberian version is much decayed in form, it is doubtful whether it formed part of the poem in its original ancient shape.

A Little Russian legend declares that the last bogatýr was caught by the recruiting officer, and turned into a soldier.

When Yermák returned to Kíef town, courteous Prince Vladímir inquired of him: "How shall I reward thee now, beloved nephew mine? Wilt thou have estates, or golden treasure?"

And young Yermák made answer: "Grant me only, uncle, that I may drink beer and wine without price in all the pot-houses." And so Vladímir granted it.

But Ilyá of Múrom the Old Cossáck of the Don was caught away from those accursed Tatars, and with his good heroic Cloudfall was turned to stone. And the bones of the Old Cossáck have become holy relics.[1]

And so the race of Russian heroes came to an end forever.

---

[1] See Appendix: *Ilyá of Múrom.*

TZAR SOLOMON AND TZARÍTZA SOLOMÓNIDA.[1]

BEYOND the glorious blue sea, in Imperial Tzargrád,[2] Tzar Vasíly Okulóvich made a great and honorable feast to many princes, nobles, errant-knights, stout and mighty heroes, and all the bold warrior-maidens, Tatars, body-guards, and merchants from other lands.

The white day drew to even, the feast waxed merry, the sovereign was well diverted, and paced the banquet-hall, shaking his yellow curls. He spoke:

"Oh, ye my princes, boyárs, mighty heroes, damsels-errant, Tatars, and body-guard! All in Tzargrád are wedded, every maid and widow is given in marriage; and I, your prince, most fair Tzar Vasíly Okulóvich, alone go unwed. Know ye not, therefore, a spouse for me? Stately of form must she be, of equal understanding; her eyes like the falcon clear, her brows of the black sable, the sable of Siberia; gracious her speech must be, as of the white migratory swan, her face white as the snow, her cheeks like the poppy in hue, her gait like that of the golden-antlered stag,

---

[1] See Appendix. [2] Constantinople: literally, "Tzar's town."

and in all this world must none be found her equal."

— All at the feast fell silent. The great hid behind the lesser, and he, in turn, behind the small, and from that little Tatar, the Tzar had no reply. Then from a side table, from his seat of precious fishes' teeth, rose Tarakáshko, a guest from over the sea, came very close to the Tzar, did him lowly reverence, and spoke with all softness:

"Bless, my liege, the word I shall utter! I have journeyed afar, beyond the blue sea; in the royal town of Jerusalem dwelleth the Tzarítza Solomónida. Such another have I never beheld upon this earth. She sitteth, lord, in a lofty castle; the red sun burneth her not, the frequent, drizzling rains wet her not, and good men scoff not at her."

Then answered Tzar Vasíly: "Thou art foolish, Guest Tarakáshko from over the sea! How may a wife be taken from a living husband?"

"I know, in sooth, how to take a wife with cunning and wisdom. Build me now three scarlet ships; fashion their prows like wild beasts, and their sides in the semblance of dragons. In place of eyes, set a whole fox of the cavern, in place of black brows a whole Siberian sable. Set a tree of cypress, and on it place birds of paradise that they may sing imperial songs. Prepare a couch of ivory, and at its head place, lord, a little gúsly, which will sing, hum, breathe forth delicate tones of itself — all the airs of Tzargrád; that they may be a solace to Jerusalem, and may sing reason and understanding into the turbulent head — the turbulent head of a human being. Roll on board food, my liege lord, noble vódka,[1] and the drink that bringeth oblivion of all things. Give me skippers, lord, and work-people; so will I bring thee Solomónida, my liege."

Then the Tzar did all as commanded, and Guest Tarakáshko made ready and sailed out upon the blue sea, and drew near to the city of Jerusalem.

— Solomon went forth upon the open plain, and came to bid farewell to the Tzarítza Solomónida.

"Most fair Solomónida, I go now to the open plain," he said. And the Tzarítza made answer:

"Most wise Tzar Solomon Davídovich! Last night I slept but little, and beheld many things in my dreams. Methought, lord, that the golden ring upon thy right hand did melt, and the Nóvgorod setting rolled away, and was scattered about thee."

"Thou hast but slept, and had a dream," spoke Solomon.

"Nay, lord," the Tzarítza said: "I slept but little, and had many visions. Methought they bore thy white swan far away from thy green garden."

This Solomon could interpret. "Most fair Tzarítza Solomónida! yield not to manly charms."

---

[1] Brandy.

Then took he leave of her, and went forth upon the open plain to collect tribute for twelve years.

— Guest Tarakáshko from beyond the sea entered the harbor, and paid a tax; he cast anchor, and paid dues, lowered his sails, and paid yet more.

Then he took noble and precious gifts, and came to the Tzarítza in her lofty castle, crossed himself as enjoined, did reverence as commanded, and spoke these words:

"Most fair Tzarítza Solomónida! Receive from my hand these honorable gifts, and give me scribes and surveyors, to write down the wares upon my vessels, that thou mayest take due tribute, and grant me leave to trade in Jerusalem."

So the Tzarítza appointed scribes and surveyors according to his desire, and Tarakáshko led them to his first vessel, and gave them lordly vódka; led them to the second, and brought them the liquor of oblivion. The scribes all drank, and lay about upon the ships.

Guest Tarakáshko wept sore thereat, came to the Tzarítza and made complaint. "Most fair Tzarítza Solomónida! no scribes and surveyors hast thou given me, but pot-house sots. Methinks they cannot have tasted of green wine for an age, for they lie like Christian beasts about my decks."

Then the Tzarítza rose, and took a force of five hundred men, and went to the first vessel to view the matter. There Tarakáshko brought lordly vódka, and on the second treated her to the wine of oblivion; and the Tzaritza drank too much. For Guest Tarakáshko was crafty, and had made her, for his purpose, pass through these two first vessels as he led her to the third where stood the couch of ivory. The Tzarítza lay down upon the fair couch, the little harp sounded softly, the birds of heaven sang, and the Tzarítza fell asleep.

Guest Tarakáshko beheld, and shouted in a hissing voice:

"Ho there, my skippers and sailors all! Hoist the linen sails, run far out upon the blue sea!"

When the Tzarítza wakened from her deep slumber, and all the skippers were hastening to and fro, hoisting the linen sails, and steering out to sea, she roused herself, and said:

"Guest Tarakáshko from over the sea! if thou bearest me away for thyself, I will not go with thee!"

But Tarakáshko was cunning, and knew right well how to shape his answer: "Not for myself do I bear thee, lady, but for Tzar Vasíly Okulóvich. And in sooth our faith is better than thine: Wednesday and Fridays are like all other days with us, and we eat meat." And this faith seemed good to the Tzarítza, and she resisted not.

Quickly they ran to Tzargrád, and cast anchor in the ship harbor. Tzar Vasíly came to meet them, took Solomónida by her white hands, kissed her sugar mouth, and led her to the cathedral where they straightway took the golden crowns. Then they began to live and pass the time in mirth.

— Solomon returning from the open plain found not his Tzarítza. Then the most wise Tzar gathered a force of forty thousand men, all clad in chain mail, and marched around the blue sea to Tzargrád. When he came to a green grove, he halted, and left all his host beneath the trees, and commanded them:

"All ye, my well-beloved host! I go now alone to Tzargrád. If I be near to speedy death, I will blow one blast upon my aurochs horn: then saddle your good steeds in haste. If a second time I sound, then mount your good steeds quickly. If a third blast I blow, then ride, ride with what speed ye may, to the oaken gallows, and defend me from sudden death."

Then Solomon took leave of his men, and went alone to Tzargrád, on foot, and so came over against the royal palace, and shouted in a ringing voice:

"Most fair Tzarítza Solomónida! give alms to a wandering psalm-singer!"

The little lattice window was opened wide: no white swan it was which twittered, but the Tzarítza, who spoke these words: "I look — lo! 'tis no wandering psalm-singer I see — 'tis Solomon the most wise Tzar. Prithee, Solomon, enter my lofty palace. That which I have done, lord, was against my will."

So Solomon entered the lofty palace, crossed himself as commanded, did reverence as enjoined, bowing on all sides. Fair Solomónida seated him at the white oak table, gave him all manner of savory viands and pleasant liquors, and showed him great honor.

But then came Tzar Vasíly from the open plain, and knocked at the silver ring, and Solomon said: "Solomónida most fair! is there not some place where I may hide?"

"Creep into this iron-bound chest, Solomon."

She undid the double locks, and when Solomon had entered she made them fast again, admitted Tzar Vasíly, and sitting upon the chest, spoke thus: "Most fair Vasíly Okulóvich! Solomon is reputed both wise and cunning. But of a truth, there is none more foolish; for lo! a woman now sitteth upon him!"

"Show me Solomon most wise, fairest Solomónida," quoth Vasíly.

Then she undid the twofold locks, and besought Vasíly: "Give speedy death to Solomon, fair Vasíly! Cut off his turbulent head; for, of a truth, Solomon is both wise and crafty."

Solomon sprang to his nimble feet, seized Vasíly by his white hands, and said: "With us 'tis not the usage to cut off the heads of Tzars. Make now, therefore, a lofty scaffold, and hang upon it three great nooses; the first of rope, the second of bast, the third of silk."

"Ho there, Tzar Vasíly!" cried the Tzarítza then, "full time is it for thee to execute judgment upon Solomon, and sever his turbulent head, else will he yet escape by his craft and wisdom."

Nevertheless the Tzar did all as Solomon had commanded, and they all went forth to the gallows of white oak — Solomon the most wise Tzar, Solomónida the fairest Tzarítza, Tzar Vasíly, and Guest Tarakáshko from over the sea.

When they were come to the gallows, Solomon spoke this word: "Tzar Vasíly Okulóvich! the horse draweth the forward wheels; why, then, should the devil bear the hind wheels?" But no one could read that riddle.

Then Solomon mounted the first step, and said:

"Most fair Tzar Vasíly Okulóvich! in my youth and childhood I fed the peasant flock. Grant me now, lord, to blow my aurochs horn once more."

"Blow, Solomon, as much as thou wilt," said Vasíly.

But Solomónida urged speedy death. "He is in my hands now," quoth Vasíly. Solomon blew the first blast upon his horn, and all his force was tossed about. Right quickly did they saddle their good steeds, while Tzar Vasíly feared and was disquieted.

"What marvel is this that hath been wrought, Solomon?" he asked. "On the open plain there is stamping, and clinking of metal."

"Fear not, Tzar Vasíly," Solomon made answer, "and be not disquieted. My horses in Jerusalem have fled from their stalls to the gloomy forest, and would fain recall Solomon most wise."

Then he mounted the second step. With Vasíly's good leave, and against the will of Solomónida, he blew a second blast upon his horn. All his host was thrilled to motion, as his men mounted their good steeds in haste. And Vasíly trembled thereat, and was afraid.

"What wonder hath been wrought in the plain, Solomon? For there is a clanging and a beating of hoofs."

"Fear thou nothing, Tzar Vasíly! My bird in Jerusalem hath flown from the garden to the dusky grove, and beateth the grove with its wings, recalling Solomon most wise."

Then he mounted the third step, and craved leave to sound his horn for the last time. He blew a battle call, and all his great host was moved, as though clear falcons had flown overhead, or gray wolves had sped swiftly past. With all speed they rode to the oaken gallows, and took Tzar Solomon most wise therefrom. Then they set Tzar Vasíly in the silken noose, Tzarítza Solomónida the Fair in the rope, and Guest Tarakáshko in the noose of bast. And having taken captive all Tzargrád, they journeyed back around the blue sea to Jerusalem, and began again to live and to pass their days in pleasure.

THE CYCLE OF NÓVGOROD.
(1. VASÍLY BUSLÁEVICH. 2. SADKÓ.)

EPIC SONGS OF RUSSIA. 295

VASÍLY BUSLÁEVICH, THE BRAVE OF NÓVGOROD.

IN glorious Nóvgorod the Great, dwelt old Buslái for the space of ninety years. He dwelt in peace with Nóvgorod, challenging it not, and had no dispute with the men thereof. At length he died, being full of years, and left great possessions, a widow, and an amiable son, young Vasíliushka Busláevich,[1] the child of his old age.

When Vasíliushka had attained to seven years, his mother sent him to learn to read and write. In this he succeeded well, likewise in church singing. in all Nóvgorod the Glorious there was no singer equal to him. Then he began to roam the city, to loiter in princely courts, to consort with foolish fellows and many pot-house sots, and to jest in rude fashion with noble and princely children. When he plucked at a hand, it was torn away from the shoulder; each foot he pulled dropped off with the leg attached; heads at his touch spun round like buttons; when he knocked two or three children together, they lay as dead.

Then came people from the Princes of Nóvgorod to the very honorable widow, to make complaint

---

[1] See Appendix.

of her son; and they besought her to put a stop to his crippling the children. Thereupon she reprimanded and upbraided Vasíly, weeping bitterly the while:

"My sweet child," she said, "why goest thou about Nóvgorod making cripples? At thy age thy father had not a hundred rubles in his pocket, but he had a brave body-guard. — But thou hast neither brother nor brave guards, and thou wilt never be able to settle matters with any one."

Vasíly liked not this word, and ascended to his lofty tower. There he sat himself down in his folding-chair, and wrote many a scroll with speed, and wisely were the words ordered therein. "Whoso will eat savory viands all ready to hand, drink green wine without price, and wear flowered raiment of divers hues, let him repair to Váska's court."

Then he bound these scrolls to stout arrows, and shot them into Nóvgorod. As the men of Nóvgorod came from church, they gathered them up in the streets and lanes; and some who could read chancing there, they looked upon the scrolls, and interpreted them: "Vasíly commandeth us to an honorable feast."

Young Vasíly Busláevich made ready for his guests. He rolled a cask of green wine of forty buckets from his vaults, and set it in the midst of his court, and took to himself a cudgel of red elm.

"Whosoever shall lift in one hand a cup of this

wine, in weight a pood and a half, and shall quaff it at a breath, and shall likewise withstand a blow from my red elm upon his turbulent head, he shall make one of my brave body-guard," quoth Vasíly.

That night he slept in his lofty tower, on a bed of down laid upon a little couch of smoothed planks.

The next morning, very early, the honorable widow Avdótya Vasílievna paced her palace, and looked out upon her spacious court-yard; and lo! it was black with the assembled host. In haste she went to her dear son, and said:

"Thou sleepest, Vasíliushka, and takest thine ease, and knowest not the evil that standeth even now at thy gates. Lo! a force black as the raven is in thy court."

Vasíly, when he heard that, sprang quickly to his nimble feet, grasped his red elm in his white hands, and went forth into the spacious court.

"Aï, Vasíliushka Busláevich!" cried the men of Nóvgorod, "we stand now within thy court, and are minded to devour all thy viands, drink up all thy liquors, wear out all thy flowered garments, and drag forth thy golden treasure."

But this discourse pleased not Vasíly. He leaped forth into the court, grasped his red elm more firmly, and began to brandish it. Where he swung it a lane appeared, where he drew it back, an alley; and he slew the men of Nóvgorod like a thunderstorm, so that they lay dead in heaps. And Vasíly returned again to his lofty, golden-crowned tower.

Then came Kóstya[1] New-trader, took a cup of green wine, raised it with one hand, drained it at a single draught. Thereupon Vasíly sprang forth from the new hall, grasping his red elm, and smote Kóstya a deadly blow; but the child stood firm and moved not, the black curls on his turbulent head waved not, the full cup in his hand was not spilled.

"Is my strength less than of old?" quoth Vasíly: "doth not my red elm serve me as of yore?"

And lo! a little stone lay there, white and burning: on this he essayed his strength — and the stone was shivered to atoms.

"Aï, Kóstya New-trader!" he cried, "be thou of my brave body-guard, and enter now my palace of white stone."

Then came Lame Potányshka, lifted the great cup in one hand, drained off the green wine at a breath, and when he had withstood Vasíly's stern assault he likewise became one of the body-guard; and in like manner also, Kómushka the Hunchback.

These three went not forth from the new hall.

"Enter now my palace of white stone," quoth Vasíly. "There we will quaff sweet liquors, and

---

[1] *Kóstya*, diminutive of *Constantine*.

eat sugar viands; and there is none in Nóvgorod whom we must fear."

Thus did Vasíly choose his brave body-guard, and chose these three, no more.

After that, Vasíly made an honorable feast for the men of Nóvgorod. But when they came to it, he gave meat and drink to his guards, and gave neither meat, drink, nor honor to the men of Nóvgorod.

So when the men of Nóvgorod perceived that things were not well with them they said: "Cursed be thou, Vasíly Busláevich! We have come at thy bidding, yet have neither fared sumptuously, nor worn fine apparel. Therefore is eternal strife engendered." Then they took counsel together, and said:

"Children! let us turn Vasíliushka into a laughing-stock: let us make an honorable feast for Vasíly, and let us not bid him to it — this miserable little Vasíly!"

So they made their feast. And when Vasíly heard of it, he said: "My lady mother, I shall go to that feast."

Avdótya Vasílievna, that honorable widow, would have dissuaded him. "My dear child," she spoke, "there is room for the guest who is bidden, but not for him who is unbidden."

Nevertheless Vasíly hearkened not to his mother's counsel. He took his brave body-guard, and went to the feast. He asked no leave of the gate-keepers, nor yet of the lackeys at the doors, but entered straight the banquet-hall. He set his right foot in the hall, his left on the oaken table in the great corner, and flung himself on the wall-bench in the corner by the oven, stretching out his right hand and his right foot.

The guests all came to the oven-corner; and Vasíly moved to the corner by the door, and stretched out his left hand and left foot. Thereupon the guests went to the new hall, and some fled to their homes in terror.

Then Vasíly went to the oaken tables with his body-guard, and all the guests assembled again, and said: " Though thou hast taken thy seat in the great corner, Vasíly Busláevich, yet art thou an unbidden guest, while we are bidden."

Thereto Vasíly made answer: " Though I be an unbidden guest, where I am placed, there will I sit; and what cometh under my hand, that will I eat and drink."

The red sun declined to even, the feast waxed mirthful; all the guests grew drunken and merry, and began to make great brags. Thereupon Vasíly, with drunken and stupid mind, laid a great wager, even his turbulent head, that he would go on the morrow to the bridge over the Vólkof, and there, with the sole aid of his good guard, hold his own against all Nóvgorod.

When he left the feast, and returned home to his princely palace with drooping head, and eyes fixed on the ground, his mother inquired the cause of his sadness.

"Did they pass thee with the cup, or did some drunken churl jeer at thee?"

Vasíly could make no reply, but his brave bodyguard told her all. Then Avdótya Vasílievna put her shoes in haste upon her bare feet, cast her mantle of sables upon one shoulder, took her golden keys, and went to her deep vaults. There she heaped a bowl with red gold, another with pure silver, and yet a third with fair round pearls, and came to the honorable feast. She crossed herself as prescribed, did reverence in courteous wise, and said:

"Hail, ye men of Nóvgorod! Forgive now Vasíly his fault."

But they refused to accept her gifts, or to pardon Vasíly. "If the Lord help us to take Vasíly, we will ride his good steeds, wear his flowered garments, and squander his golden treasure. We will pardon him when we shall have cut off his head!"

Then Avdótya[1] Vasílievna went home in grief and sadness, scattering the red gold, pure silver, and fair round pearls over the open plain, saying: "Not this is dear to me, but the turbulent head of my beloved son, young Vasíly Busláevich!"

---

[1] Popular for *Evdokia*, Eudoxia.

So when she was come to her own dwelling, she gave Vasíly to drink of the cup of forgetfulness, led him to a deep dungeon, and locked him securely therein. Then she loosed his good steed in the open plain, and hid his red-elm cudgel of forty poods, his sharp sword, and heroic garments.

Early the next morning, Vasíly's brave troop took their stand by the Vólkof river, and began to contend with the men of Nóvgorod.

All that day they fought without eating; a second day and night they fought without drinking, and yet a third day without pausing to rest.

In the mean while Vasíly slept, and took his ease, knowing naught of the evil that was come upon them. But a brave, black-visaged handmaiden, who went with her oaken buckets and her maple yoke to the stream for fresh water, beheld the evil case of the bold youths. She seized her yoke, and began to brandish it, and slew four hundred men therewith. Then she ran very quickly, and came to the dungeon, and cried:

"Sleepest thou, Vasíly, and wilt not waken? Upon yon Vólkof bridge thy brave guards stand up to their knees in blood, and captive, their heads broken with whips, their hands bound with their girdles."

Thereupon Vasíly entreated the black-visaged maid: "Release me from this dungeon, and I will give thee golden treasure as much as thou desirest."

So she undid the door, breaking the lock with her maple yoke, and let Vasíly out into the white world. And since he could not find his warlike harness, his mace and sharp spear, he wrenched the iron axle from a cart which stood near by (its length was two fathoms, and its weight forty poods), — threw it over his heroic shoulder, and said:

"I thank thee, damsel, that thou didst not let my brave body-guard perish. I will reckon with thee hereafter, but now I must not tarry," and therewith departed.

When he came to the Vólkof bridge, and found all as the maiden had told him, he shouted:

"Aï, my brave body-guard! Ye have breakfasted, now let me dine. 'Twas not I, brothers, who betrayed ye, but my own mother. Go now, my well-beloved brothers, and rest, while I play with these children."

Then he began to stride about upon the bridge, brandishing his axle, and the men of Nóvgorod fell in heaps before him. The princes perceived that their pitiless inevitable fate was come upon them, and that Vasíly would leave no man alive of all Nóvgorod, and so went with the Voivóda and the Elder to his lady mother, and spoke this word:

"Aï, thou honorable widow, Avdótya Vasílievna! Curb thy dear child, young Vasíly Busláevich; soften his heroic heart, that he may leave but a handful of our men alive." But she replied:

"I dare not, ye princes of Nóvgorod. I have done him grievous wrong, in that I confined him in a deep dungeon. But my dear child hath a godfather, the Ancient Pilgrim, who dwelleth in the Sergiéi monastery. He hath great power; ask him."

So the princes went to the Ancient Pilgrim, and told him all; and he sorrowed greatly, but made ready to go. He leaped into the lofty belfry, tore down the great bell of St. Sophia, in weight three thousand poods, and set it on his head, as a good cap. When he set out for the Vólkof bridge, he leaned upon the clapper for a staff, and the bridge bent beneath him as he went.

Straight up to Vasíly's clear eyes he strode, and spoke: "My godchild! Restrain thy heroic heart; spare at least a remnant of these men."

But Vasíly's heroic heart grew hot at this speech.

"Aï, my godfather!" quoth he. "If I gave thee no egg at Easter-tide, yet take thou this red one now at Peter's day. Christ is arisen!"[1]

Thereupon he smote the Ancient Pilgrim upon the great bell of Sophia, with his axle; and after that one blow, the Pilgrim's praise was sung.[2]

But Vasíly seized the great clapper, and continued to slay the men of Nóvgorod. At length the princes prevailed upon his mother to make

---

[1] The Easter greeting in Russia.   [2] He was dead.

intercession for them. So she arrayed herself in a robe of black, threw a cloak of sables about her shoulders, set a helmet on her turbulent head, and went to her dear child. The old woman was wise, and approached him not from before, but crept up behind him, fell upon his mighty shoulders, and entreated him. Vasíly dropped his arms, the axle fell from his hands to damp mother earth, and he said:

"Fair lady mother! thou art a cunning old woman and a wise! Thou hast known how to break my great power, by coming upon me from behind; for if thou hadst approached me from before, I should not have spared thee, my lady mother, but should have slain thee in the stead of a man of Nóvgorod."

Then came the Princes, the Voivóda,[1] and the Elders of Nóvgorod, and fell at Vasíly's feet, and prayed him to be their guest.

And they besought him also to gather up the bodies of the slain, and give them to damp mother earth; for the waters of the Vólkof ran blood for a full verst.

Vasíly gave command that all this should be done, and went to the banquet, but felt ill at ease there, and so returned to his palace of white stone, to his lady mother, and his brave bodyguard.

---

[1] The military leader.

There he lived at ease, healing the wounds of his good guards, and restoring them to their strength of former days.

By glorious Nóvgorod the Great, and on famous Ílmen Lake, swam and floated a gray drake, and dived like a fearless duck: — there floated the red ship of young Vasíly Busláevich, and thereon Vasíly and his brave troop. Kóstya held the helm, little Potányshka stood on the prow, and Vasíly paced the vessel, uttering these words: "My bright bodyguard and brave, all my good youths and bold! Set our vessel against Ílmen, and sail to Nóvgorod."

With anchors they caught the shore, threw out gangways to the bank, and Vasíly went to his lordly court, followed by his brave troop, leaving but a watch behind.

When he came to his lady mother, he wound about her like a convolvulus vine, and besought her great blessing to go to Jerusalem town with his band; there to pray the Lord, to worship at the holy of holies, to visit the grave of the Lord, and bathe in the Jordan river.

"Aï, my dear child," his mother made answer, "if thou goest for a good purpose, I will give thee my great blessing, but if thou goest to rob, I will not give it; and may the damp earth not bear Vasíly!"

Stone softeneth in the fire, steel melteth in the glow, her mother's heart gave way: she gave Vasíly stores of bread, and far-reaching weapons.

"Defend thy turbulent head, Vasíly!" she said.

Then in haste he assembled his good youths, and when they had taken leave of his widowed mother, they embarked on their scarlet vessel, raised the delicate linen sails, and ran out upon Lake Ílmen.

They had sailed a second day, and e'en a second week, when there came to meet them mariner guests.

"Hail, Vasíly Busláevich!" they said. "Whither, O youth, art thou pleased to journey?"

"I journey, O mariners," Vasíly made answer, "an unwilling way. In my youth I killed and stole much: in my old age I must save my soul. Inform me, good youths, the straight way to the holy city of Jerusalem."

Then they told him that the straight way demanded a seven-weeks' journey, and the way about, a year and a half. But upon the glorious Caspian sea was a stout barrier; for the chieftains of the Cossácks, three thousand in number, made their lair on the Island of Kumínsk, robbing barks and galleons, destroying scarlet ships.

"I believe neither dream nor vision," quoth Vasíly; "I trust in my red elm alone: haste now, my children, by the straight way!"

When Vasíly espied a lofty mountain, he ran quickly in to the steep shores, and ascended that Sorochínsky[1] hill, and after him flew his brave troop.

At mid-ascent, an empty human skull lay in the road, and human bones; Vasíly spurned them from the path, whereupon the skull addressed him: "Hey, Vasíly Busláevich! Why dost thou cast me aside? I was no worse than thou, O youth! And I know how to defend myself. On this Sorochínsky mountain, where lieth this empty skull of a youth, shall lie likewise the head of Vasíly."

Vasíly spat and passed on. "Either the Enemy speaketh in thee, thou skull, or an unclean spirit!" he said, and proceeded up the mountain. On the very peak thereof stood a stone, three full fathoms broad; across it only an axe might be hurled: its length was three arshíns[2] and a quarter; and on it was written this inscription, "He who shall solace himself at this stone, and divert himself by leaping along this stone, shall break his turbulent head."

This Vasíly believed not, and began to divert himself with his brave guards, by leaping across the stone. Nevertheless, lengthwise they did not dare to leap.

At length they descended from the Sorochínsky mountains, embarked again upon their scarlet ships,

---

[1] Saracen. [2] An arshín is equal to twenty-eight inches.

spread their sails of fine linen, and ran across the Caspian sea to that barrier to shipping where the robber Cossácks with their aged chieftains held their stand. At the landing stood a hundred men; nevertheless, young Vasíly approached, cast out landing-stages upon the steep shore, and sprang to land, leaning upon his red elm.

Then all the bold and goodly youths, the guard, were terrified, and did not long await his coming, but fled to the chieftains of the Cossácks.

The atamáns sat, marvelling not, and said:

"We have defended this isle these thirty years past, and have beheld no great terror. 'Tis young Vasíly Busláevich who cometh with falcon flight, and youthful daring."

Vasíly and his band strode up to the Cossáck chiefs, and stood in a single ring. Then Vasíly bowed low, and spake this word: "Hail, ye Cossáck chieftains! Tell me now the straight road to the holy city of Jerusalem."

Said the atamáns: "Ho, Vasíly Busláevich! We pray thee to eat bread with us at one table."

And Vasíly refused not, but sat with them at one table.

When they poured out green wine, he grasped the cup in one hand, and emptied it at a single draught: — and the measure of the cup was a bucket and a half. Thereat the chieftains marvelled greatly, for they could not drink so much as half a bucket. And when they had broken bread, Vasíly betook himself once more to his scarlet ships; and the chieftains gave him gifts — a bowl of red gold, a bowl of pure silver, and a third bowl of fair round pearls. For these Vasíly returned thanks, and did them reverence, craving a guide to Jerusalem. This they refused not, but having given him a young guide they took their leave of him.

Then Vasíly and his brave troop hoisted their sails of fine linen, and ran out upon the Caspian sea. When they came to Jordan river, they threw out strong anchors, and landing-stages upon the precipitous banks; and Vasíly and his bold youths entered Jerusalem town.

He came to the cathedral church, served a mass for his mother's health, and for himself, and a mass with service for the soul of his father and all his family. On the next day was celebrated a service with prayers for the bold good youths, who from their young years up had slain and stolen much. Vasíly prayed before the holy of holies, bathed in Jordan, reckoned with the popes and deacons, gave gold without stint to the aged people who depended on the church, and embarked again with his band on his scarlet ships.

Then the guards bathed in Jordan river, and an aged crone came to them, and said:

"Wherefore bathe ye naked in Jordan? None

must bathe naked therein save only Vasíly Busláevich! For Jesus Christ the Lord himself bathed in Jordan river. And ye shall lose your great chieftain, Vasíly Busláevich."

"Our Vasíly will not believe that, either in dream or vision," said they.

A little space thereafter, Vasíly came to his men, and gave order that the ships should be sent out of the mouth of the Jordan river.

So they sailed across the Caspian sea, and came to the Island of Kumínsk where he bowed before the Cossáck captains. With them he talked not much, when they inquired if he had journeyed in safety to Jerusalem; but gave into their hands a writing which laid many labors upon them, and held a service with prayers for the youths. Then those Cossack chieftains bade Vasíly to eat with them; but he consented not, and taking leave of them shortly, set out upon the Caspian for Nóvgorod.

When they had sailed a week, and yet a second, Vasíly espied the Sorochínsky mountain, and was fain to view it once again. So they ran up to it, threw out their landing-stages, and began to ascend.

On the summit lay the stone with its inscription, which Vasíly believed not. And after he had made merry and diverted himself with his bodyguard, leaping across the stone, he was minded to essay a leap lengthwise. He leaped but a quarter way, and falling, was killed upon the stone. And where the empty skull had lain, there they buried Vasíly.

Then his good body-guard sailed home to Nóvgorod, and coming to his mother, the honorable widow, they did homage, and laid a letter in her hand. When she had read it, she wept, and said: "Aï, ye bold and goodly youths! There is nothing now which I may do for ye. — Yet go ye into my deep vaults, and take golden treasure without stint."

So the black-visaged handmaiden led them thither, and when they had taken a little gold they came and gave thanks to Avdótya Vasílievna for her hospitality, in that she had fed, clothed, and shod the good youths. Then she commanded that a cup of green wine should be given to each, and when they had drunk it, they bowed low before her.

And after that, the good youths went their way, each youth wheresoever he listed.

EPIC SONGS OF RUSSIA. 313

MERCHANT SADKÓ THE RICH GUEST OF
NÓVGOROD.

In the glorious city of Nóvgorod dwelt Sadkó[1] the gúsly-player. No golden treasures did he possess; he went about to the magnificent feasts of the merchants and nobles, and made all merry with his playing.

And it chanced on a certain day, that Sadkó was bidden to no worshipful feast; neither on the second day nor the third was he bidden. Then he sorrowed greatly, and went to Lake Ílmen, and seated himself upon a blue stone. There he began to play upon his harp of maple-wood, and played all day, from early morn till far into the night.

The waves rose in the lake, the water was clouded with sand, and Sadkó feared to sit there: great terror overcame him, and he returned to Nóvgorod.

The dark night passed, a second day dawned, and again Sadkó was bidden to no worshipful feast. Again he played all day beside the lake, and returned in terror at nightfall.

And the third day, being still unbidden of any

[1] See Appendix.

man, he sat on the blue burning stone, and played upon his harp of maple-wood, and the waves rose in the lake, and the water was troubled with sand.

But Sadkó summoned up his courage, and ceased not his playing. Then the Tzar Vodyanói[1] emerged from the lake, and spake these words:

"We thank thee, Sadkó of Nóvgorod! Thou hast diverted us of the lake. I held a banquet and a worshipful feast; and all my beloved guests hast thou rejoiced. And I know not, Sadkó, how I may reward thee. Yet return now, Sadkó, to thy Nóvgorod, and to-morrow they shall call thee to a rich feast. Many merchants of Nóvgorod shall be there, and they shall eat and drink, and wax boastful. One shall boast of his good horse, another of his deeds of youthful prowess; another shall take pride in his youth. But the wise man will boast of his aged father, his old mother, and the senseless fool of his young wife. And do thou, Sâdkó, boast also: 'I know what there is in Lake Ílmen — of a truth, fishes with golden fins.' Then shall they contend with thee, that there are no fish of that sort, — of gold. But do thou then lay a great wager with them; wager thy turbulent head, and demand from them their shops in the bazaar, with all their precious wares. Then weave thou a net of silk, and come cast it in Lake Ílmen. Three times must thou cast it in the lake, and at

---

[1] The Water-King.

each cast I will give a fish, yea, a fish with fins of gold. So shalt thou receive those shops in the bazaar, with their precious wares. So shalt thou become Sadkó the Merchant of Nóvgorod, the rich Guest."

Then Sadkó returned again to Nóvgorod. And the next day he was bidden to a worshipful feast of rich merchants, who ate and drank, and boasted, one of this thing, and the other of that thing. And as the rich merchants of Nóvgorod sat there, they spoke thus to Sadkó.

"Why sittest thou, Sadkó, and boastest not thyself? Hast thou nothing, Sadkó, whereof to boast?"

Sadkó spoke: "Hey, ye merchants of Nóvgorod! What have I, Sadkó, that I may boast of? No countless treasures of gold are mine, no fair young wife; there is but one thing of which I may boast; in Ílmen's Lake are fishes with fins of gold."

Then began the rich merchants to contend with him; and Sadkó said: "I stake my turbulent head upon it, and more than that I have not to wager."

Said they: "We will stake our shops in the bazaar, with their precious wares — the shops of six rich merchants."

Thereupon they wove a net of silk, and went to cast it in Lake Ílmen. At the first cast in Ílmen, they took a little fish with fins of gold, and likewise with the second and the third cast.

Then the rich merchants of Nóvgorod saw that there was nothing to be done, for it had happened as Sadkó had foretold; and they opened to him their shops in the bazaar, with all their precious wares. And Sadkó, when he had received the six shops, and their rich goods, inscribed himself among the merchants of Nóvgorod; he became exceeding rich, and began to trade in his own city, and in all places, even in distant towns, and received great profit.

Sadkó the rich merchant of Nóvgorod married, and built himself a palace of white stone, wherein all things were heavenly. In the sky, the red sun burned, and in his palace likewise a fair red sun; and when shone the lesser light, the moon, in heaven, in his palace it shone also; and when the thick-sown stars glittered in the sky, stars thickly sown gleamed within his towers. And Sadkó adorned his palace of white stone in all ways.

After this was done, lo! Sadkó made a banquet and a worshipful feast, and called to it all the rich merchants, the lords and the rulers of Nóvgorod, and the rulers were Luká Zinoviéf and Thomá Nazariéf. As they sat and feasted, after they had well eaten and drunken, they began to boast,— one of his good steed, one of his heroic might, another of his youth; the wise of his aged parents, the foolish of his young wife. But Sadkó, as he walked about his palace, cried out: " Ho there, ye rich merchants, ye lords, rulers, and men of Nóvgorod! ye have eaten and drunk at my feast, and made your boasts. And of what shall I vaunt myself? My treasures of gold are now inexhaustible, my flowered garments I cannot wear out, and my brave body-guard is incorruptible. But I will boast of my golden treasure. With that treasure will I buy all the wares in Nóvgorod, both good and bad, and there shall be none for sale any more in all the city."

Then sprang the rulers, Thomá and Luká, to their nimble feet, and said: " Is it much that thou wilt wager with us?" And Sadkó answered: " What ye will of my countless treasure of gold, that will I wager." Then said the rulers, for the men of Nóvgorod: " Thirty thousand, Sadkó, shall be thy stake against us." So it was agreed, and all departed from the feast.

The next morning, right early, Sadkó rose, and waked his brave body-guard, and gave them all they would of his treasure, and sent them to the marts. But he himself went straight to the bazaar, and bought all the wares of Nóvgorod, both good and bad. And again, the next morning he rose, and waked his troop, and giving them great treasure, went to the bazaar; and finding wares yet more than before, he bought all, of whatever sort. And on the third day, when he came to the market, he found, to the great glory of Nóvgorod, that vast store of goods had hastened thither from Moscow, so that the shops were full to overflowing with the precious stuffs of Moscow.

Then Sadkó fell into thought: "If I buy all these goods from Moscow, others will flow hither from beyond the sea; and I am not able to buy all the wares of the whole white world. Sadkó the merchant is rich, but glorious Nóvgorod is still richer! It is better to yield my great wager, my thirty thousand."

Thus he yielded the thirty thousand, and built thirty great ships, thirty dark-red ships and three. Their prows were in the likeness of wild beasts, their sides like dragons; their masts of red wood, the cordage of silk, the sails of linen, and the anchors of steel. Instead of eyes were precious jacinths; instead of brows, Siberian sables; and dark brown Siberian fox-skins in place of ears. His faithful guards, his clerks, loaded these red ships with the wares of Nóvgorod, and he sailed away down the Vólkof to Lake Ládoga, and thence into the Néva, and through that river to the blue sea, directing his course towards the Golden Horde. There he sold his wares, receiving great gain, and filling many casks of forty buckets, with red gold, pure silver, and fair round pearls. They sailed away from the Golden Horde, Sadkó leading the way in the Falcon ship, the finest of all the vessels. But on the blue sea the red ships halted; the waves dashed, the breeze whistled, the sails flapped, the ships strained, — but could not move from that spot.

Then Sadkó the merchant, the rich guest, shouted from his good Falcon ship: " Ho there, friends, ship-men, lower ye iron plummets, sound the blue sea, whether there be any reefs or rocks or sand-bars here ! " So they sounded, but found nothing.

And Sadkó the merchant spake to his men: " Ho there, my brave body-guard! Long have we sailed the seas, yea, twelve full years, yet have we paid no tribute to the Tzar Morskói,[1] and now he commandeth us down into the blue sea. Therefore, cast ye into the waves a cask of red gold." And they did so; but the waves beat, the sails tore, the ships strained, yet moved not.

Again spake Sadkó the rich guest: " Lo, this is but a small gift for the Tzar Morskói, in his blue sea. Cast ye another cask, a cask of pure silver, to him." Yet the dark-red ships moved not, though they cast in also a cask of seed pearls.

Then spake Sadkó once again: " My brave, beloved body-guard, 'tis plain the Tzar Morskói calleth a living man from among us into his blue sea. Make ye therefore lots of alder-wood, and let each man write his name upon his own, and the lots of all just souls shall float. But that man of

---

[1] Sea-King.

us whose lot sinketh, he also shall go from among us into the blue sea." So it was done as he commanded: — but Sadkó's lot was a cluster of hop-flowers. And all the lots swam like ducks save Sadkó's, and that went to the bottom like a stone.

Again spake Sadkó the rich merchant to his troop: "These lots are not fair. Make ye to yourselves others of willow-wood, and set your names thereon, every man." This they did; but Sadkó made his lot of blue damascened steel from beyond the sea, in weight ten poods. And it sank while all the others swam lightly on the blue sea.

After that he essayed divers woods, choosing ever for himself the lighter when his men's heavy lots swam, and the heavier when his light lot fell to the depths. Nevertheless, his lot would by no means float, and the others would not sink.

Then said Sadkó the rich guest: "'Tis plain that Sadkó can do nothing. The Tzar Morskói demandeth Sadkó himself in the blue sea. Then ho! my brave, beloved guards! fetch me my massive inkstand, my swan-quill pen, and my paper."

His brave, beloved men brought him his inkstand, pen, and paper; and Sadkó, the rich merchant of Nóvgorod, sat in his folding-chair, at his oaken table, and began to write away his possessions. Much gave he to God's churches, much to the poor brethren, and to his young wife. And the remainder of his possessions he bestowed upon his brave body-guard.

After that he wept, and spake to his men: " Aï, my men, well loved and brave! Place ye an oaken plank upon the blue sea, that I, Sadkó, may throw myself upon the plank; so shall it not be terrible to me to take my death upon the blue sea. And fill ye, brothers, a bowl with pure silver, another with red gold, and yet a third with seed pearls, and place them upon the plank."

Then took he in his right hand an image of St. Mikóla, and in his left his little harp of maplewood, with its fine strings of gold, and put on him a rich cloak of sables; and bitterly he wept as he bade farewell to his brave company, to the white world, and Nóvgorod the glorious. He descended upon the oaken plank, and was borne upon the blue sea, and his dark-red ships sped on and flew as they had been black ravens.

Then was Sadkó the rich merchant of Nóvgorod greatly terrified, as he floated over the blue sea on his plank of oak; but he fell asleep, and lo! when he awoke it was at the very bottom of the ocean-sea. He beheld the red sun burning through the clear waves, and saw that he was standing beside a palace of white stone where sat the Tzar Morskói, with head like a heap of hay, on his royal throne.

The Tzar Morskói spake these words: " Thou art welcome, Sadkó, thou rich merchant of Nóvgorod! Long hast thou sailed the seas, yet offered no tribute to the Lord of the sea. And now thou art come as a gift to me. I have sent for thee that thou mayest answer me, which is now of greater worth in Russia: gold or silver or damascened steel. For the Tzarítza contendeth with us on this matter."

"Gold and silver are precious in Russia," Sadkó made answer; "but damascened steel no less. For without gold or silver a man may well live; but without steel or iron can no man live."

"What hast thou there in thy right hand, and what in thy left?"

"In my right hand is an ikón [1] of St. Mikóla; in my left, my gúsly."

"It is said that thou art a master-player on the harp," said the Tzar Morskói then; "play for me upon thy harp of maple-wood."

Sadkó saw that in the blue sea he could do naught but obey, and he began to pluck his harp. And as he played, the Tzar Morskói began to jump about, beating time with the skirts of his garment, and waving his mantle; fair sea-maidens led choral dances, and the lesser sea-folk squatted and leaped.

Then the blue sea was churned with yellow sands, great billows surged over it, breaking many ships asunder, drowning many men, and ingulfing vast possessions.

---

[1] Holy image.

Three hours did Sadkó play; and the Tzarítza said to him:

"Break thy harp of maple-wood, merchant Sadkó the rich guest! It seemeth to thee that the Tzar is dancing in his palace, but 'tis on the shore he danceth, and many drown and perish, all innocent men."

Then Sadkó brake his harp, and snapped its golden strings; and when the Tzar Morskói commanded him to play yet two hours, he answered him boldly that the harp was broken; and when the Tzar would have had his smiths to mend it, Sadkó said that could only be done in Holy Russia.

"Wilt thou not take a wife here?" the Tzar Morskói said, "wilt thou not wed some fair maid in the blue sea?"

And Sadkó answered: "In the blue sea, I obey thy will."

Then the Tzarítza said to him: "Choose not, merchant Sadkó the rich guest, any maid from the first three hundred which the Tzar shall offer thee, but let them pass; and the same with the second three hundred; and from the third, choose thou the Princess who shall come last of all: she is smaller and blacker than all the rest. And look to it that thou kiss not, embrace not thy wife; so shalt thou be once more in Holy Russia, so shalt thou behold the white world and the fair sun. But if thou kiss her, never more shalt thou behold the white world, but shalt abide forever in the blue sea."

So Sadkó let the first three hundred maidens pass, and likewise the second, and of the third he chose the last of all, the maiden called Chernáva.[1]

Then the Tzar Morskói made him a great feast; and afterwards Sadkó lay down and fell into a heavy sleep. And when he awoke, he found himself on the steep banks of the Chernáva river. And as he gazed, behold, his dark-red ships came speeding up the Vólkof, and his brave body-guard were thinking of Sadkó under the blue sea. When also his brave troop beheld Sadkó standing upon the steep bank, they marvelled; for they had left him on the blue sea, and lo! he had returned to his city before them.

Then they all rejoiced greatly, and greeted Sadkó, and went to his palace. There he greeted his young wife; and after that, he unloaded his scarlet ships, and built a church to St. Mikóla, and another to the very holy mother of God, and began to pray the Lord to forgive his sins.

And thenceforth he sailed no more upon the blue sea, but dwelt and took his ease in his own town.

---

[1] Black-visaged.

APPENDIX.

APPENDIX

EPIC SONGS OF RUSSIA. 327

THE ALÁTYR STONE.

THIS stone, so often referred to in Russian song and legend, is elektron, amber, the precious merchandise of the first Phœnician traders, and of their successors, the Greeks and Romans. From very ancient times, it has been found on the Baltic, where it still abounds on the whole southern shore, from Copenhagen to Courland. The Slavs inhabited these shores at the date of their first appearance in history, and it is in those portions of Russia which border on this sea or whose inhabitants traded on it in early times, that the most vivid images and epithets applied to the Alátyr stone are still preserved. In ancient times also, the name of the Baltic among the Slavs was the "Látyr Sea." As amber was esteemed not only for its beauty, but as a medicine, it was worn as a protection to the throat, chest, and the whole body. Numerous spells and charms attest this fact.

It is generally spoken of as situated on the "Ocean-Sea," the "Blue Sea," or the "Island of Buyán;" and it is called "white and burning," or "cold." *White* refers to its brilliance, as in the case of the "white day." *Burning* is the epithet applied to it in the frozen North, while *cold* is the favorite epithet in the South.

According to the popular notion, the Ocean is the source of all rivers; on this Ocean lies Alátyr which is healing; — hence, from beneath this stone proceed all rivers, and all healing.

The sea in which it lies varies with the locality in which the song is sung or the legend narrated. As all interests of the Archangel government centre in the White Sea, there lies the Alátyr stone. For the dwellers in the South, it is situated in the Black or Caspian Sea, while far inland it becomes synonymous with a boundary stone, and as such figures at cross-roads and so forth.

As Christianity spread, and the *stiks* or religious songs developed, the Alátyr stone acquired a new meaning. It became the stone on which Christ was crucified, and through which his blood trickled upon the head of Adam, and of all born on earth. Pilgrims returning from Jerusalem declared it to be the source of all healing, spiritual gifts, and new life. It is also said to be the stone from which Christ preached, despatched his disciples, and distributed *books* to all the world.

EPIC SONGS OF RUSSIA. 329

VOLGÁ VSESLÁVICH.

VOLK or Volgá Vseslávich, corrupted from Svyatoslávich, is the Prince Óleg (*Olg, Volg, Volgá*) who succeeded Rúrik early in the tenth century. Though this *bylína* undoubtedly preserves a dim memory of the Vseslávich of the Chronicles and the "Word of Igor's Troop," most of Volgá's traits are purely mythical. His name of *Volk* (the Wizard) corresponds to that won by Prince Óleg through his knowledge of the Black Art — *vyétchi*, the Wise Man, or Sorcerer. The history of Óleg in the Chronicle of Nestor, a monk of Kíef, 1050–1114, is almost as fantastic as the *bylína*. Like Volgá, he made a trip to "The Turkish Land," in 907. On this expedition, he is said to have placed wheels under his ships, and spreading their canvas, to have sailed thus across the plains of Thrace to the gates of Constantinople. The two heroes also begin their military career at the same age.

In the songs of the Turkish tribes of Siberia, the figure of the sorcerer and hunter who catches game and feeds his followers is very common, these peoples being still in the shepherd and hunter stage of civilization.

The signs and wonders accompanying Volgá's birth have their parallel in many other mythologies. Similar omens preceded the incarnation of Vishnu and the birth of Indra the Thunderer and Lightning-bringer.

A similar disturbing approach of the Thunder-god must be taken for granted in all epic accounts of marvellously born heroes. The omens are also often appropriated for the use of historical characters in the legends which crystallize about striking individualities, as in the case of Alexander of Macedon.

The dragon father in these myths is the Thunder-god; for the clouds, in which primitive man saw dragons, — the robbers of the living water, and of the gold of the sun's rays, — were regarded also as an external covering, a garment or cloak, in which the bright gods and goddesses wrapped themselves. Enveloping themselves thus in their cloudy garment, the gods clothed themselves, as it were, in a dragon's skin, and assumed the monstrous dragon form. The Thunder-god, slumbering within the frost-fettered clouds, invisible until the spring in the radiance of his beauty, the lightning, transformed himself into a dragon. All Volgá's transformations refer, therefore, to changes in the shape of the rain-bearing thunder-cloud.

As the representative of sorcery, Volgá holds the place in Slavic epics, held by Maugis or Malagis in the Carlovingian epos, especially in *Renaud de Montauban*.

Thirty is the favorite epic number for the body-guard (*druzhína*). In the *Chanson de Roland*, for instance, Roland's guard at the court of Charlemagne numbers thirty, while the traitor Ganelon is defended by the same number of relatives. As the ancient Slavs had no other organization than that of the patriarchal commune, this idea would seem to have been borrowed from the Scandinavians. The tests for admission to these brotherhoods, and the manner of their formation among the latter people, are well known. Princes, bishops, and even wealthy private individuals, like Churílo and Sadkó, had these guards, which owed allegiance to no one but their leader.

VOLGÁ AND MIKÚLA.

MIKÚLA represents the intermediate stage between the embodiment of purely physical and of moral power — the stage between Svyatogór and Ilyá. He partakes of Ilyá's nature, as the Thunder-god, and his nightingale mare signifies, probably, the thunder-cloud. The assistance rendered to agriculture through the rain by the Thunder-deity led in course of time to his being regarded as the god of agriculture also, who opened the plains of heaven with his whirlwinds, ploughed them with his lightning darts, and scattered his seed broadcast over them.

The dependence of man on the seasons early suggested the idea that the gods had set the example of ploughing. Many ceremonies and traditions are preserved in various countries, which point to such a mythical significance of the plough. The Siamese, for instance, celebrate a festival in its honor, of Buddhistic origin.

Herodotus, in his description of the customs and beliefs of the ancient Scythians, the ancestors of the Slavs, gives a tradition of a plough which fell from heaven in supernatural wise. With the possession of this plough and of a golden axe, yoke, and cup which had also fallen from heaven, went the imperial power. It may safely be affirmed, that the tradition of the golden implements of agriculture proceeding from heaven comes down to us from the most remote antiquity.— The Russian peasant still sees the plough which Mikúla hurled heavenward, in the constellation of Orion.

Mikúla, like Ilyá, is a glorification of the peasant. Some of the Germanic chieftains were prevented from accepting Christianity, by the thought that they should be obliged to enjoy heaven in the mixed society of common people, and even of slaves. On the other hand, Slavic traditions all represent the princely powers as derived from simple tillers of the soil; and in the Bohemian Chronicle of Kosmá of Prague, dating from the twelfth century, it is asserted that "we are all made equal by nature" (*Quia facti sumus omnes æquales per natura*) — a characteristically Slavic utterance in the midst of feudal Europe.

St. Nicholas, always called *Mikóla*, has taken Mikúla's place as the Christian deity of agriculture, and is a very great favorite among the peasant brethren of the "Villager's Son."

The affair of the bridge strongly resembles one at the bridge of Ovruch, related in the Chronicles, where perished Óleg Svyatoslávich — the Volgá Vseslávich of the epic song.

SVYATOGÓR.

SVYATOGÓR was the last of the Elder Heroes, that is to say, of the prehistoric, purely mythical giants of the cycle preceding the Vladímirian. The only songs belonging to this cycle which have come down to us are those relating to Volgá, Mikúla, Svyatogór, and the "One and Forty Pilgrims," who are thought to be nameless heroes belonging to that epoch. One or two others are slightly mentioned, as will be seen in "Ilyá and the Idol," where Ivániusho is a representative of the older race. Svyatogór's name is derived from his dwelling in the Holy Mountains (*na svyatýk gorák*), but what these Holy Mountains represent on earth is not known. Mythologically considered, they are the clouds. Hilferding found one very good rhapsodist who persisted in using the name *Svyatopólk*, on the usual ground, that "it was sung so." This suggested to Hilferding that Svyatogór might be identical with the giant of that name from Great Moravia — a legendary hero, and the representative of Slavic might. The Chronicle of Kosmá of Prague states that Svyatopólk concealed himself in the mountains, and there died a mysterious death. Svyatopólk also, like Svyatogór, was the only giant hero who did not war against Holy Russia.

The adventure with the pouches is often credited to

"Hero Samson," Mikúla being replaced by two angels sent by the Lord to rebuke the hero's arrogance.

A boast similar to that of Svyatogór was attributed to Alexander of Macedon in the manuscript legends of him which reached Russia from Byzantium in very early times.

The "Elder Heroes" make way for the Younger, typified in Ilyá, as the Titans made way for the Gods in Greek, or the Jotuns for the Asa in Norse mythology. The Younger Heroes superseded the Elder when men became convinced that in the battle constantly waged between light and darkness, summer and winter, light and summer always conquered at last. The distinction between the Elder and Younger Heroes has ceased to exist among the people, who regard them merely as representatives of different kinds of heroic, not divine, forces.

Svyatogór, the giant cloud-mountain, dies, i.e., becomes fettered with cold, and falls into his winter sleep. Popular fancy has likened the action of the frost to bands of iron, upon the frozen, stone-like earth. Svyatogór's huge sword, the lightning, which in spring and summer parts the heavens, prepares during the heavy autumnal storms the iron bands which the cold hand of winter lays upon the cloud.

Svyatogór's father belongs to the same class of easily tricked giants as Polyphemus. Instances, almost exactly similar, of the substitution of iron for the giant to grasp, are to be found in modern Greek and Swedish legends, and in the eleventh book of the Mahabharata. The crystal casket in which the hero carries his wife suggests an incident in one of the tales contained in the Arabian Nights' Entertainment.

ILYÁ OF MÚROM.

No one of the heroes has left so many proofs of his existence, no one is so popular or so firmly believed in, as the great peasant hero Ilyá of Múrom. A race of peasants called Ilyá's peasants (*krestyánye Iliúshini*) regard themselves as direct descendants of the renowned *bogatýr;* and it is a noteworthy fact, that, according to local testimony, the people who inhabit the primeval forests of Múrom are celebrated for their great stature and strength. To this day, the peasants of the village of Karachárof, Ilyá's birthplace, point out a chapel built upon the spot where a fountain burst forth beneath the hoofs of Ilyá's good steed Cloudfall, as did the springs at a blow from the hoof of Pegasus. The chapel is dedicated to Ilyá the Prophet; and "to the fountain fierce bears still come to quaff the waters and gain heroic strength," so the legend runs.

He is bound up with the religious legends of Kíef. Erich Lassota of Steblau, who made a trip to Kíef in 1594, states in his diary, that he saw in a chapel of St. Sophia, the tomb, now destroyed, of "Elia Morowlin, a distinguished hero and bohatér," and of another hero; and Kalnoforsky, a Pole, in a book published in 1638, says that Ilyá lived about 1188. His portrait was published in the XVII. century among the saints of Kíef, with an inscription to the effect that his body was still uncorrupted — which corresponds to the statement in the epic poems, that he was turned to stone.

In this portrait he appears as a gaunt ascetic, with masses of hair and beard, barely covered with his mantle, and with hands outstretched. One of the rhapsodists who sang the lay of the heroes' end to Hilferding in 1870, said that he knew Ilyá was turned to stone in Kíef, because some people had once made a pilgrimage thither to see how his fingers were placed for the sign of the cross — great importance being attached to this point. They saw Ilyá, but his hand was broken, and the question remained unsettled.

The antiquity of the legends about Ilyá is shown by the mention of his name in the cycle of *Dietrich of Berne*, which was compiled in the XIII. century from songs already existing. He appears as the brother of the Russian King Voldemar, Ilyá the Greek, referring to his religion, or in the Russian form of *Iliás* von Riuzen; the German would be *Elias*. His exploits in *Dietrich of Berne* have, however, nothing to do with those attributed to Ilyá in the epic songs.

Notwithstanding all this tolerably strong evidence of his actual existence, Ilyá is a purely mythical personage, an incarnation of the Thunder-god, the successor of heathen Perún. In the Christian mythology of the peasants, he appears as "Ilyá (Elijah) the Prophet," probably on account of the fiery chariot in which Elijah was translated to heaven. The mythical allusions are confined to a very restricted circle of natural phenomena — the clear heaven, the lightning, the rain, the thunder-clouds, and the powers of darkness in general. Like Thor and Indra, he wages incessant battle against the evil powers, and there are few episodes in his career to which a parallel does not exist among the various Indo-European races.

One of the most widely disseminated of traditions is that concerning the tardy development of the hero's strength, his late entrance upon active life, or long obscurity under persecution or in exile. Cinderella (Slavic *Pópeliuga*), and the youngest of three Princes who carries every thing before him at last, after years of ridicule or ill-treatment from his brothers, are some of the best known. It is hinted that the renowned Siegfried passed his youth in obscurity, as Ilyá sat for thirty years upon the oven. All these legends refer to the absence of the Thunder-deity in winter.

The wandering psalm-singers who heal Ilyá, and bestow upon him his vast strength, are the rain-bearing clouds, and their miraculous draught the life-giving dew. The hero and his horse are but two myths of the same phenomenon, originally independent, and only combined at a much later epoch.

In the riddles of which the people are so fond, the horse signifies the wind, and his neigh is the thunder.

Another embodiment of the whirlwind is Nightingale the Robber, whose historical prototype is supposed to be the Mogut, pardoned by Vladímir. The whirlwind chases the dark clouds through the heavens, and obscures the sunlight, i.e., bars the road to Fair Sun Vladímir, — troubles the sea with its whistle and roar, and uproots century-old oaks, like the giant Hraesvelgr in the Elder Edda, who sits on the border of heaven in eagle's plumage, and by the flapping of his wings produces the tempest.

The supernatural birds with iron feathers which Hercules drove from the Stymphalian swamp, one of

EPIC SONGS OF RUSSIA. 339

whom was named Aella — the whirlwind, and the two storm-birds of the Ramayana, who by waving their wings shake the mountains, raise great billows in the sea, and overthrow trees, are also forms of the same myth. In Latin also, *aquila* and *vultur* furnish names for stormy winds, *aquilo* and *vulturnus*. The Smoródina is a mythical river — the rain ; and the bridge built by Ilyá is the rainbow.

In his contest with Falcon the Hunter, Ilyá represents the heavens, Falcon being the lightning which turns its sharp blade against its mother from the realms of darkness, the clouds. To this lightning Ilyá opposes his own, and having conquered shines forth again clear and radiant. Falcon's mace cast heavenward, and returning always to his hand, is the lightning flash.

The Russian examples of the very common legend concerning the conflict of father and son are remarkable for their number and variety; some versions substitute Ilyá's daughter,[1] a "bold *polyánitza*," for Falcon ; most of then have preserved their tragic ending.

Idol, like the robbers and the Tatars who effaced, in course of time, the memory of the tribes who really warred against Vladímir, must be accepted as another embodiment of the dark and hostile principle. The gluttony ascribed to him constitutes a sort of distinction in a great number of legends. In ancient Hindoo myths, it appears to be the special attribute of the evil powers. Thor in the Edda and Indra in the Rig-Veda are credited with a great capacity for drinking, and Ilyá is represented as intoxicated. Owing to his connection

---

[1] Several heroes decline to fight her, because they doubt their ability to conquer her.

with the rain, drunkenness is the special attribute of the Thunder-god.

Ilyá's conduct in his quarrels with Vladímir is much more moderate than that of many epic heroes in disputes with their sovereigns. — The paladins of Charlemagne's court pulled the Emperor's beard, beat him, and called him a fool, with the same readiness which they displayed in humiliating themselves before him and kissing his footsteps when circumstances rendered it advisable.

Many epic personages disappear from the scene in a mysterious manner which renders their death uncertain, their return probable at any moment. Then arises the legend of their return on the fulfilment of certain conditions, as in the case of Frederic Barbarossa. As the Russian heroes were known to have been killed in battle or turned to stone, with Ilyá's tomb in two or three places in Kíef to prove his death in particular, this legend has become the special property of Stenka Razin, the famous Cossack chief of the XVII. century, and his return is still awaited by the peasants.

A fragmentary *bylína* represents Ilyá, Dobrýnya, and other heroes as sailing in the " Falcon ship," to some unknown region, whence they do not return.

EPIC SONGS OF RUSSIA. 341

THE FAIR SUN PRINCE VLADÍMIR.

Two noted historical personages are combined in the courteous Prince Vladímir of the *bylínas* — Saint Vladímir Svyatoslávich, who established Christianity in Russia in the year 988, and died in 1015; and Vladímir Monomáchus, who was born in 1053, and died in 1125. Both are celebrated in the Chronicles for their feasts, and the latter's courtesy is frequently referred to. His name Vladímir, *Vladýki-Mirí*, Ruler of the World, chances to express his most ancient mythical signification. His peculiar title, "*Fair Sun*," renders it even more apparent. It has taken the place in Russian tradition of the most ancient name of the divinity of the heavens and the Sun. If not identical with the Volós [1] of the Chronicles, it stands at least in close philological relationship with him, and with the Semitic Baal or Bel.

He does not represent the active principle of light and warmth, however, but the passive. He paces his banquet-hall, the heavens, and serves his guests with wine, but relegates all active duties to his heroes. His distinctive appellation is *courteous*, as *good* is that of French and Spanish epic kings (*le bon roy, el buen rey*), or of King Arthur. But as the Sun can be not only clear or courteous, but burning and oppressive, so Vladí-

---

[1] St. Vlásy (Blasius) in the Christian calendar. For some account of the ceremonial songs connected with this patron saint of flocks and herds, see *Songs of the Russian People* (p. 251), by W. R. S. Ralston.

342 EPIC SONGS OF RUSSIA.

mir is, on occasion, both oppressive and discourteous, as these songs show. In one omitted here, Prince Vladímir despatches young Sukmán Odikmántievich to shoot game for his table. Sukmán finds none, but destroys an innumerable host of Tatars. When he reports to Vladímir on his return, the Prince does not believe him, orders him to be thrown into a dungeon, and sends heroes to examine into the truth of the story. Convinced at last, he releases Sukmán, who kills himself for grief at his prince's treatment.

Many marriages of heroes are mentioned in these epic songs besides Vladímir's, and in the epics of other nations marriage is a frequent topic. Students of comparative mythology are agreed in regarding these marriages as variations of the same theme; viz., the union of a bright and beneficent male principle with an obscure and noxious female principle, taken from the realm of darkness.

QUIET DÚNAÏ IVÁNOVICH.

DÚNAÏ is the name borne by one of Prince Vladímir Vasílkovich's voivódes, and is mentioned in the Chronicles of the years 1281 and 1287. Like Mikáilo he was a rover, and probably not a Russian.

Geographical accuracy is not to be looked for in these epic lays. Dúnaï and Nastásya, as rivers, bear various names, and their courses are as fantastic as in the version selected.

EPIC SONGS OF RUSSIA. 343

STAVR GODÍNOVICH.

STAVR, whom we meet with in the Chronicle of Nóvgorod in the year 1118, was not a *boyár*, as stated in the songs, but a *sótsky*, — the ruler of a hundred; Nóvgorod and its suburbs being divided into hundreds according to their different trades. The courteous Prince was Vladímir Monomáchus, who summoned all the nobles of Nóvgorod to Kíef, and made them take an oath of allegiance to him. Some he permitted to return home; others, among them Stavr, he sent into exile in wrath at some of their exploits.

Ryabínin, one of the best of epic singers, explained Vasilísa's easy victory over Vladímir's heroes, by saying that Ilyá of Múrom had not arrived in Kíef at that time. Consequently, as a daughter of Mikúla, a representative of the Earth and the Elder Heroes, she was superior to all the Younger Heroes.

Such wrestling and shooting matches were not uncommon at feasts, as the Ipatiéf Chronicle of 1150 informs us, and even horse-racing, as in the song of " Iván the Merchant's Son."

BOLD ALYÓSHA POPÓVICH.

SEVERAL references are made to Alyósha in various chronicles, under the name of Alexander Popóvich. The most important, from the Nikonof Chronicle of the year 1224, states that "Alexander Popóvich with his servant Torop" (*Akím* of the song), "Dobrýnya Golden Belt of Ryazán, and seventy great and brave bogatýrs were slain in the battle of Kalká, by the Tatars, through the wrath of God at our sins."

This is the famous battle described in "Ilyá Múrometz and Tzar Kálin," where Russian chivalry perished.

What relation the character of the Alyósha of epic song bears to that of the actual historical personage, it is impossible, with our meagre information, to decide. It is probable, however, that his name of Popóvich, *pope's son*, determined the characteristics of the epic hero, rather than his personal traits. — Numerous tales (*skázkas*)[2] bear witness to the unpopularity of popes and their relatives in Russia. His language and deeds in some short poems justify Dobrýnya's description of him as a scorner of women in "Dobrýnya and Alyósha." He bears some resemblance to the Loki of Northern mythology, the mischief-maker.

An incantation, "The Patrol of the Flocks," mentions among evil spirits, wild beasts, and other noxious

---

[2] See W. R. S. Ralston: *Russian Folk Lore*, p. 351.

influences to be guarded against, "popes and their popesses, monks, nuns," and so forth.

Tugárin, adapted from Tugár-Khan, is the spirit of the storm, the fire-flashing cloud, one of the dragons combated by Dobrýnya as well as by Alyósha.

346   EPIC SONGS OF RUSSIA.

DOBRÝNYA THE DRAGON-SLAYER.

Two historical Dobrýnyas are united in the person of this hero. The first, mentioned in the Chronicles towards the end of the tenth century, was uncle to Prince (Saint) Vladímir, and brother to Malúsha the Princess Ólga's housekeeper (*kliúchnitza*), Vladímir's mother. In the *bylínas* he becomes Vladímir's nephew and steward (*kliúchnik*).

The second, Dobrýnya of Ryazán, surnamed "Golden Belt," was a hero who perished in the battle of Kalká in 1224.

Marína is to a certain degree an historical reminiscence of the heretic, Polish wife of the False Dmítry, Marína Mníshek. It is evident that her name must have superseded the original one in the seventeenth century. That name was in earlier times probably "Márya the White Swan," as her character is identical with those of the treacherous wives of Mikáilo the Rover, and Iván Godinóvich : in some versions of the latter, she is called Márya instead of Avdótya. *Mora* or *Morena*, the goddess of serpents, death, sleep, and cold, was no doubt the original heroine.

Marína Mníshek, like the Marína of the song, was reputed a witch among the common people, and like her the latter is sometimes designated as the " heretic."' This Slavic Circe typifies the dark and hurtful female principle which is united to a bright and beneficent male principle.

It often happens in mythology, that one deity is divided into two or more distinct persons, in accordance with his various attributes. This is the case here. While Vladímir is the passive, inactive principle of the Sun, and pursues his way tranquilly through the sky, the active, warlike principle is embodied in Dobrýnya.

Dobrýnya wages incessant war with darkness, triumphing over it every morning, and with winter, whose fetters he strikes asunder every spring with the sword of his rays. Like Krishna, Apollo, Hercules, Frey, Siegfrid, and Yegóry the Brave, the St. George of the religious ballads, he is a slayer of dragons; like Perseus and Yegóry, he rescues captive women.

He possesses traits in common with Ilyá, also. For the Sun-god and the Thunder-god are both descendants of *Svaróg*, the Heaven, the father of all gods. Hence their brotherhood in arms was originally a mythical bond. Dobrýnya corresponds to Odin, Ilyá to Thor, in Northern mythology.

The marriage round the bush is undoubtedly the ancient heathen rite against which early Russian writers inveigh.

Dobrýnya's long absence from Nastásya, the Russian Penelope, has the same mythical signification as Mikáilo Rover's imprisonment in the stone, or Ilyá's long confinement to the oven — the night and winter repose of the deities of light and warmth. Dobrýnya's transformation into an aurochs likewise represents the obscuration of the beneficent summer deities in winter, and his golden horns are an intimation of his bright origin.

These Russian poems treating of the return of the long-absent husband are more complete and perfect in form, and, from an epic point of view, more original, than either the oral traditions of Western Europe which are chiefly in prose, or than the literary versions which go back to the thirteenth century.

EPIC SONGS OF RUSSIA.   349

IVÁN GODINÓVICH.

PULLING off the bridegroom's boots, in token of wifely submission, was one of the ceremonies which were regularly performed after a wedding. Apparently, in the oldest versions of this song, Avdótya's refusal to pull off Iván's boot was the direct cause of her death.

Iván's experience with Avdótya the White Swan is supposed to reflect that of Prince Vladímir with Rognyéd, daughter of Rogvólod, Prince of the Polotzkí. "I will not marry the son of a slave," she said, in answer to Vladímir's proposal of marriage, and prepared to wed his half-brother Yaropolk. Koschéi represents Yaropolk. This was in allusion to Vladímir's mother, who had been a servant of his grandmother, Ólga. Vladímir slew Rogvólod and Yaropolk, and forced Rognyéd to wed him.

After several years, so runs the legend, Rognyéd attempted to kill Vladímir in his sleep, by way of avenging her father's death and her own wrongs. Vladímir woke, and seized her hand as she held the dagger over him. Then he ordered her to dress herself in her wedding garments, and wait for him, intending to kill her with his own hand. But she put a sword into the hands of her little son, and bade him greet his father with the words: "Father, thou thinkest that thou art alone here!" Touched by the sight of his son, Vladímir summoned his boyárs, and begged them to judge the matter. On their advice, he sent Rognyéd and her son back to her native land. Her descendants thenceforth reigned over the Polotzkí, and warred against the descendants of Vladímir by other wives.

Iván's wooing, as well as Dúnaï's wooing for Prince Vladímir, furnishes a picture of that rough, forceful manner of courtship which prevailed in the old patriarchal days. The memory of it is preserved in a great many wedding songs, which represent the bride as purchased or stolen away by an entire stranger. There is a striking likeness between the birds which surround Avdótya, and the two peacocks which hover over the head of Hilda in *Dietrich of Berne*. This is a very ancient trait, pointing to a supernatural being.

CHURÍLO PLENKÓVICH.

CHURÍLO's name does not appear in any of the old chronicles.

The epithet applied to old Plenkó, *surozhánin*, indicates his business of silk-merchant or trader on the *Suróg Sea* — the Sea of Azóf. Another explanation professes to include Churílo's mythical significance, by deriving the term from the same Sanskrit root as *Svaróg*, the Slavic Saturn.

The numerous attendants credited to Prince Vladímir belong to the Moscow epoch, and present a strange contrast to the plainness and simplicity of the court of Kíef. Churílo met his death at the hands of an enraged husband, the Bermyág mentioned in the song.

DIUK STEPANOVICH.

Diuk's unflattering description of the lack of elegance at Kíef is confirmed by an ancient account of one of Saint Vladímir's feasts. This narrative of the year 996 says that there was a great abundance of all sorts of food, flesh of domestic and wild animals. But "when the guests had drunk freely, they began to murmur against the Prince, and to say: 'Woe be upon our heads! for we are given wooden spoons to eat with and not silver.' Vladímir heard them, and commanded silver spoons to be brought, for he loved his druzhína, and reflected that a good body-guard might acquire silver and gold, but could never be purchased by either."

Nevertheless, Burhard, the ambassador of the Emperor Henry IV. at the court of Svyatosláf in 1075, was amazed at the quantity and magnificence of the treasures he saw there.

In the same manuscript with the " Word of Ígor's Troop" of the twelfth century, was found an " Epistle from Tzar Iván the Indian to Tzar Manuel the Greek," which reads as follows: "If thou desirest to know all my power, and all the wonders of my Indian realm, sell thy kingdom of Greece and purchase paper, and come to my Indian realm with thy learned men, and I will permit thee to write down the marvels of the Indian land; and thou shalt not be able to make a writing of the wonders of my kingdom before the departure of thy spirit."

Which of these two fictions, the epic poem and the epistle, is derived from the other, it is impossible to say.

VASÍLY THE DRUNKARD AND TZAR BÁTÝG.

THIS song resembles an episode narrated in the Chronicles, which has been idealized and transferred to the favorite epoch of Vladímir, and the siege of Kíef by Bátyg in 1240.

In 1381, Toktámysh besieged Moscow. "Taken unawares," says the Chronicle, "and deprived of all power of defending themselves, nearly all the inhabitants gave themselves over to drunkenness. A few, however, fought the enemy from the city wall, among them a certain cloth-dealer, Adam by name, who shot an arrow from the Frolóf gate, and slew one of the horde, a son, and a person of distinction, causing thereby great grief to Tzar Toktámysh, and to all his princes."

EPIC SONGS OF RUSSIA. 353

SWEET MIKÁILO IVÁNOVICH THE ROVER.

IN some versions of this poem, Márya the White Swan is the Dragon of the under-world, transforming herself into that shape in the coffin, in order to kill Mikáilo. This malicious view is the one adopted in many legends and tales; Mikáilo cuts his bride in bits, when he discovers her character, cleans out the snakes and other reptiles concealed within her body, sprinkles her with the living water, marries her, and lives happily ever after.

In the myth, the White Swan signifies a cloud: the living water is the rain. The dragon is, as usual, a cloud, but larger and darker than the first. Mikáilo's roaring in the grave is the thunder, and the bursting of the coffin denotes the bursting of the cloud.

Mikáilo's candles are the lightning. His wife not only denotes a single cloud, but the cloudiness common in summer, which is capable of entering into beneficent union with the thunder and lightning, but in winter remains sterile in the heaven, and, dying with idleness, conceals within itself, as though entombed, the Thunder-power, its husband. For it appears that Mikáilo's mythical foundation is the same as that of Ilyá of Múrom, and of Dúnaï also, to a certain extent.

Mikáilo's rods and pincers point him out as the heavenly smith, the forger of the lightning, which is represented by those weapons. A corresponding instance of double burial in case of death, as a condition of marriage, and of the visit of a serpent to the grave, is found in a German tale (Grimm, *Kinder- und Hausmärchen*). Mikáilo sometimes appears as the leader of the " One and Forty Pilgrims " instead of Kasyan.

EPIC SONGS OF RUSSIA. 355

NIGHTINGALE BUDÍMIROVICH.

ALL authorities are agreed as to the foreign element in Nightingale Budímirovich. He was not a hero of Kíef. Some regard him as a Norman pirate, others as one of the prehistoric Slavs who dwelt on the shores of the Baltic. The "land of Ledenétz," or *Vedenetz* as it appears in some variants, has led to the suggestion that he was a merchant from Venice, or one of the Italian architects who came to Russia in the twelfth century.

One variant represents Nightingale's mother as opposed to the marriage until her son has proved himself in a long voyage. During his absence, young David Popóf arrives, and, stating that he had seen Nightingale imprisoned for smuggling in Ledenétz, seeks Love's hand in marriage. Nightingale returns in time to claim his bride at the wedding feast. The incident, and the treacherous suitor's name, recall the story of Alyósha and Nastásya.

Nightingale Budímirovich's mythical signification is probably the reverse of that of Nightingale the Robber. They represent the opposite sides of the same atmospheric phenomenon; the Robber being the rude and boisterous gales, while fair Love's wooer is the breeze, gentle and seductive as a minstrel.

The description of his ships recalls the famous dragon ships of the ancient Scandinavians. An Eastern tale describes the ceiling of a rich man's house as " covered

356   EPIC SONGS OF RUSSIA.

with figures of all sorts of wild beasts, seam-onsters, and fishes. When the wind blew, they moved about, and were reflected in the floor." This exaggerated description of bas-reliefs explains the decoration of Nightingale's bower with sables, and so forth. Nightingale is not an historical character. His palace suggests that of Aladdin.

TZAR SOLOMON AND TZARÍTZA SOLOMONÍDA.

AMONG the traditions common to all Aryan races, the quest of a bride in a marvellous ship, with the aid of wondrous song or music, is one of the most widely disseminated. This legend seems to have reached the Russians through the medium of books, as it is recorded in some of the Chronicles, though not the most ancient. It received its present poetical form from the people, and offers a very rare and noteworthy example of a poem purely popular in style, though derived from foreign and literary sources.

In one version, Tzar Vasíly lives in Nóvgorod, and Solomon in Tzargrád (Constantinople).

VASÍLY BUSLÁEVICH.

THIS doughty hero, a representative of the nobility and, as some think, of the *ushkúiniki*, the noted river-pirates, was a contemporary of Sadkó. Only one mention is made of him in the Chronicles: his death is recorded in 1171. As this was considered worthy of record amid events of the greatest moment, some idea may be formed of his importance. He was, in fact, a *posádnik*, — lord mayor or president of the popular assembly.

It has been suggested that the "black-visaged maid" is identical with the Iris of Greek mythology. The fact that she had an arched yoke, and that she was in the service of Avdótya Vasílievna, forms the foundation for the comparison with Iris's rainbow and position as handmaid to Juno.

MERCHANT SADKÓ, THE RICH GUEST OF NÓVGOROD.

THE hero of this poem, whose adventure with the fish of Lake Ílmen is suggestive of the Arabian Nights, and whose later experience with the Tzar Morskói recalls Jonah, and the men of Nineveh or Arion in Greek mythology, is not a purely imaginary being.

The Chronicles state that he founded a church in

Nóvgorod, though they differ as to the particular edifice. He probably lived in the twelfth century, and in the song preserves the type of the great traders of that Venice of the North in the middle ages, Nóvgorod the Great.

He must have been a prominent figure in his day, for frequent reference is made to him in the Chronicles, in connection with the church which he built, for about hundred years.

ST. MARY'S COLLEGE OF MARYLAND
ST. MARY'S CITY, MARYLAND

45804